Studies in Graduate & Professional Student Development

Context and Content in the Preparation of Future Faculty

Edited by Laura L.B. Border

NEW FORUMS
Stillwater, Oklahoma
U.S.A.

NEW FORUMS PRESS INC.

Published in the United States of America
by New Forums Press, Inc.1018 S. Lewis St.
Stillwater, OK 74074
www.newforums.com

Library of Congress Cataloging-in-Publication Data Pending

This book may be ordered in bulk quantities at discount from New Forums Press,
Inc., P.O. Box 876, Stillwater, OK 74076 [Federal I.D. No. 73 1123239]. Printed in the
United States of America.

ISSN: 1068-6096   Volume 13, 2010, ISBN: 1-58107-207-4

Contents

Editor's Introduction .... *xi*
    Laura L. B. Border

**Section 1— How Graduate Students View the Graduate
    School Experience** **1**
Chapter 1—Doctoral Students Make Meaning of Their
    Experience: A Constructivist Inquiry 2
    Katherine Vahey, Patricia Witkowsky, Jessica Rehling, & Sarun Saifah
Chapter 2—Instructional Concerns of Kinesiology Basic Instruction
    Program Graduate Teaching Assistants 23
    Jared A. Russell

**Section 2—Educating Graduate Students for Their Roles
    as College Instructors** **43**
Chapter 3—A Prep Course for Graduate Teaching Assistants:
    Building a Community 44
    **Gili Marbach-Ad, Patricia A. Shields, Bretton W. Kent,
    Bill Higgins, & Katerina V. Thompson**
Chapter 4—A Pedagogy Course's Influence on Graduate
    Students' Self-Awareness as Teacher-Scholars 59
    **Lauren Miller Griffith, Valerie Dean O'Loughlin,
    Katherine D. Kearns, Mark Braun, & Isaac Heacock**

**Section 3—The Challenges Involved in the Education
    of Future Faculty** **83**
Chapter 5—Student Engagement Challenges in Teaching
    about Controversial Issues 84
    Jacki Fitzpatrick, Jeremy Boden, & Erin Kostina-Ritchey
Chapter 6—Students' Perceptions of Lesson Objectives in
    Introductory Mathematics Courses Taught
    by Teaching Assistants 103
    Jeff Meyer, Matt Elsey, & Vilma Mesa
Chapter 7— The Effectiveness of Online Case-based Instruction
    on International Teaching Assistants' Presentation and
    Active Listening Strategies 122
    Shenghua Zha & Gail Fitzgerald

**Section 4—Models in Context: Educating Graduate Students
   for Future Roles as Academics** **137**

Chapter 8—An Interdisciplinary Approach to Graduate TA Training:
   A Reflection of Best Practice 138
   **Barbi T. Honeycutt, Miriam Ferzli, Tamah Morant,
   & Sarah Egan Warren**

Chapter 9—One Process, Two Contexts: Collaborating to
   Design Professional Development for Graduate
   Student Educators 153
   Michele M. Welkener

Studies in Graduate & Professional Student Development

Editor

Laura L. B. Border
Director, Graduate Teacher Program
201 ATLAS, 362 UCB
University of Colorado at Boulder
Boulder, CO 80309-0362
Laura.Border@colorado.edu

Associate Editor

Linda von Hoene
Director, GSI Teaching and Resource Center
301 Sproul Hall #5900
University of California, Berkeley
Berkeley, CA 94720-5900
vonhoene@berkeley.edu

Tuesday L. Cooper
Walden University

Sandra L. Courter
Adjunct Assistant Professor
Engineering Professional Development
Wisconsin Center for Educational Research
University of Wisconsin - Madison

Daniel Denecke
Director, Best Practice
Council Graduate Schools

Nanda Dimitrov
Associate Director, Teaching Support Centre
University of Western Ontario

Maureen Dunne
Manager, Instructional Development
Memorial University of Newfoundland

Chris M. Golde
Associate Vice Provost for Graduate
Education
Stanford University

Linda C. Hodges
Director, McGraw Center for Teaching
& Learning
Princeton University

Trevor Holmes
Education Associate
Teaching Support Services
University of Guelph

Jeff Johnston
Assistant Director, Center for Teaching
Vanderbilt University

Kevin M. Johnston
Director, TA Programs
Michigan State University

Katherine Dowell Kearns
Campus Instructional Consulting
Indiana University

Michele Marincovich
Associate Vice Provost of Undergraduate
Education,
Director, Center for Teaching and Learning
Stanford University

Jeanette McDonald
Manager, Educational Development
Teaching Support Services
Wilfrid Laurier University

Kathryn M. Plank
Associate Director
Faculty & TA Development
The Ohio State University

Brian Rybarczyk
Director, Graduate Student Academic &
Professional Development
University of North Carolina at Chapel Hill

Stephanie Rohdieck
Instructional Consultant for GTA Programs
University Center for the Advancement
of Teaching
The Ohio State University

Kathleen Smith
Director, Center for Teaching & Learning
University of Georgia

Mary C. Wright
Assistant Director, Evaluation
and Assistant Research Scientist
Center for Research, Learning & Teaching
University of Michigan

A peer-reviewed book series on the research, issues, and programs that address the education and development of graduate and professional students.

Publisher: Douglas Dollar
Circulation: Jean McKinney

Studies in Graduate and Professional Student Development is published once per year by New Forums Press, Inc., P.O. Box 876, Stillwater, Oklahoma 74076, to highlight those aspects of graduate education and the development of graduate and professional students to prepare them for the multiple roles they play on their campuses and for the professional roles they will fill upon leaving graduate school. The full range of issues involved in the development, programming, research projects, and administration of such programs is addressed by the series.

PRICES & STANDING ORDERS: Beginning with volume 11, this publication's content was broadened and the title was changed to ***Studies in Graduate and Professional Student Development*** (see page *ix* for details). Prices beginning with volume 11 are:
    List for existing single issues... U.S. $22.95
    Standing orders may be placed by emailing contact information
    to sales@newforums.com. You will be contacted prior to shipment.
    Overseas and Canada ....add U.S. $9.00 to above
          rates for each year.
    Call for information about bulk rates.
Please make payment with a check for U.S. funds drawn on a United States Bank in the Federal Reserve System, or with a U.S. Dollar World Money Order, or with a Postal Money Order imprinted in U.S. currency, or through your subscription agency. Send subscription requests to New Forums Press, Inc., P.O. Box 876, Stillwater, OK 74076 U.S.A.

SUBMISSIONS: See "Call for Papers," page *ix*.

ADVERTISING: Requests for classified and display advertising space rates and deadlines should be sent to the publisher.

Call for Papers

Studies in Graduate and Professional Student Development
Laura L. B. Border, Editor
Linda von Hoene, Associate Editor

Studies in Graduate and Professional Student Development is a peer-reviewed book series designed to provide a platform for the discussion of the research, issues, and programs that address the professional development of graduate and professional students. Areas addressed include:

- Research on teaching, professional development, curricula, assessment and evaluation, training, certification, and career planning
- Research on effective disciplinary and interdisciplinary programs and workshop design, implementation and evaluation for teaching and learning
- Research on the transition from graduate school to full-time faculty positions
- Basic research on teaching and learning

The intended audience for this journal comprises:

- Disciplinary societies and their subcommittees on teaching and learning
- Personnel in the Office of the Graduate Dean
- Administrators, chairs, graduate faculty, and graduate directors
- Administrators, chairs, graduate faculty, and professional advisors in the professional schools
- Research faculty, research associates, and postdoctoral fellows at research institutions
- Faculty who teach departmental discipline-specific teaching methodology courses
- Faculty who serve as teaching assistant coordinators or supervisors
- TA development personnel at research institutions
- Preparing future faculty personnel at research institutions
- Graduate and professional student development personnel at research institutions

(Continued on page x.)

- Faculty development personnel at research, four-year, and two-year institutions
- Faculty who teach courses on postsecondary teaching and research on higher education in any department or in the School of Education
- Centers for Teaching and Learning
- Career development personnel who focus on nonacademic careers for master's and doctoral graduates
- Administrators and faculty at two-year and four-year institutions who hire candidates into faculty positions
- Graduate and professional students in all fields
- The Council of Graduate Schools
- The National Association of Graduate-Professional Students

To view authors' guidelines and subscription procedures, please visit the New Forums Press website at: http://www.newforums.com/

If you would like to submit your name to become a reviewer, please contact: Laura L. B. Border, Editor, at laura.border@colorado.edu

Introduction

Context and Content in the Preparation of Future Faculty

Graduate education occurs within a context that is quite different from that of undergraduate education. Undergraduate students attend classes, choose a major, complete the required number of credit hours, achieve a grade point high enough to graduate, and graduate. Graduate students enter an educational environment that is much more complex, harder to understand, and more difficult to navigate. Success is not dependent simply on the completion of credit hours in the major field, rather it is the result—on the content-mastery side—of an in-depth engagement with the content of the discipline, a choice point on one's own research project, mastery of appropriate research procedures and data analysis, the ability to work independently and in coordination with a faculty committee of experts in the field, the perseverance and commitment to complete an in-depth study that is well supported by data and evidence, and the ability to write up one's scholarly work for publication. The culmination of one's efforts is judged by a panel of experts to be worthy of the doctorate or not. Simultaneously, the aspiring doctoral candidate must learn to teach at the college level, maintain his or her current relationships, and continue to engage in the demands of a typical adult life. Additionally, graduate students must participate in appropriate professional development activities that will help them to select a career path in which they might maximize their talents and which is most suitable for their interests and life goals. Thus, the recruitment and retention of graduate students is indeed difficult.

The thirteenth volume of this journal (formerly entitled *The Journal of Graduate Teaching Assistant Development*), which is devoted to research on the experiences and education of graduate students, shows that progress is being made in better defining contexts—graduate students' needs and perceptions, TA training, the actual challenges of classroom practice, and professional development—in which graduate students might benefit from support, training, and guidance. As these contexts become clearer, faculty, departments, and institutions as a whole are developing disciplinary and interdisciplinary (college-wide) support for training large numbers of future faculty, more effective pedagogical approaches, and mechanisms to assess the work accomplished.

Section 1, "How Graduate Students View the Graduate School Experience," presents the context of graduate school from the viewpoint of graduate students as researchers on the graduate experience and as teachers in college classrooms. Section 2, "Educating Graduate Students for Their Roles as College Instructors," offers a perspective gained from research on college pedagogy courses as faculty in departments attempt to support graduate students while improving undergraduate education. Section 3, "The Challenges Involved in the Education of Future Faculty," pierces more deeply into the context and challenges of the classroom that novice future faculty encounter. Finally, Section 4, "Models in Context: Educating Graduate Students for Future Roles as Academics," looks at the broader university context and provides effective models for graduate student development.

Section 1—How Graduate Students View the Graduate School Experience

In Chapter 1: "Doctoral Students Make Meaning of Their Experience: A Constructivist Inquiry" the authors, Katherine Vahey, Patricia Witkowsky, Jessica Rehling, and Sarun Saifah, who are graduate students themselves, used a constructivist case study to unveil the importance of mentoring for doctoral students, the challenges doctoral students face trying to fulfill multiple roles, and the characteristics they attribute to their success. Their analysis points to the need for more research on the doctoral student experience to reduce attrition rates and increase degree completion.

In Chapter 2: "Instructional Concerns of Kinesiology Basic Instruction Program Graduate Teaching Assistants," Jared A. Russell studied graduate teaching assistants' instructional concerns and perspectives, and attempted to determine if demographic characteristics affected the ranking of their concerns. He used the Teacher Concern Questionnaire with GTAs who teach in basic instruction programs (BIPs) maintained by the graduate academic programs in the American Academy of Kinesiology and Physical Education (AAKPE). Prominent concerns included motivating unengaged students and finding support and respect for quality teaching from faculty.

Section 2—Educating Graduate Students for Their Roles as College Instructors

In Chapter 3: "A Prep Course for Graduate Teaching Assistants: Building a Community," Gili Marbach-Ad, Patricia A. Shields, Bretton W. Kent, Bill Higgins, and Katerina V. Thompson focused their investigation on a course that highlighted three key components of graduate student teaching development: faculty engagement, teaching center involvement, and graduate student participation. They evaluated a team-taught course for new graduate teaching assistants (GTAs), which focused on building community and preparing GTAs for their teaching responsibilities in a biological sciences program at a Research University. Most GTAs reported that the course exceeded their expectations and they particularly valued discussions of authentic teaching scenarios. The course provides a model for other graduate programs in which GTAs come from diverse backgrounds and have significant teaching responsibilities.

In Chapter 4: "A Pedagogy Course's Influence on Graduate Students' Self-Awareness as Teacher-Scholars," Lauren Miller Griffith, Valerie Dean O'Loughlin, Katherine D. Kearns, Mark Braun, and Isaac Heacock explored the lasting effects of a pedagogy course on graduate student instructors' evolving orientations towards teaching. Using interviews, their study confirmed an alignment between students' perceived learning outcomes and course objectives. Graduate students said they became more reflective, gained confidence in the classroom, and developed a greater understanding of their undergraduate students' learning. However, they struggled with methods to assess their teaching effectiveness and to justify time spent on teaching development. The authors conclude with programmatic recommendations to facilitate graduate students' transition from novice instructor to scholarly teacher.

Section 3—The Challenges Involved in the Education of Future Faculty

In Chapter 5: "Student Engagement Challenges in Teaching about Controversial Issues," Jacki Fitzpatrick, Jeremy Boden, and Erin Kostina-Ritchey examined common challenges faced by college instructors, such as student resistance, inhibition, or even defiance that may be based on students' view of culture, religion, politics, media, family, or friends. The discussion of controversial issues in college classrooms forces instructors to develop strategies, such as working from a principle of acceptance, for addressing such challenges. The authors provide a review of the literature that unveils typical reasons for the dilemma and common instructor responses.

In Chapter 6: "Students' Perceptions of Lesson Objectives in Introductory Mathematics Courses Taught by Teaching Assistants," Jeff Meyer, Matt Elsey, and Vilma Mesa investigated the alignment of teaching assistants' stated lesson objectives with students' perceptions of those objectives. Their study of calculus reform courses reveals discrepancies. Their results lead the authors to make suggestions that will assist teaching assistants as they build their own lesson plans for reform-oriented classes.

In Chapter 7: "The Effectiveness of Online Case-based Instruction on International Teaching Assistants' Presentation and Active Listening Strategies," Shenghua Zha and Gail Fitzgerald used a quasi-experimental study to compare the effectiveness of online case-based instruction using asynchronous peer discussion with face-to-face instruction using peer discussion. Results reveal that online case-based instruction using asynchronous peer discussion is as effective as its face-to-face counterpart in improving international teaching assistants' effective use of presentation and active listening strategies. Based on the positive results of this study, the authors recommend the use of online case-based instruction facilitated through asynchronous peer discussion in training for international teaching assistants.

Section 4— Models in Context: Educating Graduate Students for Future Roles as Academics

In Chapter 8: "An Interdisciplinary Approach to Graduate TA Training: A Reflection of Best Practice," Barbi T. Honeycutt, Miriam Ferzli, Tamah Morant, and Sarah Egan Warren discuss the implementation of a collaborative interdisciplinary model for GTA training based upon recommendations from current literature. The model integrates a centralized university-wide developmental program with individualized discipline-specific training programs to address GTA training at a research institution not only more effectively but also more efficiently. The current program is now sustainable, scalable, and repeatable to other departments across campus.

In Chapter 9: "One Process, Two Contexts: Collaborating to Design Professional Development for Graduate Student Educators," Michele M. Welkener explores ways to guide graduate students to develop new habits of mind that will help them realize their potential. Changing graduate students' habits of mind calls for a qualitatively different type of meaning making than what they needed to be successful undergraduate students. Welkener provides a process grounded in theory and set of principles that can be used to promote graduate students' growth, and specifies the outcomes that can be derived from employing this strategy in two different institutional settings.

The articles selected for this volume demonstrate that graduate education is emerging as a field to be studied both quantitatively and qualitatively. Models for best practice need to be shared, as do discussions of issues that all college and university instructors encounter in their postsecondary classrooms. Data from the Council of Graduate Schools show that time to degree has decreased significantly over the last two decades in most disciplines, excluding engineering and education particularly (Bell, 2010). Is it possible that shifts in the preparation of graduate students may be having an effect on time to degree nationwide? The authors who have contributed to this volume demonstrate the rich terrain of graduate education. In the future, a fruitful area of investigation might be the connection between time to degree and the presence and effectiveness of teacher training, preparing future faculty, and professional development programs for graduate students on our university campuses. Other fertile ground for research lies in developments in preparing future faculty in science, technology, engineering and math (STEM), modifications in the preparation of international graduate teaching assistants, progress in introducing technology in the classroom at the graduate instructor level, and teaching graduate students to integrate the assessment of student learning into their own classrooms and practice. The field of graduate and professional student development mirrors the larger context of graduate education and research in which it occurs: change is a constant; new developments and new challenges are always present; and we as professionals can build on each other's knowledge and success.

Laura L. B. Border, Editor

References

Bell, N.E. (March 2010). *Director, Data sources: Time-to-degree for doctorate recipients.* Communicator, Washington, DC: Council of Graduate Schools.

Section 1

How Graduate Students View the Graduate School Experience

Chapter 1

Doctoral Students Make Meaning of Their Experience: A Constructivist Inquiry

Katherine Vahey, Patricia Witkowsky, Jessica Rehling, & Sarun Saifah

University of Northern Colorado

A holistic understanding of the doctoral student experience is needed to improve doctoral student attrition rates and contribute to their degree completion. The findings of this constructivist case study include the importance of mentoring doctoral students, the challenges they face trying to fulfill multiple roles, and the characteristics students attribute to their success. Implications for research and practice are discussed.

In 2007, there were approximately 375,000 doctoral students in the U.S. (U.S. Department of Education, 2007) with more than 40,000 doctoral degrees granted each year (Nerad, 2007; Walker et al., 2008). Of the 42,155 degrees granted in 2004, 8,819 were in life sciences, followed by 6,795 in social sciences, 6,635 in education, 6,049 in physical sciences, 5,776 in mathematics and engineering, 5,476 in humanities, and 2,614 in business and other professional fields (Nerad, 2007). From its 419 doctoral-granting higher education institutions, the U.S. produces the largest number of doctorates of any country in the world (Nerad, 2007). Not only does the U.S. system educate its own citizens, but also it has an impact on the global economy through the training of international students.

Without context, these seemingly impressive numbers would indicate a successful doctoral education system in the U.S. However, the current state of doctoral education is undergoing strict scrutiny as doctoral student attrition rates of upwards of 50% have continued for at least the last decade (Council of Graduate Schools, 2008; Walker et al., 2008). Although doctoral education has been studied since the middle of the twentieth century (Bieber & Worley, 2006), attention to doctoral education has increased dramatically in the past 15 years (Walker et al.). In comparison to the research and practical focus given to the undergraduate student experience at higher education institutions across the nation (Cheatham & Phelps, 1995), research on the doctoral student population and experience is scarce and long overdue (Isaac, Pruitt-Logan, & Upc 1995). Because little is known about the doctoral student experience from a holistic perspective, developing a more comprehensive understanding of it may significantly influence students' success in their pursuit of the doctorate.

The doctoral student experience differs drastically from that of undergraduate students with whom they share campus resources (Pontius & Harper, 2006). Socialization into a profession, dissertation processes, and competing roles and responsibilities are among the unique experiences of the student seeking the terminal degree. Doctoral work challenges the mind, is affected by many facets of life such as emotions, stamina, and finances, and requires an unwavering and absolute dedication (Hadjioannou et al., 2007). High rates of attrition in doctoral education call for attention to the doctoral student experience, which as Smiles (2004) notes can be less than ideal:

> While some might imagine the life of a [doctoral] student as one with certain luxuries, that of sleeping late, hanging out in coffee shops, traveling around the world to conferences and seminars, cashing in on grant money—all in the name of research, the actual image is far from ideal. All those who have stood by a PhD student know the truth—coffee is addictive, the library or lab is often the travel destination, and the grant dollars are difficult to come by.

In addition to understanding the vast differences between the undergraduate experience and the doctoral experience, briefly exploring international doctoral education helps to put the experiences of our participants in a global perspective as well. In general, there are few constants when trying to compare doctoral education throughout the world (Powell & Green, 2007). One of the few "universal givens" is that a doctorate is the highest attainable degree within a program of study and indicates that the recipient is capable of independent scholarship, usually resulting in a piece of work which is publicly defended (Powell & Green, p. 234). However, the purpose of attaining a *professional* doctorate, such as the doctorate of education, (and the potential subsequent career paths) not only differs by country, but also by institution and discipline, making comparison difficult (Powell & Green). Unfortunately, obtaining a doctorate of philosophy (PhD) versus a professional doctorate is valued differently in various countries, and may pressure the doctoral student to focus on obtaining a particular type of degree, rather than finding the program best suited for their field (Powell & Green).

Doctoral students throughout the world face other challenges, such as time to completion of the degree (Powell & Green, 2007), primary instruction in a secondary language such as English (Powell & Green), and financial constraints (Powell & Green; Most, 2008). All of these factors influence the attrition of doctoral students, which varies greatly between countries. For example, South Africa's doctoral completion rate is very low at approximately 12 percent (Powell & Green), while the Netherlands has a completion rate of approximately 70 percent (Bartelse, Oost, & Sonneveld, 2007). The country with the highest completion rate is China with more than 99 percent (Zhuang, 2007), while the U.S. rests in the medium range of 50–60 percent (Denecke, Frasier, & Redd, 2009; National Research Council, 1996; Nerad, 2007), similar to Australia (Evans, 2007) and Canada (Maheu, 2007). Though the U.S. rate is on par with other North American and European countries, attrition remains a concern as we are continually losing students who have been deemed some of the "brightest and most talented in the world" (Denecke, Frasier, & Redd, 2009, p. 36).

As researchers, we acknowledge the similar challenges faced by many types of doctoral degree seekers, however, the scope of this study focuses on the full-time PhD student experience and is limited to degrees offered by a single institution, that is, the one where our study was conducted. Following a review of the literature on the doctoral student experience, we explain the theoretical backgrounds and methods of the study. Findings from individual interviews and a focus group are discussed in depth as well as conclusions about specific patterns and themes identified by participants' experiences. Finally, implications for institutions of higher education are presented, as well as suggestions for further study.

Understanding the Doctoral Student Experience

Understanding the doctoral student experience begins with a purposeful exploration of the aspirations and potential sacrifices of a prospective doctoral student. From the admissions process through the dissertation, doctoral students face unique challenges. Previous researchers have explored various aspects of the doctoral student experience that are of interest to us, including socialization, transition issues, mentorship, and attrition in an attempt to understand the diverse experiences that may contribute to universities' efforts to retain doctoral students.

Socialization

Once admitted to a doctoral program, students can be as confused and anxious as many new undergraduates (Poock, 2004). Doctoral students are faced with the significant challenge of navigating a dual-socialization process involving both graduate study and specific academic disciplines or professions (Austin, 2002; Mendoza, 2007; Poock). While some programs attempt to facilitate this process with an orientation (Poock), doctoral students must adjust to their new environment to be successful (Nesheim et al., 2006). Unfortunately, doctoral student success is not usually viewed as an institutional endeavor, but rather the responsibility of overwhelmed academic departments (Nesheim et al.).

Doctoral education encompasses socialization into both the current roles of a graduate student on campus—teacher and researcher—and the roles and responsibilities of a future faculty member or professional in a specific field (Weidman, Twale, & Stein, 2001). This dual socialization process requires doctoral students to understand the values of academic and professional life both from the point of view of a student and from that of an aspiring faculty member (Weidman et al.). Practically, socialization and success are linked in a positive doctoral student experience (Turner & Thompson, 1993), which includes orientation (Gardner, 2009b; Poock, 2004), research and teaching assistantship experiences (Austin, 2002; Nettles & Millett, 2006), and interaction with peers and faculty (Weidman et al.).

Faculty who take the responsibility of creating positive experiences and learning, both in and out of the classroom, decrease the fragmentation of the graduate student experience, limit their feelings of isolation, improve their social integration, and lower student attrition (Guentzel & Nesheim, 2006). Furthermore, encouraging and supporting a sense of community among doctoral students is an important factor in their completion of the doctorate (Hadjioannou et al, 2007; Hesli, Fink, & Duffy, 2003). Participation in academic communities is fundamental to the transformation of doctoral students into professionals (Hadjioannou et al.; Sweitzer, 2008). As students struggle with anxiety, fear, isolation, and agitation (Golde, 2005; Williams et al., 2005), those who survive are likely to have benefited from the support of their faculty mentors.

Transition Issues

Doctoral students, many of whom have had work experience, enter their programs with a different foundation from which to grow than do undergraduate or master's students. Many programs find doctoral students to be more mature, more able to think critically, more able to handle multiple responsibilities, and to have more well-developed communication and leadership skills (Phillips, 1996). However, along with doctoral students' expected higher level of academic ability comes the assumption that attention need not be given to their personal development during their doctoral student experience (Gardner, 2009b). Nevertheless, despite their higher levels of experience and commitment, graduate students struggle with the transition to doctoral work.

Deciding to pursue a doctoral degree means facing unavoidable life changes in work, finances, living conditions, and school and social relationships (Hesli et al., 2003; Longfield, Romas, & Irwin, 2006). Facing life changes can strain students' self-worth and adaptation to the required role, thus influencing their perception of the experience (Crocker et al., 2002). Developing the ability to adapt and to find balance in their work and life relationships are important early tasks for doctoral students (Golde, 2006).

In an exploration of the challenges doctoral students experience and the orts needed to promote their psychosocial, cognitive, and social identity ~velopment during their journey toward the doctorate, Gardner also (2009b) found students' transition challenging during the initial phase of their programs. Through interviews with 177 doctoral students, transitioning to a new educational environment and leaving one's social network or previous workplace was met with "enthusiasm and trepidation" (Gardner, p. 44). Up to 40% of student attrition is noted to occur during the first year of doctoral education, which places great importance on the need to focus on guiding successful transitions for students (Gardner).

Mentorship

Lack of mentoring by their faculty or others is one of the most significant reasons for doctoral student attrition, while the presence of effective mentoring can counteract the negative aspects of the graduate student experience (Krueger & Peek, 2006). In fact, students who are mentored by faculty or their fellow students typically have more positive perceptions of institutional climate and are more likely to be academically successful (Kelly, 1999). An examination of advising and mentoring in doctoral attrition studies suggests that it is important to look at the quality of the relationships between students and their faculty advisor, and the resulting influence on the doctoral experience (Pontius & Harper, 2006).

Faculty (Mendoza, 2007) and peer mentoring (Rose, 2005) are the most typical forms of mentoring. Good mentoring is developmentally focused (Rose, 2005), that is, it is a "collaborative, dynamic, and creative partnership of co-equals, founded on openness, vulnerability, and the ability of both parties to take risks with one another beyond their professional roles" (Hadjioannou et al, 2007, p. 165). There are five essential aspects to being an effective mentor: (1) providing reliable information, (2) encouraging departmental socializing, (3) advocating for students, (4) serving as a role model, and (5) encouraging professional networking (Rose, 2005). Many graduate students "regard their relationships with faculty as the single most important aspect determining the quality of their graduate experience" (Rose, p. 56). However, when asked who acts as a primary mentor, less than a quarter of the students reported their initially assigned advisor (Rose). As such, faculty can help facilitate student interactions with other faculty on campus to expose them to additional mentors. Peer mentorship has yet to be explored in depth (Gardner, 2009b; Sweitzer, 2008), but the interactions students have with peers, particularly those more advanced in their programs, are thought to have a significant influence on students' development and ultimate success (Weidman, Twale, & Stein, 2001).

Attrition

Unfortunately, a key factor of attrition is the mismatch between student's expectations and the realities of the educational experience (Golde, 2005). For example, many students choose to pursue a doctoral degree to emulate a faculty member who mentored them as undergraduates, only to find an unbalanced faculty life and a tenuous job market for full time, tenure seeking faculty. This perceived dissonance may deter graduate students from striving toward a career as a faculty member (Bieber & Worley, 2006; Golde).

Research suggests that there is little to no academic difference between students who persist and those who drop out (Smallwood, 2004), though departments often place an increased focus on the inabilities of the departing student rather than on potential problems in the educational environment (Golde, 2005). Scholars and practitioners need to explore other factors that have an impact on student attrition and address how tailoring doctoral student services to address these needs might increase graduate students' persistence and satisfaction (Rose, 2005). Attrition rates ranging from approximately 40% to 50% (Golde; Walker et al., 2008) demonstrate the perilous nature of the pursuit of the doctorate. Unfortunately, the loss of students can be fiscally detrimental to the academic program and institution (Gardner, 2009b). Student attrition also has an impact on the morale of students who remain in the program. Knowing how to enhance the learning environment appropriately might foster healthy socialization (Hadjioannou et al., 2007), successful transition (Hesli et al., 2003; Hyun, Quinn, Madon, & Lustig, 2006), and strong mentorship (Kelly, 1999; Kluever, 1997).

Attrition rates may also be related to the fact that many graduate classrooms look strikingly different than they did 50 years ago due to the diversification of doctoral students. The graduate student population now consists of students from all genders, racial/ethnic minorities, sexual orientations, abilities, ages, and nations of origin (Brus, 2006; Walker et al., 2008). Despite the increase in the visibility of women and U.S. minorities in doctoral education, experiences of continued discrimination may explain why these students have higher attrition rates than their white peers (Lovitts, 2001). Attributing attrition to a lack of academic aptitude (Gansemer-Topf, Ross, & Johnson, 2006; Haworth, 1996) detracts from far more likely factors, such as, "student frustration with academic policies and procedures, student disappointment with program offerings and faculty advising, and student experiences with an inhospitable department climate" (Haworth, p. 94).

Structural and cultural aspects of doctoral education have been explored in relationship to attrition (Gardner, 2009a). In interviews with 60 doctoral students and 34 faculty members from six departments at a single institution, the findings demonstrate differences between faculty and students in their perceptions of why students do not persist and attain a degree (Gardner). Faculty reasons included, (1) students' lack of ability, both in motivation and academic aptitude, (2) personal problems often related to mental health, and (3) a misunderstanding of their professional goals (Gardner). While graduate students agreed personal problems often contributed to other students' departure, they attributed students' reasons for leaving more often to outside responsibilities than to mental health issues (Gardner). Students also mentioned (1) programmatic issues, such as poor advising, (2) financial concerns, (3) faculty mismatch, (4) politics, and (5) graduate school not being a good fit for certain students (Gardner). Clearly, the reasons for doctoral student attrition are multi-faceted and perceived differently by various constituents involved in doctoral education (Gardner).

Most of the research on doctoral education addresses the environment in which graduate students find themselves. Thus, this study was designed to explore what it means to be a doctoral student, to understand how doctoral students process the meaning of their experience from the point of view of graduate students themselves, and to contribute a fresh perspective to the discussion.

Methodology

Based on constructivist theory (Crotty, 1998), the case study approach (Merriam, 1998) used in this research project seeks to understand how doctoral students at an undergraduate-focused institution make meaning of their educational experience. Thus, our research poses the question, "How do doctoral students make meaning of their experience?" Our question is important because from a constructivist point of view how "participants construct their reality and understand the meaning they make of it are important elements in research" (Schwartz, Donovan, & Guido-DiBrito, 2009, p. 7). A constructivist paradigm is appropriate when exploring complex human phenomenon (Broido & Manning, 2002). At its foundation, constructivist research is value-bound (Guido-DiBrito et al., 2008); that is, it is impossible for the researchers to separate themselves from the research and research participants because values and biases are present throughout the research process (Mertens, 1998). Knowledge in a constructivist approach is "co-constructed" by participants and researchers (Creswell, 2007). We found this to be an appropriate framework given that the researchers and participants share the commonality of being full-time doctoral students.

Using a case study method, we focused on the doctoral student experience in the bounded system of a mid-sized, undergraduate-focused university with some graduate programs in the western United States (Creswell, 2007). It is an instrumental case study because it "is less about the case itself and more directed toward understanding of an issue" (Jones, Torres, & Arminio, 2006, p.

55). Because the attempt is to discover the experience of doctoral students, diversity in participant sampling is required to contribute to a broader understanding of the issue (Merriam, 1998). Thus, interview data from a diverse sample of doctoral students helped to share our findings, along with a case description and case-based themes.

Institutional Context

This exploration of the doctoral student experience occurred at a four-year, undergraduate-focused university. During the fall of 2008, graduate students comprised approximately 19% (2,389) of the 12,4978 on-campus student population. Of the 2,389 graduate students, 18.7% (446 students) were doctoral students from one of the institution's four colleges (Performing and Visual Arts, Education and Behavioral Sciences, Natural and Health Sciences, and Humanities and Social Sciences) (Institutional Fact Book, 2009). Academic and student support services available at the institution are focused on the undergraduate student population, which may contribute to the experience of doctoral students at the university.

Selection of Participants

The researchers intentionally sought out participants to obtain a diverse sample using purposeful sample techniques (Patton, 2002). Each of the four researchers individually recruited two doctoral students to participate in the study. At the time of this study, the eight participants were pursuing their doctoral degrees full-time in various academic areas, including education, behavioral sciences, sports administration, and music. Five of the participants identified as Caucasian, one as African-American, and two were international students. Three of the participants were women, four had children, and all identified as heterosexual. The age of doctoral students ranged from 27-54 years of age. The scope of our study did not address religious affiliation or ability level. Although we sought doctoral students who openly identified as gay, lesbian, bisexual, or transgender (GLBT) through contacts with peers, faculty, and the GLBTA Resource Office, we were unable to find willing participants.

The researchers instituted two primary limits to narrow the scope of this study: (1) to interview only full-time doctoral students, and (2) to interview doctoral students in current programs only from the single four-year, undergraduate-focused university used in this study. Since four colleges at this university offer doctoral degrees (Performing and Visual Arts, Education and Behavioral Sciences, Natural and Health Sciences, and Humanities and Social Sciences), the researchers did not seek participants working toward varied types of doctoral degrees not offered at this institution, including doctoral students of medicine or divinity. Similarly the researchers chose to interview only full-time time doctoral students to better understand the holistic experience of participants who identify as a student in their primary professional role. While part-time time doctoral students may have similar characteristics and face similar challenges, the researchers sought to have all full-time doctoral students as participants. As the four researchers are also full-time doctoral students, for a constructivist study, this delimitation is methodologically consistent.

Role of Researchers

The four researchers are doctoral students in a Higher Education and Student Affairs Leadership program, which focuses on leadership, research, and social justice. Learning more about the doctoral student experience inter-ests us because of the unique, challenging, understudied, and diverse experi-ences of doctoral students. As second-year doctoral students, we each have unique experiences. Three of the four researchers are White U.S. females and one is a Thai male, who maintains his Thai citizenship. The researchers are in their late-20s or early 30s, are unmarried, and do not have children. All are full-time students who have completed a master's degree, with the female re-searchers holding graduate assistantships, and the male researcher supported through a fellowship. Our interest in the study arose as we witnessed various experiences among our peers and ourselves.

As fitting to a constructivist study, the researchers were integrally in-volved in the data collection forming relationships with the participants and together, meaning was made in the shared doctoral student experience. Each of the four researchers individually interviewed the two participants they iden-tified for this study. One researcher served as the lead facilitator during the focus group while the other three took notes and assisted with logistics.

Autoethnography is an expanding methodology in the field of qualitative research. Although this study does not specifically employ autoethnographic methods, such as doctoral students researching a population of which we are a part, we possess a positionality not held by most other researchers of this topic. We are able to contribute to the literature about the doctoral student experience in a unique way because of participants' openness to peers as researchers. Additionally, the themes highlighted in the research parallel our experiences, further validating the findings.

Data Collection Techniques and Procedures

After initial identification of participants, the doctoral student participants read and signed a consent form outlining the voluntary nature of their participa-tion, the assurance of the confidentiality of their identities through the use of pseudonyms, and the time commitment. Students participated in one individual interview lasting approximately 60 minutes. The semi-structured interviews al-lowed the researchers to deviate from a set of pre-determined questions to explore participants' initial responses in more depth. Interview questions explored students' educational background, as well as the positive and negative aspects of their doctoral experience. Researchers transcribed the data following their two interviews and shared the data electronically with fellow researchers.

A 90-minute focus group with four of the participants was conducted as a member check and follow-up to the individual interviews allowing the participants to uncover similarities and differences in their experiences, as well as brainstorm ideas for improving their doctoral student experience. Although rich data can be obtained from individual interviews, the use of a focus group in this study provided an opportunity for the participants to interact with other doctoral students and to use the guided questions to further explore ideas they may not have thought about on their own (Krueger & Casey, 2000). One researcher facilitated the focus group, while the other three researchers took notes on themes emerging from the exchange of ideas. The focus group was digitally audiotaped and transcribed for use in the data analysis stage of the research.

Data Analysis

To remain consistent with the tenets of constructivist research, the recordings of the interviews were transcribed by the interviewer and shared with all members of the research team. Following the review of the individual interviews, the four researchers came together to share their understanding of the data and determine emerging themes used to guide the focus group inquiry. Conflicting data and frequent themes provided the framework for the focus group questions. Following the focus groups, which all members of the research team attended, the transcription was completed and reviewed by the researchers, thus providing further depth to the initial patterns seen in the individual interview data.

Following immersion in the data through another comprehensive review of the transcripts (Marshall & Rossman, 2006), each member of the research team individually developed themes and then came together to negotiate the final themes, mentorship, role conflict, and characteristics of success, represented in this text to reflect the researchers' shared understanding of the data (Glesne, 2006). This inductive approach to data analysis allowed for discovering themes and patterns through participants' voices (Patton, 2002). Further, the differing perspectives of the researchers engaged in the development of the themes promoted the rigor of the study. The representation of the findings described the participants and the setting, analyzed the commonalities and anomalies, and finally interpreted the findings to provide practical knowledge for faculty and administrators who work with doctoral students (Wolcott, 1994).

Trustworthiness

Trustworthiness, which includes credibility, transferability, dependability, and confirmability (Lincoln & Guba, 1985), is dependent upon the implementation of various techniques employed throughout the research process to ensure quality (Creswell, 2007; Jones, Torres, & Arminio, 2006). As doctoral students ourselves, we are immersed in the environment of our undergraduate-focused university. Although the sample was comprised of doctoral students possessing some demographic characteristics different from those of the researchers, the extensive exposure to the university as doctoral students contributes to our ability to have "prolonged engagement in the field" (Creswell, p. 203), thus establishing credibility (Lincoln & Guba; Shank, 2006). Also contributing to credibility is the member-checking process by which the focus group partici-pants reviewed preliminary findings. To develop transferability of the study's findings and conclusions for readers, "thick description" (Creswell, p. 204) pro-vides information about the setting of the case, as well as the backgrounds of the participants. Finally, dependability and confirmability were established through auditing, that is, a procedure in which the researchers kept detailed notes about how decisions were made and how we were affected in the process of con-ducting the research (Lincoln & Guba; Shank).

Authenticity

The five components of authenticity include fairness and ontological, edu-cative, catalytic, and tactical authenticity (Lincoln & Guba, 2000). The inclu-sion of perspectives from each of the members of the diverse sample within this case study represented fairness as we sought "to act with energy to ensure that all voices in the inquiry effort [had] a chance to be represented in any texts" (Lincoln & Guba, p. 180). By reflecting on their experiences, partici-pants gained an increased understanding of their journey toward a doctoral degree, thus promoting ontological and educative authenticity. Recommenda-tions for change emerged from the data, thus upholding catalytic authenticity. Tactically, the goal of the research is to share our findings with members of the U.S. educational community through publication. The impact of this research was considered throughout the process to ensure that it would be appropriate in terms of its recommendations (Shank, 2006).

Overview of Participants

The findings of our study were developed from the experiences shared by the eight participants, who are identified in this document under pseudonyms. A description of each of the participants is necessary to understand the context of the meaning they make of their doctoral student experience. Rachel, a White, married, 51-year old mother of two grown children, transferred to the Univer-sity from another institution to finish her degree in Education. Suma, also 51 years old, is an international student in Psychology and has two high school-age children with her in the U.S. Also a Psychology doctoral student, Kevin is a married White male. Jay, in his late twenties, is an international student and studies Sport and Exercise Science. Adam is a married, White male in the same program as Jay, and has a young daughter. Miles is a married, middle-aged, Black male studying in the area of Music. Charles, a Caucasian student in his mid-twenties, single and without dependents, is pursuing a degree in Neuropsychology. Jane has similar demographics characteristics to Charles as a Caucasian, single, mid-twenties student, but is studying Science Education. Figure 1 provides a summary of the study participants.

Emergent Themes

Following the interviews and focus group, three themes emerged: faculty mentorship, role conflict, and characteristics of success. Faculty mentorship influenced the participants' academic and personal satisfaction with their educational and individual experience. Respondents expressed challenges associated with their multiple roles outside of doctoral student responsibilities. Finally, participants reflected on personal characteristics that aided their success in their doctoral programs.

Mentorship

Mentorship of doctoral students from faculty contributes to students' transition process, academic progress, and ability to address challenges that arise. The following quotation reflects how one participant, Rachel, valued the mentorship she received as a doctoral student: "I think my experience is that those mentors, good mentors are able to, walk that path with you and transition with you."

Jay, a student from Southeast Asia, mentioned his relationship with his advisor is much like a marriage. Their relationship is an essential part of his

Figure 1. Summary of Study Participants

Participants	Program	Age	Ethnicity/Citizenship	Marital Status	Dependents
Rachel	Education	51	White	Married	2 grown children
Suma	Psychology	51	International (African)	Single	2 dependent children
Kevin	Psychology	late 20's	White	Married	
Jay	Sport & Exercise Science	late 20's	International (Asian)	Single	
Adam	Sport & Exercise Science	early 30's	White	Married	1 child
Miles	Music	middle-aged	Black	Married	Children
Charles	Neuro-psychology	mid-20's	White	Single	
Jane	Science Education	mid-20's	White	Single	

doctoral experience and he feels that it has had a strong influence on his development and the outcome of his professional and personal goals. He reflected:

> I believe that regardless of your program, your educational level, or when you are in the program, you are unofficially married [to] your advisor and the relationship with your advisor must be a good combination.

Suma stated that a mentor could provide advice on curriculum and research issues. Mentors can facilitate doctoral students' growth, development, thinking, and problem-solving skills. She reported:

> Maybe, as soon as the graduate student, especially the PhD student, comes in to the university, they should be assigned a professor. Kind of being a mentor for research purposes…Not only as the supervisor but someone you work with on her own work so that you actually learn from them. I know that the supervisor should already be helping you, but sometimes that is not the case.

Jane believes her research advisor is also her mentor and plays an enormous role in her doctoral education. Advisors or mentors' role in professional life are evident, but out-of-class activities also influence her education and progress towards the doctoral degree. She stated:

> [My advisor] is also like my mentor and my friend and everything. She pushed me. She allowed me to get out of my comfort zone. I am really grade oriented and I needed to get an A all the time. She kept saying that it is ok to get a B as long as you're learning something.

Mentoring can assist doctoral students in advancing learning about their discipline, navigating their field of research, and refining necessary skills needed to conduct research and practice their profession. A mentor also supports doctoral students in purposefully developing their research focuses. Adam explained: "I've always gravitated toward the person who says 'Let's get it focused, Adam, and now you run with it.' And I think that's just good mentoring."

The active involvement of mentors is one of the most pivotal aspects of a fulfilling doctoral educational experience. Mentors' genuine concern for doctoral students appears to be reflected in students' educational success and internal drive. Participants stressed the importance of ongoing mentoring programs, which often provide needed support services for doctoral students. This finding supports the well-known idea of faculty members serving necessary roles in the lives of doctoral students as both advisors and mentors in their development as researchers and professionals (Lovitts, 2001). However, students did not mention the influence of peers, other faculty, university administrators, family, or friends, which have also been found to contribute to their development (Sweitzer, 2008).

Role Conflict

Doctoral students have concerns— such as financial and family responsibilities—beyond their ability to complete their degree requirements, which cause further challenges. The multiple responsibilities and roles of doctoral students require effective stress and time management skills to ensure a positive experience. For doctoral students within the academy, Adam shares how conflicting roles occur when priorities of teaching and learning are not well balanced.

> But [teaching] could be overwhelming because it's 'here's your job and you prioritize how you want,' so it could go teaching, and then your classes and then your research, and if you keep that order too long, you're kind of scrambling around...what am I really doing here? Am I an instructor or am I a student?

Miles also recognized the difficulty of balancing being a student and teacher, along with supporting oneself and family financially by stating, "There are so many different hats you have to fill, and I think that it could be streamlined in a way to make things a little easier." Although the roles are challenging, Adam sees them positively as well as he says "so you teach quite a bit, and juggling being a teacher and being a student and a father and all these different things are difficult and challenging, but exciting as well."

As adult learners, doctoral students frequently have multiple responsibilities outside their academic and teaching roles. The role of spouse or parent commonly affects educational demands and responsibilities and has been found to contribute to attrition (Gardner, 2009a). As a husband, Kevin recognized that "it's very time consuming being committed to another person." While some students delay having children until they have completed their degree, many doctoral students are juggling the role of parent with their role as a student. As Suma explained,

> Another experience I have come across is that being a mother is something else. I brought my two kids [from my native country]. I thought I understood what I would do and how I would do it. But, I find myself overwhelmed right now by the kids because the kids need attention.

Miles agreed by stating "when you have children, you don't have the luxury of staying in the library all day, all night. You have to really make time for them even when you know you should be studying."

Understanding the importance of multiple roles is necessary to be successful in all aspects of life as a doctoral student, both those related to and separate from the ultimate goal of completion of their degree. For Adam, balance is the key, "I guess it goes back to balance. Be willing to try to balance the different things out, as a doctoral student...whether it be family, or more work, or working with more people, or more teaching duties, or all the above."

Characteristics of Success

Our participants identified similar characteristics to describe their own motivation to pursue a doctoral degree. They also offered advice to other individuals who are considering the pursuit of the doctorate on how to succeed. Some dynamics related to participants' personal motivation to complete the doctorate overlapped with other thematic findings, including striving to use knowledge for greater community action, believing that teaching is rewarding, and seeking to reach career goals as college level teachers.

In regards to the factors influencing a participant's decision to go into a doctoral program, Rachel noted "I have a definite desire to make a difference, especially in impacting policy to effect change." Kevin mirrored Rachel's thoughts in the focus group by saying "I love teaching, that's my biggest love, and the college environment." Charles articulated the value of positive support in faculty mentorship by stating, "When you're treated more like a peer… I think that promotes people in their creative thinking, and being more comfortable to do your best research." In his individual interview, Adam discussed the importance of having his children see him as "a father that is doing what he wants to do" as motivation for completing his educational goal. All participants expressed the importance of family support and keeping in mind the long-term benefits of achieving the doctoral degree as a significant source of motivation. In offering advice for individuals considering pursuit of the doctorate, Adam suggested students keep an "…open mind with all the information you're going to receive from your program. However, be focused…go and learn what you can from all your course work, but do have somewhat of a focus because it's hard to bring it all together in the end."

A few of the participants verbalized the difficulty of the doctoral endeavor, the inevitable sacrifices involved, and the ease with which you can get distracted without remaining cognizant of the ultimate goal of using the doctoral degree to promote positive change in society and the lives of individuals. The findings of Gardner's (2009a) study echoed the need for motivation and a clear purpose for pursuing the doctorate as both faculty and student participants noted lacking such attributes as potential causes of attrition.

Implications for Practice and Future Research

This study provides insight into the varied experiences doctoral students have with faculty mentorship, role conflict, and characteristics necessary for success. Armed with a better understanding of the importance mentorship plays in the lives of students, the role conflicts they face, and the characteristics they see as imperative for success, administrators, faculty, and student affairs practitioners may have deeper insights into the doctoral student experience. Implications for the practice of faculty and administrators are discussed, as well as directions for future research.

When faculty and staff understand the needs of their students, they can make positive changes to better support them. For example, a recurring struggle of conflicting roles among participants was balancing their student status with a teaching assistant (TA) position. The pressure and desire to teach and develop professionally often competes with other priorities of classes, family, and personal wellbeing. Since TAs are often overseen by faculty, supervisors who are aware that a student may have trouble finding an adequate life balance can play a pivotal role in reducing the student's stress. Support for TAs can come in the form of developmental supervision, regular solicitation of feedback, and consistent personal follow up. Faculty members are not the only ones responsible for finding better ways to support doctoral students; collaborative institutional support is necessary. Calls for collaboration are widespread in higher education (Kezar, 2003) and utilizing the expertise of student affairs professionals to support doctoral students can contribute to bridging the long-standing gap between student affairs and academic affairs. When the university community takes responsibility for providing support for all levels of students, all members of the campus community can benefit. After all, many doctoral students are the next generation of leaders and educators in our institutions of higher education.

This study focused on the experience of participants at the time of their interviews, so conducting a longitudinal study might provide further insight into their experience. Additionally, all participants were full-time students, though many doctoral students pursue their degree part-time. Thus, conducting additional research on the experiences of part-time doctoral students could yield different findings. Similar research could prompt an increase in discourse regarding how programs identify the needs of their doctoral students and support their education, moving beyond purely academic support to a holistic support network addressing life issues such as finances and time management. Discussion could begin with those who find the attrition of their students not representative of the students' academic ability and with efforts to identify what measures that faculty and the administrators could take to reduce attrition in the own programs. Benefits could come from future research that stimulates self-reflection for student affairs practitioners who work with doctoral students, whether as supervisors, mentors, or within an institutional support system. As these findings suggest, many doctoral students' struggles fall outside the realm of academics. Improving support to graduate students with varied needs can influence students' experience, which directly impacts available campus resources, and most importantly, a student's decision about continuing their study (Golde, 2005).

The variety of positive and negative experiences expressed by these participants highlights a variety of demands on doctoral students. For some, having a research mentor assigned at admission could be the key to success. For others, persistence and graduation may require flexible faculty who are willing to make accommodations when necessary. Above all, listening to students and identifying their challenges will make it easier to assist this student demographic in their progress toward completion of the achievement of the doctorate. To have the best understanding of doctoral students' concerns and need for support requires increased research and attention to this unique, continually changing, and frequently neglected student population.

References

Austin, A. E. (2002). Preparing the next generation of faculty: Graduate school as socialization to the academic career. *The Journal of Higher Education, 73*(1), 94-122.

Bartelse, J., Oost, H., & Sonneveld, H. (2007). Doctoral education in the Netherlands. In S. Powell & H. Green (Eds.), *The doctorate worldwide* (pp. 64-76). New York: McGraw Hill.

Bieber, J. P., & Worley, L. K. (2006). Conceptualizing the academic life: Graduate students' perspectives. *The Journal of Higher Education, 77* (6), 1009-1035.

Broido, E. M., & Manning, K. (2002). Philosophical foundations and current theoretical perspectives in qualitative research. *Journal of College Student Development, 43,* 434-445.

Brus, C. P. (2006). Seeking balance in graduate school: A realistic expectation or a dangerous dilemma? In M. J. Guentzel & B. E. Nesheim (Eds.), Supporting graduate and professional students: The role of student affairs. *New Directions for Student Services*, no. 115, (pp. 47-58). San Francisco: Jossey-Bass.

Cheatham, H. E., & Phelps, C. E. (1995). Promoting the development of graduate students of color. In M. J. Barr, & M. L. Upcraft (Eds.), Student services for the changing graduate population. *New Directions for Student Services,* no. 72, (pp. 91-99). San Francisco: Jossey-Bass.

Council of Graduate Schools (2008). *PhD completion and attrition: Analysis of baseline program data from the PhD completion project.* Washington, DC: Author.

Creswell, J. W. (2007). *Qualitative inquiry and research design: Choosing among five approaches* (2nd ed.). Thousand Oaks, CA: Sage.

Crocker, J., Sommers, S. R., & Luhtanen, R. K. (2002). Hopes dashes and dreams fulfilled: Contingencies of self-worth and graduate school admissions. *Personality and Social Psychology Bulletin, 28,* 1275-1286.

Crotty, M. (1998). *The foundations of social research: Meaning and perspective in the research process.* Thousand Oaks, CA: Sage.

Denecke, D. D., Frasier, H. S., & Redd, K. E. (2009). The Council of Graduate Schools' PhD completion project. In R. Ehrenberg & C. Kuh (Eds.), *Doctoral education and the faculty of the future* (pp. 35-52). Ithaca, NY: Cornell University Press.

Evans, B. (2007). Doctoral education in Australia. In S. Powell & H. Green (Eds.), *The doctorate worldwide* (pp. 105-119). New York: McGraw Hill.

Gansemer-Topf, A. M., Ross, L. E., & Johnson, R. M. (2006). Graduate and professional student development and student affairs. In M. J. Guentzel & B. E. Nesheim (Eds.),

Supporting graduate and professional students: The role of student affairs. *New tions for Student Services,* no. 115, (pp. 19-30). San Francisco: Jossey-Bass.

Gardner, S. K. (2009a). Student and faculty attributions of attrition in high and low-completing U.S. doctoral programs. *Higher Education, 58,* 97-112.

Gardner, S. K. (2009b). *The development of doctoral students: Phases of challenge and support.* San Francisco: Jossey-Bass.

Glesne, C. (2006). *Becoming qualitative researchers: An introduction* (3rd ed.). Boston: Pearson.

Golde, C. M. (2005). The role of the department and discipline in doctoral student attrition: Lessons from four departments. *Journal of Higher Education, 76,* 669-700.

Golde, C. M. (2006). Beginning graduate school: Explaining first year doctoral student attrition. In M. Anderson (Ed.), The experience of being in graduate school: An exploration. *New Directions for Higher Education,* no. 101, 101-106. San Francisco: Jossey-Bass.

Green, H. & Powell, S. (2007). Introduction. In S. Powell & H. Green (Eds.), *The doctorate worldwide* (pp. 3-16). New York: McGraw Hill.

Guentzel, M. J., & Nesheim, B. E. (2006). Throwing pebbles at Stonehenge: Advocating for graduate and professional students. In M. S. Anderson (Ed.), The experience of being in graduate school: An exploration. *New Directions for Higher Education,* no. 101, 101-106. San Francisco: Jossey-Bass.

Guido-DiBrito, F., Chavez, A. F., & Lincoln, Y. S. (in review). *Some underlying research paradigms for student affairs.*

Hadjioannou, X., Shelton, N. R., Fu, D., & Dhanarattigannon, J. (2007). The Road to a doctoral degree: Co-travelers through a perilous passage. *College Student Journal, 41,* 160-177.

Haworth, J. G. (1996). Assessment of graduate and professional education: Present realities, future prospects. In J. G. Haworth (Ed.), Assessing graduate and professional education: Current realities, future prospects. *New Directions for Institutional Research,* no. 92, (pp. 89-97). San Francisco: Jossey-Bass.

Hesli, V. L., Fink, E. C., & Duffy, D. M. (2003). Mentoring in a positive graduate student experience: *Survey results from the Midwest region, part I. PS: Political Science & Politics,* ONLINE, 457-460.

Hesli, V. L., Fink, E. C., & Duffy, D. M. (2003). Mentoring in a positive graduate student experience: *Survey results from the Midwest region, part II. PS: Political Science & Politics,* ONLINE, 801-804.

Hyun, J. K., Quinn, B. C., Madon, T., & Lustig, S. (2006). Graduate student mental health: Needs assessment and utilization of counseling services. *Journal of College Student Development, 47,* 247-266.

Institutional Fact Book (2006), compiled by The Office of Budget and Institutional Analysis.

Isaac, P. D., Pruitt-Logan, A. S., & Upcraft, M. L. (1995). The landscape of graduate education. In M. J. Barr, & M. L. Upcraft (Eds.), Student services for the changing graduate population. *New Directions for Student Services,* no. 72, (pp. 13-21). San Francisco: Jossey-Bass.

Jones, S. R., Torres, V., & Arminio, J. (2006). *Negotiating the complexities of qualitative research in higher education: Fundamental elements and issues.* New York: Routledge.

Kelly, S. (1999). Mentoring within a graduate school setting. *College Student Journal, 33.* Retrieved March 7, 2008 from http://findarticles.com/p/articles/mi_m0FCR/is_1_33/ai_62894066/pg_1.

Kezar, A. (2003). Enhancing innovative partnerships: Creating a change model for academic and student affairs collaboration. *Innovative Higher Education, 28*(2), 137-156.

Kluever, R. C. (1997). Students' attitudes toward the responsibilities and barriers in doctoral study. In L. F. Goodchild, K. E. Green, E. L. Katz, & R. C. Kluever (Eds.), Rethinking the dissertation process: Tackling personal and institutional obstacles. *New Directions for Higher Education, no. 99*, (pp. 47-56). San Francisco: Jossey-Bass.

Krueger, P. M., & Peek, L. A. (2006). Figuring it out: A conversation about how to complete your PhD *College Student Journal, 40*, 149-157.

Krueger, R. A., & Casey, M. A. (2000). *Focus groups: A practical guide for applied research* (3rd ed.). Thousand Oaks, CA: Sage.

Lincoln, Y. S., & Guba, E. G. (1985). *Naturalistic inquiry.* Newbury Park, CA: Sage.

Lincoln, Y. S., & Guba E. G. (2000). Paradigmatic controversies, contradictions, and emerging confluences. In N. K. Denzin & Y. S. Lincoln (Eds.). *Handbook of qualitative research* (2nd ed., pp. 163-188). Thousand Oaks, CA: Sage.

Longfield, A., Romas, J., & Irwin, J. (2006). The self-worth, physical and social activities of graduate students: A qualitative study. *College Student Journal, 40*, 282-292.

Lovitts, B. E. (2001). *Leaving the ivory tower: The causes and consequences of departure from doctoral study.* Lanham, MD: Rowman & Littlefield.

Mahue, L. (2007). Doctoral education in Canada: A valued national product facing the challenges of institutional differentiation. In S. Powell & H. Green (Eds.), *The doctorate worldwide* (pp. 120-132). New York: McGraw Hill.

Marshall, C., & Rossman, G. B. (2006). *Designing qualitative research* (4th ed.). Thousand Oaks, CA: Sage.

Mendoza, P. (2007). Academic capitalism and doctoral student socialization: A case study. *Journal of Higher Education, 78*, 71-96.

Merriam, S. (1998). *Qualitative research and case study applications in education..* San Francisco: Jossey-Bass.

Mertens, D. M. (1998). *Research methods in education and psychology: Integrating diversity with quantitative and qualitative approaches.* Thousand Oaks, CA: Sage.

Most, D. (2008). Patterns of doctoral student degree completion: A longitudinal analysis. *Journal of College Student Retention, 10*(2), 171-190.

National Research Council (NRC). (1996). *The path to the PhD: Measuring graduate attrition in the sciences and humanities.* Washington, DC: National Academy Press.

Nerad, M. (2007). Doctoral education in the USA. In S. Powell & H. Green (Eds.), *The doctorate worldwide* (pp.133-140). New York: McGraw Hill.

Nesheim, B. E., Guentzel, M. J., Gansemer-Topf, A. M., Ross, L. E., & Turrentine, C. G. (2006). If you want to know, ask: Assessing the needs and experiences of graduate students. In M. J. Guentzel & B. E. Nesheim (Eds.), Supporting graduate and professional students: The role of student affairs. *New Directions for Student Services, no. 115*, (pp. 5-17). San Francisco: Jossey-Bass.

Nettles, M. T., & Millett, C. M. (2006). *Three magic letters: Getting to PhD. Baltimore*, MD: Johns Hopkins University Press.

Patton, M. (2002). *Qualitative research and evaluation methods* (3rd ed.). Newbury Park, CA: Sage.

Phillips, D. G. (1996). A grounded theory model of adult doctoral student progression [Abstract]. Retrieved 4 March 2008 from ProQuest File database.

Pontius, J. L., & Harper, S. R. (2006). Principles for good practice in graduate and professional student engagement. In M. J. Guentzel & B. E. Nesheim (Eds.), Supporting graduate and professional students: The role of student affairs. *New Directions for Student Services, no. 115*, (pp. 47-58). San Francisco: Jossey-Bass.

Poock, M. C. (2004). Graduate student orientation practices: Results from a national survey. *NASPA Journal, 41*, 470-486.

Powell, S. & Green, H. (2007). Conclusions. In S. Powell & H. Green (Eds.), *The doctorate worldwide* (pp. 231-260). New York: McGraw Hill.

Rose, G. L. (2005). Group differences in graduate students' concepts of the ideal mentor. *Research in Higher Education, 46*, 53-80.

Schwartz, J., Donovan, J., & Guido-DiBrito, F. (2009). Stories of social class: Self-identified Mexican male college students crack the silence. *Journal of College Student Development*.

Shank, G. D. (2006). *Qualitative research: A personal skills approach* (2nd ed.). Upper Saddle River, NJ: Pearson.

Smallwood, S. (2004, January 16). Doctor dropout. *Chronicle of Higher Education, 50*, A10.

Smiles, R. V. (2004). All in the name of research. *Black Issues in Higher Education, 21*, 11.

Sweitzer, V. L. (2008). Networking to develop a professional identity: A look at the first-semester experience of doctoral students in business. In C. L. Colbeck, K. O'Meara, & A. E. Austin (Eds.), Educating integrated professionals: Theory and practice on preparation for the professoriate. *New Directions for Teaching and Learning, no. 113,* (pp. 43-56). San Francisco: Jossey-Bass.

Turner, C. S. V., & Thompson, J. R. (1993). Socializing women doctoral students: Minority and majority experiences. *The review of higher education, 16*(3), 355-370.

U.S. Department of Education (2007). Digest of education statistics: 2006. Retrieved October 25, 2007, from http://nces.ed.gov/programs/digest/d06/tables/dt06_251.asp?referrer=report

Walker, G. E., Golde, C. M., Jones, L., Bueschel, A. C., & Hutchings, P. (2008). *The formation of scholars: Rethinking doctoral education for the twenty-first century.* San Francisco: Jossey-Bass.

Weidman, J., Twale, D., & Stein, E. (2001). *Socialization of graduate and professional students in higher education.* San Francisco: Jossey-Bass.

Williams, M. R., Brewley, D. N., Reed, R. J., White, D. Y., & Davis-Haley, R. T. (2005). Learning to read each other: Black female graduate students share their experiences at a white research I institution. *The Urban Review, 37*, 181-199.

Wolcott, H. F. (1994). Transforming qualitative data: Description, analysis, and interpretation. Thousand Oaks, CA: Sage.

Zhuang, L. (2007). Doctoral education in China. In S. Powell & H. Green (Eds.), *The doctorate worldwide* (pp. 155-167). New York: McGraw Hill.

Katherine Vahey is in the final stage of writing her dissertation on workplace professional development training for student affairs practitioners for the Higher Education and Student Affairs Leadership (HESAL) doctoral program at the

University of Northern Colorado. She is currently working as the Coordinator for Cultural Programs with the Student Involvement, Activities, and Leadership Development Office at the University of Colorado-Boulder.

Patricia Witkowsky holds a Ph.D. in Higher Education and Student Affairs Leadership from the University of Northern Colorado. She currently serves as the Student Affairs Program Manager at Colorado State University-Pueblo.

Jessica Rehling is a doctoral student of Higher Education and Student Affairs Leadership at the University of Northern Colorado. She currently works as an Area Coordinator in University Housing at Georgia College.

Sarun Saifah is Ph.D candidate from Higher Education and Student Affairs Leadership at University of Northern Colorado. He is working as Assistant Director of Planning and Development Division at Kasem Bundit University, Bangkok Thailand.

Chapter 2

Instructional Concerns of Kinesiology Basic Instruction Program Graduate Teaching Assistants

Jared A. Russell
Auburn University

This descriptive research study used the Teacher Concern Questionnaire to examine the instructional concerns of GTAs who teach in basic instruction programs (BIPs) maintained by the graduate academic programs in the American Academy of Kinesiology and Physical Education (AAKPE). The survey examined general demographic characteristics, identified GTAs' instructional concerns and perspectives, and determined whether demographic characterizes affected the ranking of GTAs' instructional concerns. Prominent concerns included, (a) motivating unengaged students and (b) finding support and respect for quality teaching from faculty. Conclusions shed light on relevant GTA perspectives regarding instructional concerns related to the instruction of college-aged students.

Historically, graduate teaching assistants (GTAs) have been employed by graduate academic programs in varied instructional capacities within higher education settings (Russell, 2008; Wulff & Austin, 2004). GTA instructional roles and responsibilities have evolved in accordance with the ever-changing social mission of the universities in which they are employed (Prieto & Meyers, 2001). Instructional responsibilities can be as diverse as proctoring course exams, leading discussion and lecture groups under the supervision of a professor, and/or assuming teacher-of-record status and full accountability of course offerings (Meyers, 2001; Russell & Chepyator-Thomson, 2004). A graduate teaching assistantship affords many valuable benefits to both the graduate student and his or her respective graduate academic program. For the GTA, the graduate teaching assistantship can provide a substantial means for financing graduate studies, possibly obtaining a tuition waiver, and allow the individual to acquire meaningful "on-the-job" training in preparation for a future career in higher education. For the graduate academic department, the graduate teaching assistantship allows for the effective management of faculty course loads as well as the possibility of increasing course offerings for the respective academic program's student body. Lastly, the graduate teaching assistantship's financial benefits and inherent opportunities for faculty mentorship serve as a recruiting tool for kinesiology graduate academic programs to lure prospective talented graduate students to their respective programs.

Basic instruction programs (BIPs), also known as service or physical activity programs, have played a critical role in providing college-aged students with opportunities to acquire sport-related skills and conceptual knowledge relevant to promoting their involvement in lifelong physical activity and the establishment of individual healthy lifestyle habits (Hensley, 2000; Leenders, Sherman, & Ward, 2003). BIPs motivate college-aged students to be physically active across their lifetimes through course offerings such as weight training, bowling, wellness, stress reduction, yoga, and basketball.

GTAs are essential to the delivery of this instructional content because they are regularly employed as the sole teacher-of-record for BIP courses. Considerable research has examined various organizational, structural, and administrative aspects of BIPs (Mondello, Fleming, & Focht, 2000; Pennington, Manross, & Poole, 2001; Russell, 2006; Russell 2008). There is a need for inquiry specifically focused on GTA instructional development, support, and socialization processes. Existing research, within and outside of the academic field of kinesiology, clearly indicates that GTAs' instructional effectiveness and overall confidence as teachers are greatly improved when graduate academic programs provide appropriate, consistent, formal and systematic instructional support, mentorship, and evaluation (Russell & Chepyator-Thomson, 2004; Savage & Sharpe, 1998). The purpose of this research is to examine the instructional concerns of GTAs who teach in BIPs maintained by American Academy of Kinesiology and Physical Education (AAKPE)graduate academic programs. It is hoped that by obtaining and disseminating this information, graduate academic programs—particularly in the academic field of kinesiology—might (1) better conceptualize and implement instructional development processes within their respective programs that will assist their respective GTAs in the improvement of their teaching effectiveness, and (2) better prepare graduates for a career as future faculty in academia.

Research Purposes and Questions

Research focusing on the experiences of kinesiology GTAs can provide critical insight into their roles and functions in basic instruction program settings. Careful research and analysis of the instructional concerns of GTAs is important to determine appropriate methods of training graduate students to do their duties effectively. Because institutions of higher education are often dependent on GTAs to deliver undergraduate courses, their training as instructors must be viewed as important in order to ensure the quality of undergraduate instruction. This research project examined the instructional concerns of GTAs who teach in BIPs maintained by graduate academic programs in the American Academy of Kinesiology and Physical Education (AAKPE). The study had three primary goals: (1) to survey the general demographic characteristics of GTAs in basic instruction programs (BIPs), (2) to identify their instructional concerns and their perspectives on their teaching roles and environments, and (3) to determine whether demographic characteristics affected the ranking of instructional concerns about their teaching responsibilities. Five research questions provided direction for this study:

1. What are the demographics of GTAs within basic instruction programs?
2. Based on George's (1978) Teacher Concern Questionnaire (TCQ), in what order are GTA instructional concerns ranked in degree of concern?
3. Were there any statistically significant differences between the GTAs' responses to the TCQ based on critical variables such as terms of experience, program of study, degree aspirations, gender, having teacher certification, formal teaching experience?
4. What concerns do kinesiology GTAs have about their teaching responsibilities?
5. What recommendations do kinesiology GTAs have for improving their instructional development and support in light of expressed concerns?

Methods

Participants

Participants were GTAs (N = 504) employed to teach in the BIP of their respective programs by graduate academic programs listed in the American Academy of Kinesiology and Physical Education (AAKPE) Doctoral Program Information directory. Table 2 (see Appendix) provides the participants' general demographic characteristics. Participant recruitment was conducted through an invitation and information letter which was sent by e-mail to the department heads and graduate program officers of the 61 respective graduate academic programs listed in the directory. E-mail and accompanying documents explained the overall goal of the research, presented proof of Institutional Review Board (IRB) approval, and provided directions to facilitate the research. More specifically, the letter asked that the provided information be passed on to the faculty or staff member(s) responsible for GTA instructional development and supervision. The information packet provided the web-address of the on-line anonymous questionnaire. Lastly, the author asked that a reply be sent by either the department head or GTA supervisor or BIP coordinator confirming whether or not the respective graduate academic program would assist in the research project.

Instrumentation

In order to investigate the instructional concerns of the GTAs, the researcher utilized an instrument comprised of three sections. Section one consisted of questionnaire items that identified demographic and background participant information. The GTAs were asked to provide information including their gender, age, racial/ethnic background, current program of study, formal teaching experience, current degree program, number of students per course taught, terms of experience as a GTA, and courses taught. Section two was comprised of two qualitative-based open-ended questionnaire items that sought to identify the GTAs' instructional concerns and recommendations relevant to their assistantship responsibilities. Participants were asked to provide a written statement of the primary and secondary instructional concerns that had impact on their teaching. Secondly, participants were asked to provide recommendations for their respective graduate programs regarding enhancing relevant instructional support and development processes. The goal of this specific item was to add depth and understanding to information obtained quantitatively.

Section three utilized George's (1978) Teacher Concerns Questionnaire (TCQ). The complete instrument can be found in Table 1 (see Appendix (A). The TCQ is considered a valid and useful instrument for identifying teacher concerns and perspectives within the academic field of education (Capal, 2001; Torre & Casanova, 2008; Watzke, 2007). Three types of concerns are identified by the instrument: Self-centered concerns, Task-centered concerns, and Impact-centered concerns. A five-point scale was used to determine GTAs' levels of concern with the scale choices ranging from, "Not Concerned" on one end to "Extremely Concerned" on the other. All of the survey items were analyzed similarly. The "Self" category consisted of seven items: questions 3, 7, 9, 13, and 15. The "Task" category consisted of questions: 1, 2, 5, 10, and 14. The last category "Impact" had the following questions: 4, 6, 8, 11, and 12. Table 1 (see Appendix) provides a break-down of each category of questions. Reliability of the TCQ was .836 (Cronbach's Alpha). Reliability of the three sub-scales was: Self-centered concerns (.792), Task-centered concerns (.714) and Impact-centered concerns (.852).

Data Analysis Process

Quantitative data obtained from the questionnaire's participant demographic and background items were analyzed using the Statistical Package for Social Sciences (SPSS) 14.0. Descriptive statistics of participant responses generated and reported included frequency counts and percentages (refer to Table 6 in Appendix). Multiple one-way analyses of variance (ANOVAs) were conducted to determine if statistically significant differences existed between GTAs (independent variable) based on critical variables (dependent variables) identified in the demographic questionnaire items and responses to the TCQ.

The qualitative data analysis process involved the systematic organizing (Creswell, 2003; Merriam, 2002; Wolcott, 1999) of participant responses to the questionnaire open-ended items. Data analysis procedures were conducted concurrently with data collection as the study progressed. As a result, the primary researcher was able to identify provisional themes that provided context for future data collection processes. Collected data were analyzed in the following manner. First, participants' responses were tentatively grouped and analyzed to obtain insight into various aspects of the participants' instructional experiences and concerns as GTAs within the context of their respective teaching environments. Provisional interpretations, diverse participant statements, and common patterns across transcripts were used to generate preliminary themes. Findings in this study are considered legitimate based on the extent to which the quantitative data shed new light on the phenomenon under investigation and based on the qualitative data that provide the reader with a fresh awareness of the participants' experiences (Creswell, 2003). This study elucidates the perceptions of kinesiology GTAs in regards to their development as instructors and the impact of teaching concerns relevant to them. Thematic analysis was used to further deductively generate categories and themes which consequently led to a better understanding of the participants' experiences and perspectives. Lastly, the participants' quotations were used to provide a richness and depth to the representation of their experiences (Creswell 2003; Wolcott, 1999). The researcher strived to achieve a thorough, valid, and comprehensive description of the phenomenon under investigation.

Research Limitations and Generalizability

The research analysis and subsequent findings sought to provide perspectives for kinesiology graduate academic programs rather than test, support, or develop a hypothesis concerning the instructional concerns of BIP GTAs. The findings generated and the documentation of the participants' experiences might shed light on the experiences of GTAs in similar settings at other institutions but the experiences of those GTAs would probably be particularistic to that setting (Creswell, 2003). Consequently, the individual perspectives of the participants are their own and as a unit are bounded by space, time, location, and perhaps most importantly their current perception of reality.

Results

Participation of AAKPE Graduate Academic Programs

Currently, sixty-one graduate academic programs are listed in the AAKPE Doctoral Program Information directory. Forty-two of the sixty-one graduate academic programs replied that they would be willing to take part in this research endeavor. The author did not receive a reply regarding the research invitation from five graduate academic programs. In addition, fourteen graduate academic programs responded that they did not wish to take part in the study. Overall, there was a 69% participation rate for this study. Due to the confidential nature and self-reporting process of this study, response rates for individual basic instruction programs were not obtained.

Research question 1: What are the basic demographics of kinesiology GTAs teaching in basic instruction programs?

A total of 504 GTAs participated in this study. Research question 1 sought to determine the basic demographics of GTAs teaching basic instruction program courses. Table 2 (see Appendix) provides the participants' general demographic characteristics. Additionally, 85% percent of the GTAs were not certified to teach physical education in the pre-college setting. Sixty percent (60%) of the GTAs reported that they felt supported in their teaching by graduate academic program personnel (administrators, faculty, supervisor, etc.) Lastly, 90% of the respondents did not have teaching experience in a formal pre-college or college setting prior to beginning their assistantship experience. Nearly 54% and 21% of respondents identified themselves as instructor-of-record of 7 – 10 and 4 – 6 academic courses (2 academic credit hours per course) each year, respectively. Further, 91% of the GTAs reported 21 – 40 students typically enroll in each of their assigned courses. In addition, 56% of respondents reported they spent 1 – 5 hours weekly performing administrative duties associated with their courses such as planning for courses, preparing instructional materials, corresponding with students via e-mail or phone, holding office hours, and grading student assignments. Lastly, 68% and 16% of the GTAs responded that they were enrolled in 14 –18 and 19 – 21 academic credit hours of graduate course work respectively during the academic year.

Research question 2: Based on George's Teacher Concern Questionnaire (TCQ) in what order are GTA instructional concerns ranked in degree of concern?

Research question 2 sought to determine the overall and sub-scale rankings of the TCQ survey questionnaire items by GTAs. The mean score for total concern on the TCQ was 2.83. Further, the GTAs found the items causing the most concern related to their teaching to be "Challenging unmotivated students" ($M = 4.74$, $SD = 1.27$) followed by "Meeting the needs of different kinds of students" ($M = 3.56$, $SD = 1.27$), and "Whether each student is getting what he/she needs" ($M = 3.26$, $SD = 1.375$). Means and standard deviations for each of the TCQ's subscales (Self, Task, and Impact) were also analyzed. Results were Self ($M = 2.73$, $SD = 1.23$), Task ($M = 2.44$, $SD = 1.296$) and Impact ($M = 3.33$, $SD = 1.336$). Table 3 (in Appendix) provides the complete ranking, means, and standard deviations of each of the TCQ's questionnaire items.

Research question 3: Were there any statistically significant differences between the GTAs' responses to the TCQ based on critical variables such as terms of experience, program of study, degree aspirations, gender, having teacher certification, formal teaching experience?

No statistically significant differences were found to exist between GTAs demographic variables and their responses to the TCQ items.

Research Question 4: What concerns do physical education graduate teaching assistants have about their teaching responsibilities?

The following sections present this study's findings as pertinent to the open-ended question regarding the GTAs' primary instructional concerns. An interpretive analysis of the participants' responses revealed four primary themes that characterized the perceptions of the participants in regard to their concerns as teachers in the basic instruction program. Through the use of participants' responses, the "voices" of the GTAs will be used to illustrate and describe specific thematic interpretations. Respective themes are not to be construed as independent or unrelated to one another, but as interrelated aspects of a single overall pattern of meaning as interpreted by the researcher. Table 4 (see Appendix) shows the number and percentage breakdown of responses that comprised each of the primary themes.

Theme 1: "Motivating students unengaged in course activities or content." This theme generally focused on a particular segment of a typical class rather than the issue of motivating the entire class. Moreover, the participants' responses tended to cast these students as a negative aspect of the overall climate of their respective instructional settings. A respondent wrote:

> Getting some students to get off their butts is extremely hard...it's usually a small part of the class but a very visible part of the class. You would think if they signed up for the class, paid for it, and actually tried they would appreciate the opportunity they have. That's the biggest issue. Motivating students to fully engage the activities in the class for THEIR health benefits is my biggest concern. They can really bring down the entire class with their laziness if you let them. (Ph.D. candidate, Motor Behavior)

The GTA discussed the issue of motivating students who enrolled in BIP courses for reasons other than to work out or who lose the motivation to actively engage in the lesson. A health promotion and behavior major wrote:

> Some students are ready to go from jump while others just drag. That's what I dread the most. What am I going to do with the students who are just there to

get a passing grade or for other reasons? How do I motivate them to work hard if they just enrolled for insurance purposes or we're doing an activity they don't like? With classes of 30 you always get students who are just not into the lesson. So that's my biggest concern. Keeping everyone motivated for 15 weeks or at least keeping the unmotivated ones in check so they don't distract other students. (Ph.D. candidate, Health Promotion and Behavior)

Theme 2: "Developing and implementing a stimulating curriculum." This theme illustrated the GTAs' concern about implementing a curriculum to meet departmental goals for physical activity—while recognizing each student's individual learning needs and maintaining a stimulating classroom environment. More specifically, this theme described—the instructional concerns of GTAs who wished to develop curriculum and instructional experiences that kept the students engaged in the course content while providing a fun and enjoyable atmosphere. A master's candidate's response highlights this concern:

Coming up with lesson topics, presentations, group activities and experiences that the students will like and have fun at the same time is a major concern. Wellness is an exciting field but some of the concepts can be dull or just hard. So balancing being informative with being fun is my biggest teaching concern. I had to realize early on that the students taking the classes were not exercise science majors so they would only get into the materials to a point. (Master's candidate, Physical Education)

A second participant shed additional light on this concern when discussing the potential monotonous nature of teaching the same course topic (swimming) three times a week for 15 weeks. An exercise science Ph.D. candidate wrote:

Keeping the class moving and fun is my biggest challenge. 15 weeks of swimming can get boring real quick. We meet three times a week…How much swimming in a pool can a person do without it getting monotonous? That's what I mean when I tell other TAs that keeping the class interesting so that students keep coming to class and see improvements in their skills or bodies will be the biggest challenge. You have to come up with tournaments or contests to keep them coming back (Ph.D. candidate, Exercise Science)

Theme 3: "Being effectively assessed or evaluated to improve teaching effectiveness." Participants expressed an interest in being evaluated or assessed for teaching effectiveness as a means of bettering their teaching. Furthermore, the responses indicated a concern regarding the use of student evaluations as the sole means of evaluation and a desire for faculty involvement in the GTA teaching effectiveness process. Moreover, participants expressed that they would value constructive mentorship from faculty and peer reviews from fellow GTAs of their teaching on a consistent basis. A participant wrote:

How do I know when I'm doing a good job or not? The student evaluations aren't that accurate by themselves…that's all we use here and the students just write down anything a lot of times. I would like a faculty member to see my teaching and give me feedback so I can get better. Not just a casual observation but a real sit-down and talk about what I did right and wrong and how to improve. (Master's candidate, Sport Management)

In addition, participant responses brought attention to aspects of respective departmental teaching effectiveness assessment processes that need to be changed in order to be helpful to the development of the GTAs. More specifically, the GTAs noted the need to consider to the timing of the process, the involvement of faculty, and the use of individual consultation. A physical education major responded:

My concern is that something or someone needs to help me do a better job of teaching while I'm teaching the particular class. I want to be a professor one day so I need all the feedback I can get to improve my teaching skills. I don't have a lot of teaching experience so the group GTA-faculty meetings and student evaluations really provide me some good information to better my teaching…the process could be better if it was done the actual semester I taught the class rather than at the end of the academic year when they are deciding whether or not to renew my assistantship and on an individual basis. Also the faculty should be involved on a one-on-one basis. (Master's candidate, Physical Education)

Theme 4: "Finding support and respect for quality teaching from faculty." The last prominent theme focused on the GTAs' need to receive support for quality teaching and to have their efforts respected by faculty. Particularly, the GTAs expressed a concern that faculty were communicating the message that quality teaching was not a high priority in comparison to academics and research. A physical education Ph.D. candidate wrote:

My major concern is the lack of concern that faculty tend to have and express about me working hard to provide quality teaching for my physical education courses. I've been told to do just enough to get by and not to put a lot into preparing to teach but rather focus on grades and research projects…the message I get is that the assistantship isn't important outside of funding my graduate studies. I'm not always sure why I've been given these classes to teach…I don't want to be a subpar teacher and ruin someone's experience in my class. (Ph.D. candidate, Physical Education)

Respondents noted a lack of interaction among themselves and the faculty (particularly their respective major professors) concerning quality teaching. Further, as the following quote highlights, the respondents acknowledged that little support or formal signs of appreciation for effective teaching were demonstrated in their respective departments. A Ph.D. candidate's response summarizes this issue:

> My major professor has yet to talk to me about teaching my classes…I've been here for 3 years now. She doesn't seem to care unless I have a problem student or issue. That's my concern…where [is] the help with teaching? I've asked for ideas and tips for the class and she will provide basic information when pressed but outside of that she doesn't have any interest…other GTAs have the same issues. It would be nice to get some support or appreciation for teaching well but they will focus on what lab project you are doing or research you will present at the annual conference…no accolades for quality teaching. (Ph.D. candidate, Exercise Science)

Research question 5: What recommendations do kinesiology graduate teaching assistants have for improving their instructional development and support in light of expressed concerns?

The following sections present this study's findings as pertinent to the open-ended question regarding the GTAs' recommendations for improving their respective GTA program's instructional support and development processes. Two solid themes presented themselves during analysis. Table 5 (see Appendix) shows the number and percentage breakdown of responses that comprised each of the primary themes.

Theme 1: Provide a pre-teaching orientation that is meaningful to developing effective teaching practices. The first theme focused on the recommendation of improving the pre-teaching or August orientation. More specifically, the participants suggested that more content and time be devoted to the actual practice of teaching rather than an over-emphasis on departmental rules and regulations (i.e., grading policies, adding students to classes, accident reports, etc.). The following statement summarizes this theme:

> We need an orientation that makes sense…two days of lectures and reading over policies isn't enough. I don't have a teaching background so the rules and regulations is [sic] fine but how do I go about dealing with students and teaching them new skills. Right now the August orientation is too rushed and very little is done to help people like me learn the mechanics of teaching. Yes I need to know how to input final student grades and what to do during an accident but if you only have two days more focus should be on teaching. (Ph.D. candidate, Health Promotion and Behavior)

Theme 2: More input and support from faculty regarding teaching. The second primary theme presented the GTAs' recommendations that faculty take a more active role in the development and support of the GTAs as teachers. An exercise science Master's student provided the following response:

> Get the faculty involved with our teaching. Have some brown bag lunches or seminar speakers come in and help us to get better at teaching...and to value the classes we teach more. I want to hear their stories and suggestions for becoming a better teacher. Most of the professors here teach in the service program every summer so they must have suggestions for getting better or at least making the students feel like they got their money's worth out of the class. (Master's candidate, Exercise Science)

Demographic data illustrated the diverse educational backgrounds and teaching experience (or lack of experience) of the GTAs who are employed as lead instructors for basic instruction program courses. Moreover, the findings from the TCQ showed that the GTAs were more concerned with the actual extent to which their teaching positively impacted (*Impact-centered concerns*) the educational experiences of their students rather than successfully completing tasks (*Task-centered concerns*) related to teaching or their self-perceptions (*Self-centered concerns*) of their teaching. Using open-ended questionnaire items, responses from the participants also shed light on their desire to provide stimulating curriculum and course content, the necessity of instructional mentorship from faculty and lastly the presence of conflicting messages from potential role models (i.e., faculty, GTA supervisors, etc.) they received regarding the value of quality teaching.

Discussion and Implications

Studies that have sought to identify and assess the instructional concerns of GTAs are limited, particularly in the academic field of kinesiology (Russell & Chepyator-Thomson, 2004). In order to provide adequate support to increase graduate teaching assistants' preparedness and confidence to perform instructional duties, it is necessary to identify and assess pertinent instructional concerns that matter to them (Meyers, 2001; Wulff, Austin, Nyquist, & Sprague, 2004). The intent of this study was to give a voice to kinesiology GTAs who teach in basic instruction programs. More specifically, the purpose of this study was to identify the instructional concerns of GTAs and obtain relevant recommendations on ways to address expressed concerns. The present study's results and conclusions are consistent with existing knowledge concerning the instructional development, support, and particularly the socialization of GTAs for their immediate and potentially future roles as college-level instructors. However, it provides specific insights into kinesiology GTAs' teaching in basic instruction program courses. Lastly, this research extends the scant amount of literature found in the academic field of kinesiology focused on GTA development and support (Housner 1993; Russell, 2006).

Central to this discussion of the findings, subsequent recommendations and implications, is the question that graduate academic programs must confront: Is the focus of the graduate teaching assistantship experience simply to finance the graduate studies of academically talented graduate students while meeting the instructional labor needs of respective graduate academic programs, or to properly socialize and develop these academically talented graduate students to be effective teacher-scholars, comprehensively prepared for their initial and future roles in higher education, or is it a combination of both? Aligned with previous research outside of the academic field of kinesiology, the primary findings indicate that graduate academic programs in kinesiology are not effectively providing their GTAs with meaningful instructional development opportunities, leadership, or supervision (Prieto & Meyers, 2001; Russell, 2006; Savage & Sharpe, 1998).

More specifically, the consensus from the GTAs is that the graduate academic programs are lacking in three critical areas regarding their development and experiences as instructors: (a) the initial assignment of appropriate instructional responsibilities and instructional preparation; (b) the provision of formal teacher-scholar development and socialization processes between GTAs, faculty, and administrators; and (c) formal instructional supervision, development, and support processes. Existing research clearly documents that GTAs are often under-trained and under-supported in their teaching which has subsequently led to concerns about the overall quality of instruction that undergraduate students are receiving in courses in which GTAs are instructors-of-record (Rikard & Nye, 1997; Savage & Sharpe, 1998; Wert, 1998). Moreover, GTAs in the current study reported that they have faced a "sink-or-swim" or "call me if you need me" mentality from their supervisors or immediate superiors (including major high-ranking professors). This experience is also consistent with previous research (Prieto, 2001; Russell & Chepyator-Thomson, 2004). Perhaps this predicament is due in part to the lack of formal training that faculty and GTA supervisors (or faculty advisors) receive regarding GTA instructional supervision, development, and socialization techniques. In responses to our survey, GTAs expressed the fact that they found themselves experiencing "instructional abandonment" and questioning the true value of striving to improve their teaching. Unfortunately, research has long substantiated this troubling trend across academic disciplines (Meyers, 2001; Poole, 1991; Savage & Sharpe, 1998).

However, it was encouraging that participants expressed resiliency and a strong willingness to improve their teaching effectiveness despite a general lack of guidance and active mentorship from faculty and administrators. Significantly, "enhancing the instructional experiences and learning of their students" was a priority as indicated by four of the top five instructional concerns being from the *Impact-centered concerns* category. Moreover, it is important to note that the GTAs —regardless of their experiences and backgrounds— were willing to voice their opinions regarding their assistantship responsibilities.

It is imperative that GTAs are given the appropriate forum and opportunity to voice their concerns and issues and that they receive assistance to help them improve their individual experiences as instructors (Black & Kaplan, 1998; Russell, 2008). Because the respondents in this study were so open, their comments effectively present their expressed instructional concerns and identify reasonable and relevant recommendations for graduate academic programs to alleviate such concerns.

This research highlights multiple implications for graduate academic programs and the broader literature regarding the instructional development and socialization of GTAs. First and foremost, findings demonstrate the need for more in-depth scholarly inquiry to be focused on better understanding the instructional development and socialization concerns that GTAs face during their transition from graduate students to potential teacher-scholars. However, future research efforts should add to, but certainly not minimize, the necessity of student- or program-centered inquiry. Yet there is a substantial need for more attention to be paid to investigating the actual instructional concerns, successes, and general experiences of the GTAs. In addition, it would behoove GTA supervisors, particularly those supervising GTAs in basic instruction programs, to utilize existing literature on GTA instructional development to better develop programmatic processes for appropriately inducting, supporting, and overall developing the instructional skills and confidence of GTAs.

Further, the general consensus that GTAs in this study were not afforded adequate instructional development is puzzling because the extant literature stresses the necessity of mentorship and support as well as provides numerous excellent of examples of GTA instructional development programmatic guidelines, policies, formats, and processes that have been shown to be appropriate and effective (Davis, Smith, & Smith, 2002; Meyers, 2001; Prieto, 2001). Lastly, as discussed in recent publications such as *Envisioning the Future of Doctoral Education: Preparing Stewards of the Discipline* (Golde & Walker, 2006), *Paths to the Professoriate: Strategies for Enriching the Preparation of Future Faculty* (Wulff & Austin, 2004), and a special theme issue of Quest titled *The Academy Papers: Preparing Future Faculty* (Landers, 2003), there is an ever-present concern about the overall preparation and socialization of the future generation of higher education faculty. An inherent aspect of the graduate teaching assistantship (and doctoral education) experience is that it can serve as an invaluable opportunity for faculty to provide GTAs with the appropriate support, guidance, and mentorship as they develop quality skills and values as instructors (Austin & Wulff, 2004; Golde & Walker, 2006). Moreover, the experience provides a valuable opportunity for current faculty to facilitate the appropriate socialization of graduate students into their initial and future instructional roles and responsibilities. It would behoove graduate academic programs to put forth the effort to effectively socialize their GTAs to value teaching, research, and the many various aspects of the faculty position as part of their graduate education rather than assume the graduate students will "learn by mitosis" (Nyquist & Sprague, 1998; Russell & Chepyator-Thomson, 2004). In short, the graduate teaching assistantship experience was conceived many years ago as an apprenticeship in which graduate students could learn about their respective academic disciplines and begin to prepare for their roles as college-level teachers. Moreover, the experience has been characterized as an active process, which calls for vision, initiative, and effort from the administration, the faculty, and the graduate students themselves. Our research, findings suggest that collectively the GTAs were not provided what they perceived to be adequate and consistent mentorship and instructional development during their respective teaching assistantship experience.

This research contributes to the general discussion within higher education concerning the role of the graduate teaching experience and how most effectively processes can be implemented to prepare our students to be effective instructors and well-prepared future faculty. Although clear limitations of this research were the relatively small sample size (n = 504) of GTAs who participated and the self-reporting data collection technique, the collective responses can be seen as a "case-study" of the greater population of GTAs, particularly those in the academic discipline of kinesiology. In addition, each GTA's program is situated in its respective context which is heavily influenced by participant's background, university regulations, financial constraints, student enrollment trends, departmental policies and academic standards. It is hoped that the findings of this study will benefit graduate academic program administrators and GTA instructional leaders in the implementation of specific instructional development processes. The potential outcomes of such remediative actions by those involved in the development of GTAs would surely enhance the experiences of graduate students as they develop into effective college and university teachers and well-informed teacher-scholars.

General Recommendations

The following general recommendations are in response to the aforementioned findings and conclusions from this research:

a) Graduate academic programs and/or university-level teaching effectiveness programs should provide faculty-led seminars, brown bags sessions, and workshops that are focused on enhancing the practice of teaching. In addition, such sessions would be an invaluable opportunity for GTAs to inquire about the process of becoming college/university level faculty and other relevant academic professional socialization issues.

b) GTAs, particularly those with limited teaching backgrounds, should be provided with a faculty and peer GTA mentor who would be willing, or required to take an active role in the support, evaluation, consultation and overall development of their designated mentee. Specifically, the mentors and mentee would require consistent meetings and discussions on important instructional issues, concerns and triumphs relevant to the mentee's teaching experiences within the program. As an indication of institutional support mentors could be provided with some form of compensation (funding or release time) for taking part in the mentor program.

c) The personnel (faculty, supervisors, etc.) in graduate academic programs should be required to provide at least one individual consultation to each GTA during a given academic year. Particularly, individual consultations would be appropriate as part of a formal instructional teaching effectiveness process in which the GTA could be provided meaningful and formative evaluative feedback regarding instructional performance.

d) Pre-teaching orientations should be conceptualized and implemented to provide relevant instructional development information and strategies (for example, syllabus construction, developing exams, teaching basic physical skills, classroom management, providing appropriate feedback to students). Orientations can incorporate the perspectives of experienced GTAs and faculty, as well as ample coverage of pertinent university regulations, policies, and rules.

Additionally, it is recommended that future research initiatives should:

a) continue to assess the obstacles and barriers to effective GTA instructional socialization and training program development from the perspectives of the GTAs and their administrators;

b) investigate the impact of GTA coordinators' choice of supervisory practices and format on GTA instructional development, effectiveness and socialization; (

c) conduct longitudinal studies that examine to what extent that experiences as GTAs are beneficial and relevant to graduate students' effectiveness as faculty in academia; and

d) examine the impact of factors such as race, gender, degree program, formal teaching experiences, and degree aspirations on critical supervisory and development issues related to the socialization of GTAs as teacher-scholars.

Improved preparation of graduate teaching assistants in basic instruction programs can only enhance the undergraduate experience of college and university students and the graduate experience of the teaching assistants themselves.

References

Austin, A., & Wulff, D. (2004). The challenge to prepare the next generation of faculty. In D. Wulff, & A. Austin. (Eds.). (2004). *Paths to the professoriate: Strategies for enriching the preparation of future faculty* (pp. 3-16). San Francisco: Jossey-Bass.

Capal, S. (2001). Secondary students' development as teachers over the course of a PGCE year. *Educational Research, 41*(2), 247-261.

Creswell, J. (2003). *Research design: Qualitative, quantitative, and mixed methods approaches* (2nd ed.). Thousand Oaks, CA: Sage.

Davis, W., Smith, J., & Smith, R. (Eds.). (2002). *Ready to teach: Graduate teaching assistants prepare for today and for tomorrow.* Stillwater, OK: New Forums Press.

George, A. (1978). *Measuring self, task, and impact concerns: A manual for use of the teacher concerns questionnaire.* Austin, TX: University of Texas, Research and Development Center for Teacher Education.

Golde, C., & Walker, G. (Eds.) (2006). *Envisioning the future of doctoral education: Preparing stewards of the discipline.* San Francisco: Jossey-Bass.

Hensley, L. (2000). Current status of basic instruction programs in physical education at American colleges and universities. *Journal of Physical Education, Recreation and Dance, 71*(9), 30-36.

Housner, L.D. (1993). Research in basic instruction programs. *Journal of Physical Education, Recreation and Dance, 64*(6), 53-58.

Landers, D. (Ed.). *(2003). The academy papers: Preparing future faculty [Special Issue]. Quest, 55*(1).

Leenders, N., Sherman, W.M., & Ward, P. (2003). College physical activity courses: Why do students enroll, and what are their health behaviors. *Research Quarterly for Exercise and Sport, 74*(3), 313-318.

Merriam, S. (Ed.). (2002). *Qualitative research in practice: Examples of discussion and analysis.* San Francisco: Jossey-Bass.

Meyers, S. (2001). Conceptualizing and promoting effective TA training. In L. Prieto, & S. Meyers (Eds.), *The teaching assistant training handbook: How to prepare TAs for their responsibilities* (pp. 3-23). Stillwater, OK: New Forums Press.

Mondello, M., Fleming, D., & Focht, B. (2000). The organization, administration, and operational procedures of an elective, physical education program at a research one university. *The Physical Educator, 57*(2), 77-83.

Nyquist, J., & Sprague, J. (1998). Thinking developmentally about TAs. In M. Marincovich, J. Prostko, & F. Stout (Eds.), *The professional development of graduate teaching assistants, (61-88).* Bolton, MA: Anker.

Pennington, T., Manross, D., & Poole, J. (2001). Exploring alternative assessment in college physical activity classes. *The Physical Educator, 58(4),* 206-210.

Poole, J. (1991). Seven skills to improved teaching: Enhancing graduate assistant instruction. *Journal of Physical Education, Recreation and Dance, 62,* 21-24.

Prieto, L. (2001). The supervision of teaching assistants: Theory, evidence and practice. (2001). In L. Prieto, & S. Meyers (Eds.), *The teaching assistant training handbook: How to prepare TAs for their responsibilities* (pp. 103-129). Stillwater, OK: New Forums Press.

Prieto, L. & Meyers, S. (2001). Introduction. In L. Prieto, & S. Meyers (Eds.), *The teaching assistant training handbook: How to prepare TAs for their responsibilities* (viii-xi). Stillwater, OK: New Forums Press.

Rikard, G.L., & Nye, A. (1997). The graduate instructor experience: Pitfalls and possibilities. *Journal of Physical Education, Recreation and Dance, 68*(5), 33-37.

Russell, J. (2006). Investigating perceptions of a collegiate physical education program's organizational culture, instructional supervision practices and socialization processes: A case study. *Educational Research Journal, 21*(1), 65-92.

Russell, J. (2008). An examination of kinesiology GTAs' perceptions of an instructional development and evaluation model. *The Physical Educator, 65*(1), 2–20.

Russell, J., & Chepyator-Thomson, J. (2004). Help wanted!!! Perspectives of physical education graduate teaching assistants on their instructional environment, preparation and needs. *Educational Research Journal, 19*(2), 251-280.

Savage, M., & Sharpe, T. (1998). Demonstrating the need for formal graduate student training in effective teaching practices. *The Physical Educator, 55*(3), 130-138.

Torre, M., & Casanova, P. (2008). Expectancies of efficacy and teacher concerns in in-service and prospective teachers. *Infancia y Aprendizaje, 31*(2), 179–196.

Watzke, J. (2007).Longitudinal research on beginning teacher development: Complexity as a challenge to concerns-based stage theory. *Teaching and Teacher Education, 23*(1), 106–122.

Wert, E. (1998). Foreword. In. M. Marincovich, J. Prostko, & F. Stout (Eds.), *The professional development of graduate teaching assistants* (pp. xvii-xxi). Bolton, MA: Anker.

Wolcott, H. (1999). *Ethnography: A way of seeing.* Walnut Creek, CA: Altamira Press.

Wulff, D., & Austin, A. (Eds.). (2004). *Paths to the professoriate: Strategies for enriching the preparation of future faculty.* San Francisco: Jossey-Bass.

Wulff, D., Austin, A., Nyquist, J., & Sprague, J. (2004). The development of graduate students as teaching scholars: A four-year longitudinal study. In D. Wulff, & A. Austin (Eds.). (2004). *Paths to the professoriate: Strategies for enriching the preparation of future faculty* (pp. 46-73).San Francisco: Jossey-Bass.

Jared A. Russell, Ph.D., is an Associate Professor in the Department of Kinesiology at Auburn University. He supervises GTAs in the Physical Activities Program as well as teaches graduate and undergraduate teacher education courses.

Appendix

Table 1. Items on the Teacher Concerns Questionnaire (TCQ): Items Grouped by Concern Type

Concern Type	Questionnaire Item	
Self-Concerns	#3	Doing well when a supervisor is present
	#7	Feeling more adequate as a teacher
	#9	Being accepted and respected by professional persons
	#13	Getting a favorable evaluation of my teaching
	#15	Maintaining the appropriate degree of class control
Task-Concerns	#1	Lack of instructional materials
	#2	Feeling under pressure too much of the time
	#5	Too many non-instructional duties
	#10	Working with too many students each day
	#14	The routine and inflexibility of the teaching situation
Impact - Concerns	#4	Meeting the needs of different kinds of students
	#6	Diagnosing student learning problems
	#8	Challenging unmotivated students
	#11	Guiding students towards intellectual and emotional growth
	#12	Whether each student is getting what he/she needs

Table 2. Participant Demographic Characteristics

Demographic characteristic	Number (Percentag)
Sex	
Female	222 (44%)
Male	282 (56%)
Race/Ethnicity	
American Indian/Alaskan Native	14 (2.7%)
African-American/Black	26 (5.2%)
Asian/Pacific Islander	49 (9.7%)
European-American/White	376 (74.6%)
Latino-American/Hispanic	16 (3.2%)
Other	23 (4.6%)
Age Range	
20 – 26 years of age	399 (79.1%)
27 – 32 years of age	84 (16.7%)
33 – 39 years of age	21 (4.2%)
National Origin	
U.S. citizen/permanent resident	388 (77%)
Non-citizen	116 (23%)
Current Degree Aspiration	
Master's of Arts, Education, or Science	422 (83.7%)
Doctorate of Education or Philosophy	82 (16.3%)
Program of Study	
Exercise Science	110 (21.8%)
Exercise Physiology	39 (7.7%)
Physical Education Teacher Education	163 (32.3%)
Biomechanics	45 (8.9%)
Sport Management/Administration	48 (9.5%)
Motor Behavior	37 (7.3%)
Sport Psychology	10 (2%)
Health Promotion and Behavior	37 (7.3%)
Other	15 (3%)
Time as a GTA	
1 – 3 academic terms	243 (48.2%)
4 – 6 academic terms	201 (39.9%)
7 – 9 academic terms	42 (8.3%)
10 or more academic terms	18 (3.6%)
Teacher Certified prior to Assistantship?	
Yes	78 (15.5%)
No	426 (84.5%)
Formal Teaching Experience prior to Assistantship?	
Yes	53 (10.5%)
No	451 (89.5%)
Perceived Teaching Development Supported Graduate Academic Program Personnel?	
Yes	304 (60.3%)
No	200 (39.7%)

Table 3. Means and Standard Deviations for Individual Items on the TCQ in Rank Order

Questionnaire Item	Mean	Std. Deviation
Challenging unmotivated students (I)	3.7480	1.279
Meeting the needs of different kinds of students (I)	3.5675	1.273
Whether each student is getting what he/she needs (I)	3.2639	1.375
Guiding students towards intellectual and emotional growth (I)	3.2480	1.428
Getting a favorable evaluation of my teaching (S)	2.8869	1.264
Diagnosing student learning problems (I)	2.8591	1.326
Feeling more adequate as a teacher (S)	2.8274	1.117
Being accepted and respected by professional persons (S)	2.7579	1.327
Maintaining the appropriate degree of class control (S)	2.6488	1.306
Lack of instructional materials (T)	2.5873	1.342
Working with too many students each day (T)	2.5456	1.348
Doing well when a supervisor is present (S)	2.5317	1.143
The routine and inflexibility of the teaching situation (T)	2.5179	1.265
Feeling under pressure too much of the time (T)	2.3651	1.297
Too many non-instructional duties (T)	2.2143	1.228
*(S) Self Concern (T) Task Concern (I) Impact Concern		

Table 4. Thematic Responses to Open-ended Survey Question 1

Theme	Response N (%)
Motivating students unengaged in course activities or content	227 (45%)
Developing and implementing a stimulating curriculum	138 (27%)
Being effectively assessed or evaluated to improve teaching effectiveness	76 (15%)
Finding support and respect for quality teaching from faculty	51 (10%)
Other	12 (2%)

Table 5. Thematic Responses to Open-ended Survey Question 2

Theme	Response N (%)
Provide a pre-teaching orientation that is meaningful to developing effective teaching practices.	312 (62%)
More input and support from faculty regarding teaching.	153 (30%)
Other	39 (8%)

Section 2

Educating Graduate Students for Their Roles as College Instructors

Chapter 3

A Prep Course for Graduate Teaching Assistants: Building a Community

Gili Marbach-Ad, Patricia A. Shields, Bretton W. Kent, Bill Higgins & Katerina V. Thompson

This study evaluated a team-taught course for new graduate teaching assistants (GTAs), which focused on building community and preparing GTAs for their teaching responsibilities in a biological sciences program at a Research University. The course involved three key components of graduate student teaching development: faculty engagement, teaching center involvement, and graduate student participation. Most GTAs reported that the course exceeded their expectations and they particularly valued discussions of authentic teaching scenarios. The course provides a model for other graduate programs in which GTAs come from diverse backgrounds and have significant teaching responsibilities.

This study aimed to evaluate a team-taught course for new graduate teaching assistants (GTAs), which focuses on building a community and preparing the GTAs for their teaching responsibilities in a biological sciences program at the University of Maryland. GTAs are integral members of the academic community in most North American RU/VH Research Universities by virtue of their assistance with undergraduate science instruction (Luppicini, 2006, Luft et al., 2004; Travers, 1989). They support faculty by serving as graders and leading laboratory sections, small group discussions, and study sections. Often they are the primary point of contact for students interested in the sciences.

While graduate students are expected to take autonomous and sometimes complex teaching responsibilities (Austin, 2002; Habay & Bandik, 2006), they rarely receive any formal training for teaching and are generally expected to "sink or swim" (Boyer Commission Report, 1998; Coppola, 2009; Handelsman et al., 2003). This puts them in a difficult position at a particularly vulnerable time in their professional development, since they are usually not far removed from their undergraduate studies, yet are expected to assume the role of expert in the classroom, as well as to develop the ability to balance the competing demands of teaching, research, and personal life.

In our college of Chemical and Life Sciences there are large cohorts of new graduate students each year (about 100, with biology and chemistry combined). The new graduate students in our college are recruited into graduate programs, and their initial support is derived from teaching assistant positions. In their first year of graduate education, they can be overwhelmed by their need to adjust to the different expectations of graduate education, explore in detail their chosen discipline, perform laboratory rotations, and spend 20 hours per week as a teaching assistant in a class that they may not have taken, or took four years earlier. In many cases, new GTAs feel they need to devote more than 20 hours per week to their teaching responsibilities because they do not have any prior teaching experience.

Students in our programs come from different cultural, demographic, and teaching experience backgrounds. Around 30% are international students. Domestic graduate students come to our university from different kinds of institutions (from small liberal arts colleges to large research institutions). Some graduate students have extensive previous university teaching experience while others have none. Many first-year students do lab rotations and have yet to identify a dissertation advisor, so they are not part of a lab community or any other learning community.

Recently, educators have introduced the concept "learning communities" or "communities of practice" (Wenger, McDermott, & Snyder, 2002). Wenger suggests that, "communities of practice are groups of people who share a concern or a passion for something they do and learn how to do it better as they interact regularly" (Wenger, 2006, http://www.ewenger.com/theory/). Communities of practice theories have been used in many educational settings to bring together novice and experienced educators to discuss teaching, but there are no more than a few examples at the postgraduate level (Ash, et al., 2009; Cox, 2004). We believe that it is critical to build a community of graduate students in the first semester, so that new graduate students can form peer support networks and have their pressing teaching questions answered. This community is supported by experienced GTAs as well as experienced faculty who can provide mentoring in teaching.

A second priority is to provide more focused preparation for teaching in science disciplines. The university provides an intensive one-day orientation to all new teaching assistants. We also have a range of programs for students with an interest in gaining extensive formal training in university teaching. This includes workshops by the University's Center for Teaching Excellence (CTE), formal courses in pedagogy (some of which are focused specifically on teaching science in a university setting), and a University Teaching and Learning Program (UTLP) that enables graduate students to earn a certificate in university teaching by attending workshops, completing a teaching research project, and developing a teaching portfolio that documents their teaching philosophy and expertise. However, less than 5% of GTAs take advantage of these more formal opportunities. Therefore, in our new preparation course, we aimed to bridge the university's brief orientation program and the more formal resources of the CTE. This course was not designed to replace our existing university teaching preparation program (UTLP), but rather to provide the new GTAs with the tools and support they need to negotiate their first teaching experiences successfully and guide them towards appropriate resources should they choose to seek more training in science teaching.

Initial attempts to enhance the preparation of GTAs in our college resulted in several small, departmentally-based classes focusing on university teaching. Unfortunately, inconsistencies in format and content left both graduate students and instructors dissatisfied. Therefore, in Fall 2007, we evaluated a new approach, combining three separate classes and pooling our expertise to create a single innovative and engaging team-taught preparatory course for all new GTAs from three biological sciences departments (Cell Biology and Molecular Genetics, Biology, and Entomology). A variety of teaching approaches were incorporated, including whole group discussions, small group discussions, and individual instruction. Topics included: writing quizzes, grading using rubrics, academic dishonesty, effective time management, fostering meaningful class discussions, writing a comprehensive syllabus, and presentation skills. In addition, a panel of experienced GTAs shared their experiences and was available to answer questions. Finally, the instructors of the course visited classrooms to observe GTAs while teaching in order to provide them with constructive feedback. We evaluated the new course by incorporating researcher's observations, interviews of course instructors, and students' reported opinions. We also used a pre-post survey for affective measurement on students' expectations and feedback.

Description of the University and the Course

The University of Maryland is a research university that enrolls 25,000 undergraduate and 9,900 graduate students in 111 undergraduate and 96 graduate programs. Within the College of Chemical and Life Sciences (CLFS), there are 110 tenured/tenure-track faculty and about 2,400 undergraduates pursuing majors in the biological sciences. Every year there are about 200 graduate teaching assistants (experienced and new). In the last few years, the University of Maryland and the College of Chemical and Life Sciences specifically have made substantial investments to build excellence in the biological sciences and are committed to ensuring that undergraduate programs keep pace with the rapid developments in this field. Prospective students are drawn to our campus by the strength of its research-based science curriculum. Therefore we need to prepare our GTAs to take advantage of the cutting edge research and innovative teaching approaches in our program, and to communicate these ideas effectively to our undergraduate students.

The new course, *Teaching Biology,* is a one-credit course required for

all new GTAs in the biological sciences graduate programs at our
The course was team taught by three faculty members, one from ea
cal science department. The course consisted of seven meetings
once per week) and one-on-one instructor-student mentoring. Atten
monitored, and students who missed two or more classes earned a grade of
"Unsatisfactory." Dinner was provided at three sessions as a way of fostering
a collegial atmosphere. The first six weekly sessions followed a similar template, comprised of two parts:

(a)   Stories from the classroom: "War stories." For 15-20 minutes, the students discussed real incidents from their or the instructors' teaching experience. For example, in the first session, one instructor recounted an incident
from her class that sparked discussion about a teacher's reaction to a student's
inappropriate behavior during the class session. She described to the students how she reacted and then the students discussed additional alternative
ways to handle such a situation. In later sessions, students were provided the
opportunity to share their own stories. This usually fostered discussions, such
as what to do with an inattentive student, how to deal with students who are

Table 1: An Overview of Topics Discussed in the Course

Sessions	Topics
1	**Introduction meeting (with dinner)** • TA panel: Five experienced TAs shared their experiences with course students and answer students' questions. • Administrative campus information.
2	**Perfecting your presentation** • Strategies for teaching and structuring successful discussions. • Use of PowerPoint presentations.
3	**The development of quizzes and tests** • Awareness and sensitivity toward individuals with disabilities and discussion of special arrangements for students with disabilities. • Development of quizzes and tests. Students were introduced to Bloom's Taxonomy (Bloom, 1984) and asked as a homework assignment to formulate three questions, each falling under different Bloom's Taxonomy (1984) levels (Knowledge, understanding, application, analysis, synthesis, and evaluation).
4	**Quiz design and grading rubrics** • The instructors collected the students' questions before the class session and presented the questions to the students, discussing the quality of the questions and the taxonomy level of each question. Students were also presented with examples for grading rubrics and asked to discuss pros and cons of each rubric.
5	**Academic dishonesty and time management** • Report on confidentiality, academic integrity, plagiarism, copyrights and sexual harassment. • Time management (balancing graduate student responsibilities, such as teaching, research and personal life).
6-7	**Sessions based on students' requests and queries (with Dinner)** • How to run review sessions. • How to deal with your faculty coordinator. • How to deal with students' excuses. • Importance of the syllabus/How to prepare syllabus.

_aught cheating during tests, preferred ways instructors should interact with students (e.g., through e-mail, office hours), and appropriate places to schedule meetings with students.

(b) Discussion: Topics of the week. Following the "stories from the classroom", instructors focused on one of several topics (see Table 1). While discussing the topics of the day, they demonstrated different teaching techniques (e.g., small group discussions and think, pair, share).

Course meetings were supplemented with outside readings and assignments on active learning pedagogies and science education theory. For example, one unit focused on Bloom's Taxonomy (Bloom, 1984). After reading the relevant theory, students wrote questions suitable for an introductory biology course aimed at three different Bloom's Taxonomy levels. They posted their questions on the course website for their classmates to critique. At the subsequent class meeting, the questions were discussed and evaluated for their quality and cognitive level. Following the fifth class meeting, the students were asked to provide three different dates when it would be convenient for one of the instructors to evaluate them teaching in their classroom. This allowed the instructors to observe each student while teaching his/her class or lab session and provide feedback.

Who participated in the course?

Forty-three graduate students (28 doctoral and 15 master students) enrolled in the course. The students expressed diversity across several dimensions (Figure 1).

Gender: 29 females and 14 males

Age: 29 students were between 20 to 25 years old;

10 students were between 26 to 30 years old;

4 were between 31 to 50 years old.

Ethnicity: 12 Asian, 30 Caucasian and 1 did not report.

Degree Program 16 Cell Biology & Molecular Genetics; 8 Sustainable Development &

Conservation Biology; 5 Biology; 4 Molecular and Cell Biology; 3 Marine-Estuarine-

Environmental Sciences; 3 Entomology; 2 Neuroscience & Cognitive Science; 2

Behavior, Ecology, Evolution and Systematics.

Fourteen students were international students.

Figure 1: Demographic Background of Students in the Course

Data Collection and Analysis

Qualitative and quantitative methods were used in this study. For the qualitative data, the science educator, who serves as the director of the College of Chemical and Life Sciences Teaching and Learning Center, observed all class sessions. The observer took extensive notes that focused on documenting and interpreting the nature of the classes and the degree to which the instructional objectives were achieved. Three months after the course, the course observer interviewed the three instructors. We summarized the interview and present excerpts from their responses in the section "Interviews with the course instructors" below. We also administered a pre- and post-survey to the graduate students enrolled in the class. For the qualitative analysis of open-ended questions in the students' surveys, we used a modified content analysis strategy (Ryan & Bernard, 2000). The quantitative data was obtained from the multiple-choice questions in the pre- and post-surveys.

Students' Responses to a Pre-Survey in the Beginning of the Course

One question from the pre-survey focused on students' expectations of the course. Twenty students wrote specifically that they expected to learn how to teach science to undergraduate students (e.g., "I expect this course to teach me techniques to help me become a more organized and effective instructor," "Improve my teaching skills," and "Help think of ways to enhance the lab."). Another 12 students wrote more generally that they expected to get advice on how to be an effective TA (e.g., "To help me get through the beginning of the semester," "To become more efficient in my work," "To learn more about the role that TAs play."). Six students mentioned the word "troubleshooting" ("Troubleshooting for whatever doubts I have"). Four students reported that they expected to learn from others' experience.

Another open-ended question on the pre-survey was: "Why are you taking this class?" Students reported that they took this class because it was required (21 students), because they wanted to learn how to teach (18 students), and because they had never taught before (four students). To the question "Do you believe you need this class?" 40 students answered "Yes", one answered "No" and two students answered "Not sure".

Students' End-of-Semester Feedback

Overall the students' end-of-semester feedback for the course was very positive (Figure 2). Eighty percent of the students wrote that the course met their expectations. The others wrote that they didn't know what to expect or that it would be better if the course were parallel to their teaching. (A small number of students did not begin their teaching responsibilities until the subsequent semester.)

To be more specific on the feedback and be able to improve the course, we asked students to choose the three topics that they found most useful and the three topics that they found the least useful and to provide explanations for their choices. Figure 3 shows the list of topics and summarizes the students' responses.

War Stories. A majority of students (26) chose the stories from the classroom as one of the most useful topics in the course. They explained that the stories made them realize that they are "not the only one with problems." Students also explained that the stories were "funny," "brought up problems/solutions that I would otherwise not think of," "brought forth issues that are faced by TA's day in and day out and this kind of 'pre-warned' us to things to come," "War stories are just a good way to encourage talking/discussing in this class while encouraging us to think while we get to laugh," "It was great to hear first-hand stories of unusual situations that may arise and how people have handled those."

Academic dishonesty. Another topic identified by many students (21) as a most useful topic was academic dishonesty. Students explained that "there are

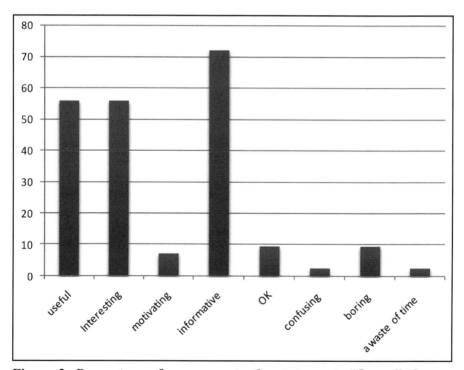

Figure 2: Percentage of responses to the statement: "Overall the course was: a. Interesting b. informative c. boring d. OK e. confusing f. motivating g. useful h. a waste of time.

a lot of legal issues surrounding academic dishonesty, [and it] would have been hard to navigate w/ no help prior," "the discussion on academic dishonesty was useful as it provided me with a clear guidance to follow in case I detected a case amongst my students."

Time management. This topic also was mentioned among the three most useful topics (17 students). Students explained that it was very useful because they needed to learn ways to balance their time between "TAing & research along with courses." Students also mentioned that they could pass on tech-

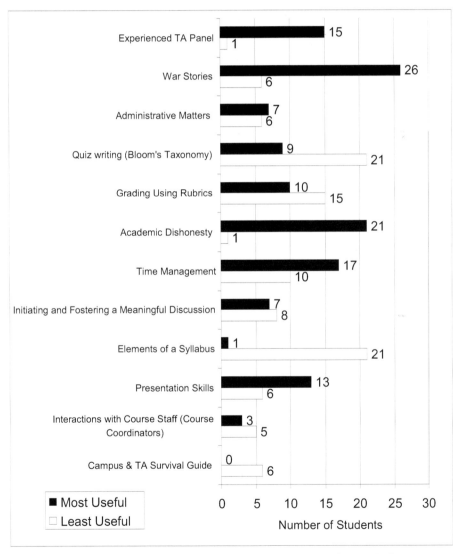

Figure 3: The three topics students found most useful and three topics found least useful in the course.

niques for time management to their own students ("My students had questions about how to do well and this was good advice to pass on").

Panel of experienced TAs. About a third of the students (15) found the panel of experienced TAs as one of the most useful topics. The students explained that the panel "was a good intro into what to expect," "passed on good advice," and "It was great to hear first-hand stories of unusual situations that may arise and how people have handled those."

Presentation skills. Thirteen students chose presentation skills as one of the most useful topics. Students' explanations included: "I never taught before so this helped me to keep my students interested," "Initiating a meaningful discussion—helped me during class period and office hours to better explain things," and "it is very difficult to get use used to standing up in front of people. Receiving some "training" advice was both helpful and comforting. I especially liked the 'what NOT to do with PowerPoint' part."

The three topics that were most chosen as the least useful topics were: quiz writing using Bloom's Taxonomy (21 students), discussion regarding elements of the syllabus, writing a syllabus, and presenting it to your students (21 students), and grading assignments using a rubric (15 students). Most students that chose these as the least useful topics did not comment that the topics were taught poorly, instead they believed that they simply did not apply to their current experience as TAs. They explained, "I didn't have to write a quiz," "not going to do it, will have one [quiz] written by instructor," "I did not have to write my own quizzes (although it was a good insightful exercise)," "I didn't have to write a [grading] rubric," "as a TA for BSCI 105 the rubric had already been created," "the syllabus was already written for us (the TAs)."

One question on the end-of-semester survey referred to the one-on-one mentoring of students by the course instructor. The question was "Towards the end of the course one of the instructors came to observe you teaching and provided you with feedback. Was this feedback helpful to you? How so? Do you have any suggestions for making this component of the course more helpful?" Most of the students responded positively to this question. They explained: "Yes, feedback from the instructor helped me identify areas where I could improve my teaching style," "It was very helpful to have someone evaluate your individual performance. This I think was the most important part of the course," "The feedback was very helpful, I was told the things I should work on in a very nice manner and I realized that they were actually very important and helpful," "This feedback was very very helpful. Dr. [name of instructor] pointed out my strengths and weaknesses and this helped me to become a better TA the next semester. This was one feature that I very much liked about the course."

One student suggested that it would be better to have the instructors observe them more than once during the semester, "Maybe have two observation periods if practical. One in the beginning of the semester to establish weaknesses and reinforce strengths and then one later at the end of the semester to see if improvement has occurred."

Interviews with the Course Instructors

The first question presented to the instructors following the course was "What were your initial expectations for the course?" The instructors mentioned their aim was to build a GTAs' community in which the students could exchange information and provide peer-support. They also wished to share their teaching experience with the students. Finally, they expected that the team teaching approach, which involved all three biological sciences departments and a larger number of students, would enhance participation and exchange of experiences.

> My initial expectations, I guess I would start with opening lines of communication and information exchange with our new grad students and TAs who formerly didn't have anybody to talk about those kinds of pedagogical and practical issues. Second, I thought that we would all learn from an exchange of experiences, and I guess the third thing is it's always good to talk specifics about strategies and ploys, and issues that maybe we do but we don't ever really recognize that we're doing. (Instructor 1)

The three instructors felt that the course met their expectations even though they had some concerns. Instructor one said, "It met my expectations and more... the discussions were great, people were interested..." Instructor two expressed her concern about the large size of the new class, "...I wondered if it would lose that therapy session feel [that they previously had] because they were going from a smaller class from between 12 and 15 up to a bigger class of 45... and it really didn't because we were able to break down into smaller groups... so it really exceeded all of my expectations."

When the instructors were asked to elaborate how the merged course differed from the departmental courses they have taught before, they mentioned some pros and cons. The major item they found lacking was to have students practice giving presentations, and this is something under consideration for future workshops prior to the course or in small groups during the course.

> The one thing we didn't do in this that I always do in my 701 class, and I really wished we had the chance to do, and it's something that my kids actually talked about was the fact that we didn't give them a chance to practice speaking before they actually talked for the first time. I always do that the week before class starts is give them a chance to talk for 10 minutes so that we can all critique them and say these are the things you need to think about, you know are you talking too fast, are you talking too slow, is your voice carrying... We didn't have the time this time when we started. And there are 40 of them. If we had a

half day workshop, we could break out into small groups and do that. (Instructor 2)

In response to questions about the positive aspects of the course, the instructors stressed that the team teaching was enriching for all and served as a model of effective collaboration for the students. They also mentioned that the dinners provided during three of the class sessions made the students feel that they were important parts of the university community. In addition, the instructors felt that they made strong connections with the students so that the students would feel comfortable approaching them with teaching or communication problems.

...I can't emphasize enough that this was a comment that came across a lot [from the students], that the three of us have very different styles and it gave them hope that people with three very different styles obviously respect one another and get along with one another and that gave them hope that... in their own work that they wouldn't have to find somebody exactly like them but they would still be able to establish some sort of a good working relationship... And they thought that transferred not only in teaching but into research and in life... Another thing I felt that they found another address if their lab coordinator is not coordinating with them and if they have a problem between two lab coordinators or between two instructors, they have the address to come to you and you are outside and you are not in this same equation. (Instructor 3)

When asked to respond to what they would change in the class, instructor 2 suggested building the course website with the course material in a way that makes it accessible for student and instructor communication during and following the course. The current website was built using the university-supported course management system, which is only accessible to students during the course term.

Observer's Overview

The three instructors attended every session. They team taught the class while dividing into small groups for specific assignments. The instructors usually followed the planned syllabus that they built prior to the fall semester, although they sometimes changed the discussed topic as a result of students' requests. The instructors started each session with a story from their teaching experience, usually about problematic situations from their classroom (e.g., student does not pay attention in class, students' cheating during tests, students' excuses, students that didn't read the syllabus well, interaction with students, and making mistakes in grading the assignment). These stories, along with the openness and the personality of the instructors, helped to create a very open and comfortable atmosphere in the class. Throughout all class sessions the instructors encouraged in-class and out-of-class students' questions, which they answered in class or through e-mails. The instructors used multiple communication channels: PowerPoint presentations, Blackboard, whole class discussions and small group discussions. One goal of the course was to provide a point of contact for the students to get advice from someone other than their lab coordinators or their course director. Therefore, the instructors encouraged students to keep in touch with them and seek them out for informal discussions following the course's conclusion. The instructors also made themselves available during the first weekend of the semester to work with individual graduate students on the graduate student's course website. Another major goal of the course was to build a community for the new GTAs, which would allow them to consult with each other and build social and professional relationships. While we did not explicitly survey students regarding whether they felt connected to a teaching community as a result of the course, many students mentioned the connection to their peers and the course instructors as among the most useful features of the course.

Conclusions and Future Plans

In a recent article, Austin et al., (2009) suggested that in order to improve the quality of undergraduate education for decades to come, we need to pay special attention to the preparation of graduate students. Graduate students initially have an integral role in the undergraduate education as teaching assistants, and later they are the ones that potentially will be faculty members. If we expect our PhD graduates to balance teaching and research in their future faculty positions, we must build this balance into their graduate training. Even for those students who pursue careers in government positions, industry or public policy rather than university teaching, the need to communicate complex scientific ideas effectively to a variety of audiences is critical.

Consequently, in the last few years GTAs preparation programs have started to emerge and most higher education institutions have adopted some form of training program for GTAs. The training programs vary in length and in content from half-day university-wide orientation sessions to more discipline-specific sessions to full semester courses with university-wide or specific departmental training (Ishikawa, Potter, & Davis, 2001; Luft, et al., 2004; Robinson, 2000).

In the College of Chemical and Life Sciences we aimed to build a community for the GTAs, not only to ensure that our GTAs are prepared for their educational responsibilities (supervising laboratories and discussion sections), but also to build a peer support system that could be supplemented by ongoing support from the GTA preparatory course instructors. To this end, we revised our three departmental prep courses and enlisted our best instructors in developing and implementing this revised course.

On the post survey, most GTAs reported that the course exceeded their expectations. The most valued course components were discussions of authentic teaching scenarios with the faculty, academic dishonesty, and the experienced GTA panel. Course observations showed that students were comfortable asking a variety of questions, from basic ones such as, "How to dress for the first class?" or "How to introduce myself?" to more weighty questions, such as "What to do with rude student?" What to do if a student is not cooperative with his/her group?" "What to do if you lose a test?" The students' feedback regarding the least useful topics (element of the syllabus, quiz writing and grading rubrics) was very informative for the course instructors. It highlighted the need to emphasize for the graduate teaching assistants that the content learned in the course could serve them in their future career, even if they are not going to pursue academic or teaching-oriented careers. Interestingly, when we asked students to report on their future career choices, most of them included teaching to some extent. In response to the question: "As you know, university careers span a continuum from exclusively research to exclusively teaching. Where along this continuum do you envision yourself in your future career?" Six students chose "exclusively research", 13 "mostly research", 15 students chose "50:50 research and teaching", four "mostly teaching", one "exclusively teaching" and four did not answer.

Most of the students reported that they appreciated the one-on-one student-instructor mentoring and felt that the course provided them an opportunity to communicate and receive support from the instructors and their peers, "Yes, it was great to be able to interact and discuss issues with fellow first timers, and find out you're not alone!" "…To me, the benefit from this course was the ability to connect with faculty who understand that you are concerned about doing well and are there to help you (the same goes for the rest of the TAs in the class). The support was reassuring…"

We did not receive many negative comments, but based on student feedback, we intend to allow more breakout sessions with small groups to give voice to the less outspoken members of the group and find ways to increase student enthusiasm towards teaching. An additional recommendation for future years is to include student presentations, which allows them opportunities to receive feedback on their teaching from their peers and instructors before they teach their first formal class session.

Many of the most successful elements of the class depend on a high level of interaction between students and individualized mentoring by the instructors. Based on this and our previous experiences, we feel there exists an optimal range of class size. In class sizes below ~10 students, discussions are less open and productive, and the range of experiences shared is more limited. Above a class size of ~50, it is difficult to maintain an intimate, collegial atmosphere and provide individualized guidance. We recommend an instructor to student ratio of 1:15.

We believe that our course could serve as a model for other graduate programs in which GTAs come from diverse backgrounds and have significant teaching responsibilities.

Acknowledgments

This research was supported in part by a grant to the University of Maryland from the Howard Hughes Medical Institute through the Undergraduate Science Education Program. This work has been approved by the Institutional Review Board as IRB Protocol #: 07-0021.

References

Ash, D., Brown, C., Kluger-Bell, B., & Hunter L. (2009). Creating hybrid communities using inquiry as professional Development for college science faculty. *Journal of College Science Teaching, 38*(6), 68-76.

Austin, A. (2002). Preparing the next generation of faculty. Graduate school as socialization to the academic career. *Journal of Higher Education, 73*(1), 94.

Austin, A. E., Campa H. III, Pfund, C., Gillian-Daniel, D. L., Mathieu, R., Stoddart, J. (2009). Preparing STEM doctoral students for future faculty careers. *New Directions for Teaching and Learning, 117*, 83-95.

Bloom, B. S. (ed.). 1984. Taxonomy of educational objectives. Handbook 1: Cognitive domain. Longman, New York: Boyer Commission Report.

Coppola, B. P. (2009). Advancing STEM teaching and learning with research teams. *New Directions for Teaching and Learning, 117*, 33-44.

Cox, M. D., (2004). Introduction to faculty learning communities. *New Directions for Teaching and Learning, 97*, 5–23.

Habay, S. A., & Bandik, G. C. (2006). The course coordinator program: An additional tool for preparing graduate student for academia. *The Journal of Graduate Teaching Assistant Development, 10*(1), 65-72.

Handelsman, J. (2003). Teaching Scientists to Teach. *HHMI Bulletin, 12*, 31.

http://scientificteaching.wisc.edu/documents/HHMIPerspective2003.pdf

Ishikawa, C. M., Potter, W. H., Davis, W. E. (2001). Beyond this week's lab: Integrating long-term professional development with short-term preparation for science graduate students. *Journal of Graduate Teaching Assistant Development, 8*(3), 133-138.

Luft, J. A., Kurdziel, J. P. Gillian, Roehrig, H., & Turner, J. (2004). Growing a garden without water: Graduate teaching assistants in introductory science laboratories at a doctoral/research university. *Journal of Research in Science Teaching, 41*, 211–233.

Luppicini, R. (2006). A study of graduate student perspectives on teaching assistantships and unionization. *The Journal of Graduate Teaching Assistant Development, 10*(1), 17-30.

Robinson, J. B. (2000). New teaching assistants facilitate active learning in chemistry laboratories: Promoting teaching assistant learning through formative assessment and peer review. *The Journal of Graduate Teaching Assistant Development, 7*(3), 147-157.

Travers, P. L. (1989). Better training for teaching assistants. *College Teaching, 37*, 147–149.

Wenger, E. (2006) Communities of practice. A brief introduction. *Communities of practice.* Retrieved from http://www.ewenger.com/theory/

Wenger, E., McDermott, R., & Snyder, W. (2002) *Cultivating communities of practice: a guide to managing knowledge.* Cambridge, MA: Harvard Business School Press.

Gili Marbach-Ad, Ph.D., is the director of the Chemical and Life Sciences Teaching and Learning Center in the College of Computer, Mathematical and Natural Sciences (CMNS) at the University of Maryland. Her research areas include science education in high-school and higher education and science teacher preparation programs.

Patricia A. Shields, Ph.D., is the Course Coordinator for Principles of Genetics and she teaches other introductory level biology classes as well as the Graduate Teaching Prep class. Her research has been focusing on the use of upperclassmen to aide in the development of curriculum.

Bretton W. Kent, Ph.D., is the Director of Undergraduate Studies (Department of Entomology), and the Associate Director of the Master of Chemical and Life Sciences graduate program (College of Computer, Mathematical and Natural Sciences) at the University of Maryland. His research areas include the dental biomechanics of fossil sharks and the analysis of oysters in archeological sites.

Bill Higgins is in his 38th year as a faculty member in the Department of Biology at Maryland. He routinely teaches freshman biology, organismal biology, and physiology. Bill has received many campus teaching awards, including the campus' Kirwan Award.

Katerina V. Thompson is Director of Undergraduate Research and Internship Programs in the College of Computer, Mathematical and Natural Sciences at the University of Maryland. In addition to facilitating student involvement in co-curricular experiences, she coordinates several externally funded teaching and learning initiatives focusing on professional development and curriculum redesign in the biological sciences.

Chapter 4

A Pedagogy Course's Influence on Graduate Students' Self-Awareness as Teacher-Scholars

Lauren Miller Griffith
Northern Arizona University

Valerie Dean O'Loughlin, Katherine D. Kearns,
Mark Braun, Isaac Heacock
Indiana University

Most studies about graduate students' development as teacher-scholars rely on surveys and short-term outcomes. We used focused interviews to explore graduate students' perceptions of the lasting effects of a pedagogy course on their evolving orientations towards teaching. The interviews confirmed alignment between students' perceived learning outcomes and course objectives. Students said they became more reflective, gained confidence in the classroom, and developed a greater understanding of their students' learning. However, they struggled with methods to assess their teaching effectiveness and to justify time spent on teaching development. We conclude with programmatic recommendations to facilitate students' transitions to scholarly teachers.

Programs and activities that prepare graduate students to teach and measures of these programs' effectiveness have been a subject of development and inquiry for over 20 years (see review by Chism, 1998). The preparation of graduate students for their teaching responsibilities can take many forms, including teaching orientation programs, pedagogy courses, teaching certificate programs, and preparing future faculty (PFF) programs (Diamond and Wilbur, 1990; Marincovich, 1998; Tice, Featherstone, and Johnson, 1998; Tice, Gaff, and Pruitt-Logan, 1998). Specific activities such as classroom observation and consultation can improve graduate students' teaching effectiveness, positively influencing their students' learning, ratings of the course, and attitudes about the discipline (Abbott et al., 1989; Black, 1995; Carroll, 1980; Levinson-Rose and Menges, 1981; Shannon et al., 1998). In addition, comprehensive initiatives, which provide teaching support throughout graduate students' programs, can have a positive impact on teaching effectiveness. Participants in these programs may become more knowledgeable about teaching topics, acquire new teaching behaviors, and develop new attitudes toward teaching and learning (Bomotti, 1994; Carroll, 1980; DeNeef, 2002; Gaff and Lambert, 1996; Gaia et al., 2003; Nyquist and Wulff, 1996; Shannon et al., 1998; Taylor et al., 2008; Tice, Gaff, and Pruitt-Logan, 1998). Teaching enhancement programs also can raise graduate students' awareness of their own progression, helping them to recognize important teaching-related skills that they have gained and components of these programs that contributed significantly to their skill development (Austin, 2002; DeNeef, 2002; Shannon et al., 1998; Wulff et al., 2004). Preparing future faculty programs seem to be particularly successful in raising graduate students' awareness of their developmental path (DeNeef, 2002).

The influence of pedagogy courses on the long-term development of graduate students as reflective teacher-scholars has received comparatively little attention. Pedagogy courses often emphasize scholarly understandings of teaching as practical tips and best practices (excellent teaching), as evidence gathering and analysis (scholarly teaching), and as "community property" (scholarship of teaching) (Hutchings and Shulman, 1999). Yet studies that have examined the outcomes of pedagogy courses have often relied on end-of-semester student satisfaction surveys and student performance measures as primary sources of data (Carroll, 1980; Jerich and Leinicke, 1993). Furthermore, when perspectives from pedagogy course participants have been investigated, these studies have focused on short-term outcomes such as reduced anxiety, increased self-efficacy, or increased confidence (Baumgartner, 2007; Prieto and Altmaier, 1994; Prieto and Meyers, 1999; Schussler et al., 2008, Williams, 1991). As suggested by Wulff et al. (2004), additional data are needed that reveal how graduate students themselves perceive the role of pedagogy courses in their long-term development as scholarly teachers. To what extent does a pedagogy course influence graduate students' awareness of their progression as teachers, and does this awareness persist after the end of the course?

In a preliminary study to address these questions, the authors used focused interviews to explore the role of a health sciences pedagogy course on graduate students' teaching development. Specifically, we conducted interviews with the graduate students no earlier than six months after the end of the course in order to examine their perceptions of the potential *lasting* impacts of the course on their progression and awareness as scholarly teachers. We were interested in the changes students realized in their own definitions, attitudes, and behaviors related to teaching and learning and explored the practices that students thought had improved their teaching and the roadblocks that they believed had hindered their teaching development.

Pedagogical Methods in Health Sciences: Course Background

Two of the authors (MB and VDO) developed and implemented a new, three-credit hour graduate level course titled *Pedagogical Methods in the Health Sciences* (MSCI M620) at a large, public research university. This course is one of about 30 discipline-based pedagogy courses on our campus, with typical enrollments of 10-20 graduate students per course. Although the course was listed in the area of health sciences, the course content was broadly based and applicable to most graduate student instructors. This course was first offered in the spring 2007 semester (January through May) and met once a week for three hours.

Our instructional approach in the pedagogy course reflected the work of Sprague and Nyquist (1989, 1991) and Nyquist and Wulff (1996) about graduate student development in that we viewed our students as colleagues-in-training who would soon transition to the position of junior colleague. Since most of our students had previous teacher training and experience, our learning goals and objectives focused on building students' teaching skills, encouraging awareness of connections between teaching methods and student learning, and promoting reflective practice. By the end of the course, we expected the graduate students to be able to:

- Construct a syllabus and choose appropriate course readings.
- Tailor instruction to students with different learning style preferences.
- Present instructional material in a clear and engaging manner (microteaching).
- Evaluate the appropriateness of different instructional methods (such as lecture, discussion, collaborative and group learning) for different learning goals.
- Become familiar with the literature in Scholarship of Teaching and classroom research literature, including journals, research design, assessment techniques, and quantitative and qualitative research methods.
- Prepare a statement of teaching philosophy that communicates and guides teaching practice.
- Prepare a course or teaching portfolio that documents assessment, reflection, and analysis of teaching practice.

The subject content for the fifteen-week semester was divided into five blocks: (1) basic educational methods and learning styles, (2) teaching styles and delivery (3) course construction and mechanics, (4) assessment and evaluation tools, and (5) classroom research and the scholarship of teaching and learning (SOTL). The last block was the longest of the five blocks, comprising five of the 15 weeks of the semester. The course dynamic consisted of group discussions, workshop-led activities, and didactic informational sessions. Each student was required to participate in one microteaching session, to conduct two classroom observations of faculty, to apply pedagogical topics from selected articles to classroom practice, and to critique the methodologies of classroom research publications. Graded written assignments included (1) a sample course syllabus (for a course the student wished to develop in the future), (2) a statement of teaching philosophy (submitted as a rough draft and later as a final version) and (3) a comprehensive teaching portfolio (also submitted as a rough draft and then as a final version). One of the authors (KDK), an instructional consultant, provided workshops to the course participants about developing a teaching statement and teaching portfolio and offered individualized assistance with these course assignments.

Participants and Methods of Study

Ten graduate students were enrolled in the pedagogy course during the spring 2007 semester. Their academic departments included anthropology, applied health, biology, kinesiology, and medical sciences. The gender distribution was seven women and three men. While some of the graduate students were relatively new to college teaching, most students had at least one year of experience as a graduate teaching assistant (TA) and/or extensive informal teaching experience such as: conducting public health workshops, leading surgical rounds groups, supervising archeological field school excavations, or mentoring undergraduate students in laboratory and clinic settings.

Beginning six months after the completion of the course (November 2007), six of the ten students participated in voluntary, focused interviews regarding the lasting effects of the pedagogy course on their scholarly teaching behaviors and attitudes. While the initial purpose of the interviews was to determine the degree to which students believed they had applied scholarly concepts from the pedagogy course to their actual teaching six months later, the richness of the interview data gave the authors a snapshot of the graduate students' self-awareness of their development as teachers. Approval for conducting these interviews was obtained from our institution's Human Research Protections Program, and students completed consent forms so we could use their anonymous comments in our study. A graduate student researcher not affiliated with the course (IH) conducted each interview separately. These sessions ranged from one to one-and-a-half hours in length and were audio recorded. Interviews were loosely structured around several general topics that included: students' motivation for taking the pedagogy course; their prior teaching experience; how they measure their teaching effectiveness; and to what extent they are currently applying their knowledge from the course. A substantial portion of the interview asked students to reflect on their experiences related to the pro-

duction of their teaching statement and teaching portfolio. The op
nature of this interviewing format allowed students to explore areas (
to them, and the interviewer was free to probe into areas that eithe
unclear or had the potential for further deconstruction.

Multiple graduate students not affiliated with the pedagogy course produced verbatim transcripts of these audio recordings, including LMG who also
inductively analyzed the transcripts. LMG identified five major themes that
occurred repeatedly across the interviews, and then created a codebook (Table
1) that contained an outline of the major themes and associated subthemes, as
well as descriptions of each for consistent coding. In this grounded theory
approach, the terms of analysis (in this investigation, themes and subthemes)
emerge from a researcher's sustained immersion in the text (see Bernard,
2006; Glaser and Strauss, 1967 for an extensive methodological review of
grounded theory and qualitative analysis). The themes that resulted from this
analysis mirrored a preliminary synthesis of the interview transcripts by VDO
and MB, suggesting a valid and reproducible analysis. Coding was done manu-
ally and, within the context of this study, codes were treated as mutually exclu-
sive. Therefore, responses could only be counted once, and the coder determined which category presented the best fit for the data in question. Each
transcript was tallied by theme and the resulting quantitative data were analyzed to identify the most commonly referenced themes emerging from the
interviews. Interview excerpts quoted in the Results come directly from transcripts and have not been altered by the authors. Furthermore, quoted excerpts give voice to the various viewpoints of the interviewees.

Results

Graduate students' reflections on their teaching development and the influence of the pedagogy course grouped into five major themes, which were
further refined into subthemes (Table 1). The themes are defined as follows:
- *Teaching:* students' definitions of teaching and the role of the pedagogy
  course in these evolving definitions;
- *Training:* the relative value students placed on various sources of teacher
  training, including the pedagogy course;
- *Outcomes:* measurable products from the pedagogy course from the
  students' perspectives;
- *Effectiveness:* students' perceptions of how their attitudes towards teaching have changed as a result of the pedagogy course;
- *Disconnects:* reasons why students may not have used tools they received in the pedagogy course and/or persistent naïve perceptions regarding teaching and learning.

Teaching

The graduate students' responses in the interviews indicated that the pedagogy course played a significant role in their evolving definitions of *Teaching* (Table 1). Interviewees mentioned a considerable amount of informal teaching experience (e.g., as camp counselors, volunteers, or laboratory or field school supervisors), stretching as far back as middle school. However, at the time of those experiences, five of the six interviewees did not categorize them as teaching. This theme arose 27 times across the interviews. The graduate students shared a common preconception of what teaching was; namely, something done formally by an older expert in a particular field in front of a classroom of students who were being graded.

A couple of interviewees, particularly one who has spent a significant amount of time in the workforce before returning to school, maintained a separation between formal and informal teaching. Speaking of the informal teaching that occurred in the workplace, this student said: "that kind of teaching is extremely practical…you're right in the middle of something. It's kind of like being in the middle of an engine repair and teaching someone how to repair an engine. You have to be very specific and very detailed and the information you give people would be very useful information, but no, it's not a classroom. There's no lesson plan or anything like that." This suggests that the individual could see the utility of informal teaching situations, but maintained a separation between this kind of learning and what would happen in a classroom.

However, in part as a result of their participation in the pedagogy class, four of the six interviewees redefined earlier informal experiences as teaching. As one subject remarked: "I look back and see that I *was* passing on knowledge, but at twenty, twenty-one…I thought teaching was something you did in the classroom…" Another student echoed this sentiment: "I think I had a different idea of what teaching was then… My idea of teaching has changed over time. In undergrad I sort of thought of being a teacher as being someone who is in front of a large group of people, not one-on-one training like you get in field school." This same student added: "Overall it [the pedagogy course] kind of allowed me to think about teaching in a broader sense, not as restrictive as the definition I had before."

Due to the pedagogy course, maturity, and the passage of time, two-thirds of the graduate students interviewed were able to reclassify many of their foundational informal experiences as teaching. Furthermore, as the students broadened their definitions of teaching, they also moved away from teacher-centered instructional approaches. One student noted: "It [the pedagogy course] made me a lot more conscientious about what I should be doing overall so that I actually am more aware of reaching out to everybody." Another student, referencing an expanded definition of teaching, was able to draw a parallel

between efforts in the classroom and more applied settings, whic' tc
clude social work, clinics, and archaeological field sites: "I believe
is really the facilitator of information and not stuffing it in…I don't
people help themselves and I offer tools. And that just transfers to teach.....

Table 1. Interview themes regarding graduate students' self-awareness as teacher-scholars

Themes	Subthemes	Description	Frequency
Teaching		Changing definitions of what constitutes teaching	23
Training		How interviewees claim to have received their training	
	Informal Teaching	Everything from summer camps to mentoring	27
	M620 Pedagogy Course	The pedagogy course described in this article	22
	Campus Resources	Other pedagogy courses, scholarship of teaching and learning events, campus consulting offices	17
	Mimicking	Copying what they have seen; following a mentor's lead	13
	TA Experience	Experience as a grader, discussion leader or course instructor	13
	Peers	Learning from other graduate students	11
Outcomes		The results of taking the M620 graduate pedagogy course	
	Interest in Pedagogy	How the pedagogy course influenced anticipated career activities	25
	Application	Using techniques from the pedagogy course in the classroom	23
	Teaching Philosophy Statement	Statement of teaching philosophy	18
	Teaching Portfolio	Teaching portfolio	15
	Self-Evaluation	Changes in students' beliefs about their teaching	
	• reflexivity	Interviewees either self-report more conscious awareness of themselves as teachers or model reflexive thinking during the interview	10
	• confidence	Interviewees report feeling more confident and comfortable in the classroom	8
	• understanding of students	Interviewees report a better understanding of their students	6
Effectiveness		How interviewees measure teaching effectiveness	
	Student Performance	Improved performance as evidence of effectiveness	16
	Evaluations	Student feedback of instructor performance	12
	Reviews	Reviews from professors and/or supervisors	4
Disconnects		Areas in which students are unable to utilize/ apply info from the class	
	Time Constraints	Interviewees report time constraints that interfere with implementation of what was learned	12
	Lack of Teaching Portfolio Materials	Interviewees have failed to produce or save components needed for the teaching portfolio	8
	Forgotten Aspects	Memory lapses	3

." Yet another student remarked: "… [the pedagogy course] changed my perspective on teaching so that I don't see it in the same way anymore. I'm more interested in the learning process as a teacher." Students' experiences in the course helped them to expand their definition of teaching to anyone who facilitates learning, thus embracing a student-centered paradigm for teaching.

Training

The graduate students interviewed identified several sources for their teaching development, including but not limited to the pedagogy course, which testifies to the multifarious ways in which today's graduate students acquire their training. These varied sources became our *Training* subthemes (Table 1) and included: *Informal Teaching, M620 Pedagogy Course, Campus Resources, Mimicking, TA Experience,* and *Peers. Informal Teaching* experience (referenced 27 times in five of the six interviews) and the *M620 Pedagogy Course* (mentioned 22 times by five of the six interviewees) were by far the most influential training experiences for these students. Four of the six interview respondents mentioned *Mimicking* professors, and five of the six mentioned *TA Experience* as ways they learned to teach. Each of these themes were mentioned a total of 13 times during the interviews.

Five of the six interviewees acknowledged having *Informal Teaching* experiences prior to their first graduate teaching assignments. The students realized these informal teaching practices contributed to their overall development as instructors by teaching them a great deal about interacting with people and directing learning. For example, one student said: "I never took any teaching or education courses in my undergraduate career to tell me how to teach, …it was more reading people and figuring out what they needed, what kinds of techniques would help them to understand the material." Another student was able to apply the knowledge gleaned from applied settings to formal teaching situations: "Being an athletic trainer and working in the clinical setting with athletes on a daily basis, you teach every day." Thus, the students used their previous experiences to inform their current teaching practices.

All but one of the interviewees cited the *M620 Pedagogy Course* as an important influence in their development as teachers. In particular, the course offered a more advanced means of training and development than other pedagogy courses they may have taken in the past. Students in the pedagogy course had already performed as teaching assistants (TAs) and, because enrollment in the pedagogy course was elective, they were already highly motivated. Like other pedagogy courses, the pedagogy course did provide students with some practical advice on teaching, and offered students a number of resources. But the pedagogy course also allowed students to "think about teaching in a broader sense," as one interviewee said. The students in the pedagogy course appreciated the faculty emphasis on both teaching *and* research. One respondent commented: "I saw [the pedagogy course] as a good way to improve teaching, but also to start thinking about educational research as a way to combine teaching and research. I like both aspects of that part of academia, but I think people tend to concentrate on one or the other. It was nice to see you could do both." In a sentiment echoed by one other interviewee, one student described the M620 pedagogy course as "a much more mature process" than other pedagogy courses she had taken and said it prepared her "to actually teach at a higher level, to teach at maybe the professor level rather than just [the TA] level." The course introduced graduate students to the idea of classroom research and provided them with an environment in which they could explore their passions for both teaching and research, something most had not encountered regularly in the general academic community. One student expressed her enthusiasm for the course as follows: "It's really encouraging just to be in a class where it's OK to be excited about teaching, that it's not just about being a good teacher because that's what pays the bills and allows you to do the research, but because that's really the exciting part of the job."

The graduate student respondents also recognized several *Campus Resources* that were significant in shaping their skills as teachers. Five of the six interviewees took advantage of regular campus workshops, scholarship of teaching and learning (SOTL) events, and a variety of services provided by campus instructional support offices, whose services are available free of charge to both faculty members and graduate students. Many students made use of the teaching consultation services available on campus, working with KDK in particular for personalized feedback on their teaching statements and portfolios. Speaking of the teaching statement, one student said: "It was new to me. I think it was very helpful because it allowed me to be reflective, to think about why I was doing what I was doing and why I could be valuable to institutions. And of course the help of [the instructors] and, in particular, [the instructional consultant], to help me convey that information to others was extremely useful…I needed some help and [the instructional consultant] was very helpful in helping me put things in a way that other people could understand." Students who did attend campus events such as workshops and the SOTL events found them to be useful, especially for practical concerns such as classroom management and academic dishonesty.

Observations of teachers were an influential source of pedagogical instruction for two-thirds of our interviewees, especially those students who had not received any previous formal instruction about pedagogy. Whether positive or negative, these observations and *Mimicking* gave students some degree of confidence in having a template to follow in their own teaching. Because of previous teaching models, one student adopted a strictly lecture format in her classes: "I didn't know any other way to do it… In my undergraduate classes, that's how they were, the professor standing up there lecturing, giving you pages and pages of notes, and I really didn't know any other way to teach the material I was going to teach." Students also mentioned influential professors whose innovative styles they have observed and would like to emulate: "That's the kind of teacher I'd really like to be someday. That kind of teacher that's *really* reaching the students and getting them excited about the material, no matter how big the classroom." Through modeling and mimicking, teaching strategies were transmitted between generations of instructors.

The graduate students interviewed also spoke of how their *TA Experience* influenced their development as teachers. Four of the six interviewees reported that they were expected to serve as TAs without any explicit teacher training. The expectations of TAs vary greatly across and within departments. There is no internal differentiation of the TA designation despite the fact that some act as graders for large lecture courses, others run their own discussion section under the supervision of a faculty member, and still others are responsible for the development and teaching of their own independent course. For the most part, the students in our study who held TA positions led sections with tightly controlled content and close faculty supervision, a situation especially common in science, technology, engineering, and math (STEM) disciplines. One third of the students interviewed said they received little direction in their teaching. One such student said she felt like they were "flying by the seat of [their] pants." Yet half of the respondents thought that they did not have enough autonomy in the classroom to justify this as a substantial teaching experience. These interviewees tended to be dissatisfied by their lack of control over the course; as one interviewee said: "I'd like to do something that would give me a little more of an opportunity to teach and less of an opportunity to observe and do grading and things like that." Others, however, saw the benefit of such a structured environment; one interviewee claimed that while "you don't have control over the content, you do have control over the way that you provide the information to the students." Yet, regardless of any limitations in their own TA experiences, all respondents cited the TA experience as a valuable way to learn the craft of teaching.

Peers exerted a significant influence on our students and their teaching. Peers helped each other learn as they progressed through their coursework together and also developed similar teaching styles when sharing responsibility for a large class. Whereas initially they perceived themselves as neophytes seeking advice from more experienced TAs, the graduate students in our study soon found themselves as the ones to whom younger graduate students turned for guidance. As one student commented: "When I first started, the people that are more senior, I would definitely go to them with questions. And I find that happening now too. Some of the people come to me sometimes with questions. So there is a lot of dialogue, but it's much more informal." Another interviewee realized she was developing teaching skills even as a s̶ think [teaching] happened even just in the classes that you take. If yo̶ more experience you do end up being a teacher to the people that d̶ experience in that area even if you're not the instructor for that class." By interacting with colleagues through teaching, the interviewees had developed an awareness of their own positioning within a constantly changing social field.

Outcomes

Due to our interest in the durational effects of pedagogy courses, the bulk of the interview data related to *Outcomes* of having taken the graduate pedagogy course (Table 1), with subthemes that included: *Interest in Pedagogy*, *Application*, *Teaching Statement*, *Teaching Portfolio*, and *Self-Evaluation*. Based on a quantitative analysis of students' comments related to *Outcomes* (Table 1), students most often referred to an increased *Interest in Pedagogy* as well as to *Application* of practical skills learned in the pedagogy course, topics that were mentioned 23 and 21 times, respectively, across all six interviews. References to the *Teaching Statement* and *Teaching Portfolio*, both class assignments, occurred slightly less frequently. Although all students discussed these themes, the former was only mentioned 16 times and the latter 13 times across all six interviews.

The lowest frequency subtheme was *Self-Evaluation*, which is defined as students' perceptions of how their attitudes about teaching and teaching behaviors have changed as a result of the course. This subtheme was further divided into three categories: *reflexivity*, *confidence*, and *understanding of students*. Five out of the six students reported an increase in being more reflective about their teaching but only three of the six reported having more confidence in the classroom. Likewise, only three of the six interviewees mentioned developing a greater understanding of their students and their different learning styles.

Because the pedagogy course was not required, the enrolled students had a preexisting *Interest in Pedagogy*. Thus, the course helped these motivated students reach even higher levels of commitment. Many students interviewed said that taking the pedagogy course "reinforced" or "cemented" the idea that teaching was their primary career goal. In a sentiment mirrored by another interviewee, one student said that the pedagogy course led her to see "pedagogy as a field standing alone." At least one student acknowledged a transition from a view of teaching as just a required part of graduate school to a goal in and of itself. The pedagogy course also exposed students to the idea of classroom research as a productive balance between teaching and scholarly inquiry and generated interest for some students, though not all, in conducting their own classroom research projects. As one student commented: "I saw the class s not just a way to improve my own teaching, but a way to really start using the classroom for research." Another student remarked: "I think it can be a real eye opener that...being a teacher doesn't mean giving up research *at all*. In fact, you're still expected to do both. Sometimes even a little bit more research because you're supposed to be paying attention and taking stock of what you're doing and what works and what doesn't work." While two-thirds of the graduate students interviewed said they were not always able to make teaching a priority because of other demands on their time, all of them reported a greater interest in reading pedagogical literature and attending events about the scholarship of teaching and learning on campus.

Regarding the subtheme *Application*, there was a high degree of variability in the extent to which the students applied their newfound knowledge from the pedagogy course. Some students reported that they were using the same teaching methods, but that the course had helped them refine those techniques. One respondent said: "I don't know that I have [applied methods from the pedagogy course]...I don't know why, if that's just because of the nature of the classes I teach or if it's because I just didn't develop any from the class. I kind of do the same things I did before, I just think I maybe do them better." Interviewees also reported that they did not have the latitude to implement new techniques not prescribed by their supervisor; one respondent predicted that the tools from the pedagogy course "will become more of a component as [they] get more and more responsibility of the class." Still other students commented that the pedagogy course had significantly affected their ability to teach to a large audience or reach students with different learning styles. All but one student interviewed said they implemented new techniques learned during the course, however two of these students reported difficulty in doing so. As one said, the process was "hard and time consuming, but a huge payoff in the end."

Because the *Teaching Statement* and *Teaching Portfolio* were course requirements requiring a substantial amount of time and effort from the students, these outcomes of the course became focal points in the interviews. Comments about the teaching statement demonstrated that the students were interested in preparing a quality product to accompany job applications. Furthermore, the students argued they had grown as teachers because they had been persuaded to articulate and analyze their teaching approaches. Again, the students became aware of themselves as dynamic individuals likely to change and grow as they progress through their careers as teachers. One respondent anticipated returning to her teaching statement and revising it as she enters the job market about a year following the interview because "there'll be some distance between [now and then] and presumably some growth." A majority of respondents admitted that they would not have written the teaching statement if it had not been a requirement of the class. As one interviewee stated: "it was kind of a catalyst for what is my teaching philosophy and what do I do in my classes that *shows* this is what I think of my teaching…It's been a really good way to try and integrate the two and to kind of make sure I'm living my philosophy when I'm teaching." Comments such as these suggest that the students in the pedagogy course were beginning to think of their teaching in terms of evidence-based practice. Despite the difficulty and what one called "weirdness" of evaluating their teaching methods through their teaching statements, students unanimously agreed that the teaching statement and teaching portfolio assignments helped them to reflect upon their strengths as teachers.

Interview responses showed the greatest diversity and idiosyncrasies for *Self-Evaluation*, the personal reflections of how taking the graduate pedagogy course six months prior to the interview shaped the students' attitudes about teaching and teaching behaviors. The three minor subthemes included under *Self-Evaluation* are *reflexivity*, *confidence*, and *understanding of students*. The minor *Self-Evaluation* subtheme referenced the most frequently (ten times) by all but one of the interviewees was *reflexivity*, which refers to the graduate students' increasing conscientiousness in the classroom. For example, one student developed an increased awareness of her minor speech impediment that might interfere with student learning. The classmates pointed out that undergraduates may be uncomfortable pointing this out to their instructor; these comments prompted her to think of how she "could deal with some of the things [she] does" when teaching. The students also began to think more critically about their ability, or lack thereof, to evaluate teaching effectiveness, a topic examined more fully below. One student said: "I would probably say that taking [the pedagogy course] made me a more conscientious teacher. I can't say if it made me more effective. I can't say, because I don't have any proof…I feel like I'm paying more attention now to how they're learning and what they're learning and what I'm doing in the classroom than I did before I took [the pedagogy course]." Although the graduate students interviewed continued to struggle with ways of measuring their effectiveness as teachers, the majority of them claimed they are now more likely to reflect upon themselves as teachers and students' understanding of material than they were prior to taking this pedagogy course. These responses indicated that students viewed improvement of their teaching as an ongoing process not to be mastered in one semester, but over the duration of their career.

Another common thread in the interviews related to *Self-Evaluation* was increased *confidence* in teaching ability as a lasting result of the pedagogy course. This subtheme was brought up by three of the six respondents, one of whom mentioned it five separate times during the interview. Increased confidence allowed the graduate students to relax in the classroom, and for at least one student, this led to increased enjoyment of teaching as well. The pedagogy course moved graduate students from the idea that there is what one student called a "good natural teacher" to the realization that there are tools appropriately suited to the college classroom that can improve any teacher's performance. Some students initially approached their TA assignments with some degree of trepidation, due in part to the misconceptions they had about teachers being older experts. Yet taking the pedagogy course imparted the confidence necessary for one graduate student to say: "I'm ready to formally teach a class on the college level." While increased confidence was reported by only half of the respondents, it was a significant outcome of the pedagogy course for those interviewees who did mention it.

The graduate students interviewed identified *understanding of students* as another lasting effect of taking the course. Although this subtheme was only mentioned by three of the six respondents, those students believed that the pedagogy course fostered a deeper understanding of undergraduates, particularly the different ways students learn. One graduate student revised her approach to student learning and introduced new study strategies based on an increased understanding of different learning styles: "I feel like I'm trying more this semester to incorporate those different learning styles that my students might have. So instead of doing just straight lecture for the most part I try to do a lot of partner activities or group activities, things like that." Another graduate student commented favorably on the maturity of the pedagogy course and its theoretical focus. Specifically, this student cited valuable classroom discussions such as those about "being able to recognize when students have different learning styles and being able to develop exercises that will appeal to multiple learning styles so that you're not having students strictly adhere to something that's only going to fit the learning style of maybe 2% of your class. You can accommodate more people with your assignments to get them to learn better." Another graduate student was able to bridge the distance between herself as instructor and the students whom she saw struggling or resisting in her classes, turning a potentially frustrating experience into a teaching opportunity. This student said she developed "a better understanding of who [sic] my students are and what they need from me." These three graduate students believed they were better prepared to respond to their students' needs as a result of their participation in the pedagogy course.

Effectiveness

Like many faculty, the graduate students continue to struggle with means of measuring their teaching effectiveness. The graduate students interviewed commonly cited three methods for measuring their *Effectiveness* as teachers: informal evaluations of their *Students' Performance* in the classroom and on examinations; *Evaluations*, primarily the end-of-course evaluations administered through the students' academic departments; and *Reviews* from professors and/or supervisors.

The graduate students most commonly mentioned *Student Performance* as a method to informally evaluate their teaching effectiveness, although one of the six interviewees made no mention of this subtheme. Interview respondents pointed to grades, effort, and application of knowledge as benchmarks of student success. One graduate student was learning to take cues from the class during lecture to determine objectively her level of effectiveness and said: "I still have to kind of learn I guess how to take that visual feedback from the students and incorporate it into my own assessment without having it really negatively impact my own assessment." Another graduate student looked to more tangible measures to gauge student performance, but made a distinction between undergraduates and upper-level medical students: "For the undergraduates, it's just how well they do on tests and things. I look at my averages versus other people who teach the same material and see if my averages are comparable or better or worse or whatever, and that's how I would assess my teaching ability at this point in time. I also assess just by feedback from the students." The graduate students rarely made reference to other formal learning measurement techniques such as Classroom Assessment Techniques (Angelo and Cross, 1993), which were explicitly discussed in the pedagogy course. These comments revealed a lack of confidence with student performance as a measurement of teaching effectiveness. One respondent stated: "I really don't know [if the technique is effective] because I don't do any evaluation on it to see if they are actually learning from it other than their tests." While recognizing that test scores do indicate a degree of teaching effectiveness, this student also realized that she had not implemented all of the tools necessary to accurately gauge effectiveness. Overall, the pedagogy course increased interviewees' awareness that assessment of teaching effectiveness is an important element of scholarly teaching, but the students often did not incorporate formal student learning assessments into their reflective teaching practice.

The students continued to rely heavily on end-of-semester *Evaluations*, particularly the open-ended responses, to assess their teaching effectiveness. All six interviewees discussed evaluations to some extent. Yet many of them remain skeptical about the validity of these instruments. The graduate students believed that standardized assessments were not the most reliable tools for measuring effectiveness, but they were a necessity, especially in large classes. As one student remarked: "When you're doing big classes, that's kind of the only way you can [measure effectiveness]." Another respondent did not put much stock in undergraduates' evaluations: "When you're an undergraduate and you don't know anything, your opinion doesn't really matter much." This respondent's perception of undergraduate students' evaluations of teaching effectiveness may be related to a teacher-centered conception of teaching.

Three of the six graduate student interviewees reported on instances when they asked peers, faculty, and consultants for *Reviews* of their teaching effectiveness through classroom observations. One of the students interviewed felt comfortable with the amount of documentation she had amassed for her portfolio, but claimed: "The one big gap I had, that I still actually really need…is I don't have a lot of people critiquing me in the classroom, and that's something I need to do one of these days… I could have one of the other [TAs] do it, but that's, you know, I don't think that's an objective eye really." The fact that the graduate students did not actively solicit their colleagues' feedback on their teaching suggests that, although they reported an increased interest in the scholarship of teaching and learning, these students may have been too intimidated to ask colleagues to evaluate their teaching. It is also possible that these students' departments did not promote the kind of direct observation by colleagues that would provide a space for critical reflection and growth and/or that the students were unaware of campus resources explicitly dedicated to these types of support for teaching.

Disconnects

Despite the changes students reported in their perspectives about teaching as a result of their participation in the pedagogy course, the graduate students also referred to *Disconnects* that prevented them from applying course aspects to their teaching, including: *Forgotten Aspects* of the course (mentioned by three students), *Lack of Teaching Portfolio Materials* (mentioned by five students), and *Time Constraints* (mentioned by four students).

Interviewees mentioned many of the theories and techniques taught in the pedagogy course, but recognized they had not retained all the information. In half of the interviews, students reported that when they returned to the classroom after taking the course, they forgot to incorporate many of the activities that they had learned. One student reported: "I don't remember the theories because I'm not a theory person, but I like having them here." While this individual continued to think of teaching in practical terms, exposure in the course to scholarship of teaching and learning literature led to the awareness that theory supports practice.

More specific disconnects surfaced when the interviewer asked the students about their *Teaching Portfolios*. Two-thirds of the students interviewed expressed gratitude that the graduate pedagogy course forced them to begin working on their teaching portfolios. As one student stated: "I wouldn't have done [the teaching portfolio] without [the pedagogy course] at this point, I'll be honest. Like I might have thought about it like a year from now. So it's really nice to know that when the time comes and I want it, that it's pretty close to looking professional and that I'll have to add a few things and tweak a few things, but for the most part, the bulk of the work is done." Another student was grateful for the opportunity to start sorting through these materials well in advance of job application deadlines, saying: "Had I waited until the semester before I'm ready to graduate with my Ph.D. and then try and amass all that stuff it would have been kind of a logistical nightmare and induced tremendous amounts of stress." However, many wished that they had been told to save these materials earlier in their graduate careers. One student said: "I guess I had never really thought of keeping things. I had never thought that you would have to put evidence of student learning in your teaching portfolio. So that was something that I really struggled with because I had never kept that."

A third concern was *Time Constraints*. The graduate students believed they did not have enough time to focus on teaching and learning because of the competing demands placed on their time such as their research, writing their dissertations, and departmental obligations. In an explanation about why it was sometimes impossible to incorporate concepts learned in the pedagogy course, one student said: "A lot of times it was more of a time constraint. Like I didn't have time to replan [sic] my lecture around an activity or something like that. So if I didn't do it, it wasn't because I didn't want to. It's just simply because timing with other things in school didn't work out to do that." Even if they knew they could do a better job of assessing their teaching effectiveness, the students were reluctant to do so because, as one student said: "Stuff like that to implement takes time." Students in the sciences particularly felt that advisors might be unsupportive of their desire to spend more time on teaching development because it would take time away from their laboratory research. In the words of one respondent: "I have the additional challenge of trying to convince [my advisor] that no, this is really something that I need to do for my own professional development and I can balance it with research."

Discussion

While end-of-course student evaluations can provide some basic information about how graduate students perceive the usefulness of a pedagogy course, in-depth interviews with the graduate students permit examination of students' self-awareness about their development as scholarly teachers, and to what extent the participants believe the pedagogy course influenced their development. Further, analyses conducted months after the course provide information about the lasting effects of a pedagogy course on this development. In response to Wulff et al.'s (2004) call for more empirical research in graduate student development, we used qualitative research methodology to take a fine-grained look at the role of pedagogy courses in graduate students' development as teachers. We gauged the enduring effects of a pedagogy course by interviewing six of the ten students who took MSCI M620 (*Pedagogical Methods in Health Sciences*) six months after the completion of the course. In designing this study, we believed that conducting interviews six months after the conclusion of the pedagogy course demonstrated ongoing effects of the course while limiting outside influences on the students' development. We believe this does demonstrate ongoing effects of the pedagogy course while limiting outside influences on the students' development. At the six-month mark, the pedagogy course was still one of the primary resources students had for improving their teaching. Conducting these interviews much later increases the odds that students would be incorporating lessons learned in settings other than the M620 pedagogy course. The open-ended nature of the interview sessions allowed the students to reflect on their experiences in the course, how their ideas about teaching had changed, what modifications they had made in their own teaching, and in what areas their views remained unchanged.

Results from our interviews indicate that the graduate students became more self-aware of their development as scholarly teachers, in part through their participation in the pedagogy course. Similar to the observations of Wulff et al. (2004), some of our interviewees acknowledged broadened and complex definitions of teaching as they progressed through their graduate careers. In particular, these students were cognizant of their own emergent definitions of teaching, which began to include many situations outside of the formal classroom. Formal and informal teaching experiences, observations of their own teachers, peer influence, campus resources, and the pedagogy course contributed substantially to these changing perceptions of teaching. Some (but not all) students integrated new student-centered techniques and teaching assessment methods in their own classes as a result of having taken the pedagogy course. And many students believed that because of the pedagogy course, they had become more conscientious and confident teachers who were attentive to students' various learning approaches.

However, there were several disconnects between the graduate student respondents' scholarly teaching beliefs and practice. As other researchers have observed with their graduate student subjects (Jones, 1993; Luft et al., 2004; Wulff et al., 2004), our graduate students received little teaching mentorship from their faculty supervisors and relied substantially on their peers for teaching support. In addition, our students grappled with conflicting and contradictory messages about the relative importance of research and teaching at a large research 1 university (Wulff et al., 2004). Much like faculty, these graduate students could not always justify, to themselves or their superiors, time spent on teaching development with the competing demands of coursework and research. Also, like many faculty, our students struggled with methods to measure and document their teaching effectiveness. Many of our interviewees said they relied solely upon standardized end-of-semester evaluation forms to determine their effectiveness, even though their interview responses indicated that they were aware of other measures such as gauging students' improvement in the course and tracking student acceptances into professional programs after taking a course with the graduate student. In addition, the students lacked some materials for their teaching portfolios because they had not been advised early enough in their career to retain evidence of effective teaching practice. These are issues many of our graduate students will continue to face, as they themselves become faculty members.

Just as academic search committees like to see candidates who can articulate their approach to teaching, the graduate students interviewed in our study valued opportunities to reflect on and assess their teaching. For them, key features of a successful pedagogy course included both foundational elements of best practices for teaching as well as reflective and evidenced-based approaches to assessing teaching effectiveness. We discovered that the interview process itself served as both an assessment tool for the investigators and as a forum for graduate students to reflect on their teaching. The students were not able to utilize all that they learned in the pedagogy course due to the limitations of their structured teaching assignments. However, the students commented that the tools they acquired would be useful when they had the opportunity to become more independent teachers.

Because our sample was small and focused on one of many pedagogy courses, we plan to conduct interviews with future cohorts of students enrolled in the pedagogy course. There are also opportunities to further this research through collaboration with other pedagogy courses on our campus and beyond. A larger sample size would necessitate multiple coders, who would be normed for interrater reliability. Though outside the scope of this study, a comprehensive analysis might also include classroom observations of teaching behavior to complement students' self-reported behavior in interviews.

Conclusions

Activities that contribute to graduate students' awareness as teacher-scholars and future faculty include regular opportunities for reflection about teaching experiences as well as a variety of programs to support graduate students at different developmental stages (Austin, 2002; DeNeef, 2002; Nyquist and Sprague, 1989; Nyquist and Wulff, 1996; Schussler et al., 2008; Shannon et al., 1998; Wulff et al., 2004). Ideally, a pedagogy course would offer both a foundation for effective teaching as well as the tools to progress along the path to becoming reflective teacher-scholars. Thus teaching enhancement programs such as pedagogy courses can contribute to graduate students' career progress as future faculty. Such programs can effectively socialize graduate students to the multitude of roles they will encounter in their future careers (Adams, 2002; DeNeef, 2002). Furthermore, these teaching enhancement activities address the changing responsibilities and concerns of graduate students throughout their teaching career (Spraque and Nyquist, 1989; Nyquist and Wulff, 1996; Wulff et al., 2004), thereby supporting a smooth transition throughout graduate school and encouraging graduate students to pursue a faculty career (Bomotti, 1994).

Graduate students want to be informed of the research, teaching, and service responsibilities of faculty (Austin, 2002; Perlman, et al., 1996; Wulff et al., 2004). It goes without saying that graduate students who develop realistic expectations of faculty responsibilities through departmental and campus opportunities for teaching development are more likely to have successful transitions to faculty careers (Smith and Kalivoda, 1998). These individuals are more likely to have higher job satisfaction and experience lower stress than their colleagues who have not been adequately socialized to academic life (DeNeef, 2002; Olsen, 1993; Olsen and Crawford, 1998). Because most new faculty members spend the first two years adjusting to their responsibilities, with teaching preparation dominating their time through the fourth semester (Boice, 1991), hiring institutions prefer new faculty who are knowledgeable about the demands of the job (Adams, 2002). Therefore, academic search committees regularly consider and value participation in a teaching enhancement program as well as teaching-related materials (e.g., teaching statements, teaching portfolios, summary student evaluations) for determining their candidates' teaching effectiveness (Bruff, 2007; Kaplan et al, 2007; Meizlish and Kaplan, 2008).

Departments can encourage this transition to independent scholarly teaching through "systematic preparation that acknowledges the holism of graduate student development" (Wulff et al., 2004, p. 65). Our findings led us to make several recommendations to departments and faculty mentors:

1) Offer forums for graduate students to talk about teaching; these programs should be tailored to the concerns of students at different points in their graduate careers and should permit discussion among graduate students and faculty both in and outside the discipline.

2) Provide graduate students with opportunities to teach their own classes or to deliver selected lectures within a larger class.

3) Pair graduate students with teaching mentors who are available throughout their graduate program. These mentors can assist graduate students with designing lesson plans and offer formative and summative feedback based on their classroom observations.

4) Encourage students throughout their graduate programs to document teaching assessments and innovations in a teaching portfolio and to reflect on teaching successes and challenges in a statement of teaching philosophy.

5) Model and facilitate the application of research tools to teaching in order to analyze teaching with a rigorous investigative process and an understanding of the relevant literature.

6) Finally, reward evidence-based assessment of teaching to a similar de-

gree as research because teaching awards and teaching leadership roles can sustain students' enthusiasm about their scholarly teaching development.

Acknowledgements

The authors wish to thank G. Rehrey and J. Robinson (Campus Instructional Consulting) for their help with the M620 course development and our educational research design. L. Plummer (Campus Writing Program) graciously provided us with graduate student assistance in this project. D. Clasby (Campus Instructional Consulting) and A. Schutte (Medical Sciences) helped transcribe interview data. Our Institutional Review Board (IRB) was invaluable in helping us secure human subjects protection. We are most grateful to the M620 students, who consented to participate in this study, who allowed us to learn much from them, and who helped us grow as educators in the process. Finally, we thank our anonymous reviewers whose comments improved the clarity and focus of this manuscript. This work was supported, in part, by an Indiana University Scholarship of Teaching and Learning (SOTL) 2007 Grant.

References

Abbott, R. D., Wulff, D. H., & Szego, C. K. (1989). Review of research on TA training. In J.D. Nyquist, R.D. Abbott, & D.H. Wulff (Eds.), *Teaching Assistant Training in the 1990s: New Directions for Teaching and Learning, no. 39* (pp. 111-123). San Francisco: Jossey-Bass.

Adams, K. A. (2002). *What Colleges and Universities Want in New Faculty*. Preparing Future Faculty Occasional Paper Number 7. Washington, DC: Association of American Colleges and Universities and Council of Graduate Schools.

Angelo, T. A. & Cross, K. P. (1993). *Classroom assessment techniques: A handbook for college teachers*. San Francisco: Jossey-Bass.

Austin, A. E. (2002). Preparing the next generation of faculty: Graduate school as socialization to the academic career. *The Journal of Higher Education, 73*(1), 94-122.

Baumgartner, E. (2007). A professional development teaching course for science graduate students. *Journal of College Science Teaching, 36*(6), 16-21.

Bernard, H. R. (2006). *Research Methods in Anthropology*. Lanham: AltaMira Press.

Black, B. (1995). TA training: Making a difference in undergraduate education. In P. Seldin (Ed.), *Improving College Teaching* (pp. 65-76). Bolton, MA: Anker.

Bomotti, S. S. (1994). Teaching assistant attitudes toward college teaching. *The Review of Higher Education, 17*(4), 371-393.

Boice, R. (1991). New faculty as teachers. *The Journal of Higher Education, 62*(2), 150-173.

Bruff, D. (2007). Valuing and evaluating teaching in the mathematics faculty hiring process. *Notices of the AMS, 54*(10), 1316-1323.

Carroll, J. G. (1980). Effects of training programs for university teaching assistants: A review of empirical research. *The Journal of Higher Education, 51*(2), 167-183.

how does this compare 4 present

, N. V. N. (1998). Preparing graduate students to teach: Past, present, and future. In M. Marincovich, J. Prostko, and F. Stout (Eds.), *The Professional Development of Graduate Teaching Assistants*. Bolton, MA: Anker.

DeNeef, A. L. (2002). *The preparing future faculty program: What difference does it make?* Preparing Future Faculty Occasional Paper Number 8. Washington, DC: Association of American Colleges and Universities.

Diamond, R. M. & Wilbur, F. P. (1990). Developing teaching skills during graduate education. In L. Hilsen (Ed.) *To Improve the Academy: Resources for Student, Faculty, and Institutional Development, 10*: 199-216.

Gaia, A. C., Corts, D. P., Tatum, H. E., & Allen, J. (2003). The GTA mentoring program: An interdisciplinary approach to developing future faculty as teacher-scholars. *College Teaching, 51*(2), 61-65.

Gaff, J. G. & Lambert, L. M. (1996). Socializing future faculty to the values of undergraduate education. *Change, 28*(4), 38-45.

Glaser, B. G. & Strauss, A. L. (1967). *The discovery of grounded theory: Strategies for qualitative research*. Chicago, IL: Aldine.

Hutchings, P. & Shulman, L. S. (1999). The scholarship of teaching: New elaborations, new developments. *Change, 31*(5), 10-15.

Jerich, K. F. & Leinicke, L. M. (1993). A comparative study of the teaching effectiveness of graduate teaching assistants in accounting. In K.G. Lewis (Ed.) *The TA Experience: Preparing for Multiple Roles* (pp. 59-67). Stillwater, OK: New Forums Press.

Jones, J. L. (1993). TA training: From the TA's point of view. *Innovative Higher Education, 18*(2), 147-153.

Kaplan, M., Meizlish, D. S., O'Neal, C., & Wright, M. (2007). A research-based rubric for developing statements of teaching philosophy. *To Improve the Academy, 26*, 242-262.

Levinson-Rose, J. & Menges, R. J. (1981). Improving college teaching: A critical review of research. *Review of Educational Research*, 51(3): 403-434.

Luft, J. A., Kurdziel, J. P., Roehrig, G. H., & Turner, J. (2004). Growing a garden without water: Graduate teaching assistants in introductory science laboratories at a doctoral/research university. *Journal of Research in Science Teaching, 41*(3), 211-233.

Marincovich, M. (1998). Preparing graduate students to teach: Past, present, and future. In M. Marincovich, J. Prostko, & F. Stout (Eds.), *The Professional Development of Graduate Teaching Assistants*. Bolton, MA: Anker.

Meizlish, D. & Kaplan, M. (2008). Valuing and evaluating teaching in academic hiring: A multidisciplinary, cross-institutional study. *The Journal of Higher Education, 79*(5), 489-512.

Nyquist, J. D. & Wulff, D. H. (1996). Recognizing and adapting to stages of graduate teaching assistants' and graduate research assistants' development. In J. D. Nyquist and D.H. Wulff (Eds.), *Working effectively with graduate assistants*. (pp. 18-32). Thousand Oaks, CA: Sage.

Olsen, D. (1993). Work satisfaction and stress in the first and third year of academic appointment. *The Journal of Higher Education, 64*(4), 453-471.

Olsen, D. & Crawford, L. A. (1998). A five-year study of junior faculty expectations about their work. *The Review of Higher Education, 22*(1), 39-54.

Perlman, B., Marxen, J. C., McFadden, S., & McCann, L. (1996). Applicants for a faculty position do not emphasize teaching. *Teaching of Psychology, 23*(2), 103-104.

Prieto, L. R. & Altmaier, E. M. (1994). The relationship of prior training and previous teach. experience to self-efficacy among graduate teaching assistants. *Research in Higher Education, 35*(4), 481-497.

Prieto, L. R. & Meyers, S. A. (1999). Effects of training and supervision on the self-efficacy of psychology graduate teaching assistants. *Teaching of Psychology, 26*(4), 264-266.

Schussler, E., Torres, L. E., Rybczynski, S., Gerald, G. W., Monroe, E., Sarkar, P., Shahi, D., & Osman, M. A. (2008). Transforming the teaching of science graduate students through reflection. *Journal of College Science Teaching, 38*(1), 32-36.

Shannon, D. M., Twale, D. J., & Moore, M. S. (1998). TA teaching effectiveness: The impact of training and teaching experience. *The Journal of Higher Education, 69*(4), 440-466.

Smith, K. S. & Kalivoda, P. L. (1998). Academic morphing: Teaching assistant to faculty member. In M. Kaplan (Ed.), *To Improve the Academy, 17* (pp. 85-102). Stillwater, OK: New Forums.

Sprague, J. & Nyquist, J. D. (1989). TA supervision. In J. D. Nyquist, R.D. Abbott & D. H. Wulff (Eds.), *Teaching assistant training in the 1990s* (pp. 37-53). San Francisco: Jossey-Bass.

Sprague, J. & Nyquist, J. D. (1991). A developmental perspective on the TA role. In J. D. Nyquist, R. D. Abbott, D. H. Wulff, and J. Sprague (Eds.), *Preparing the professoriate of tomorrow to teach: Selected readings in TA training.* (pp. 295-312). Dubuque, IA: Kendall/Hunt.

Taylor, K. L, Schonwetter, D. J., Ellis, D. E., & Roberts, M. (2008). Profiling an approach to evaluating the impact of two Certification in University Teaching programs for graduate students. In L. Border (Ed.), *Studies in Graduate and Professional Student Development: No. 11* (pp. 45-62). Stillwater, OK: New Forums Press.

Tice, S. K., Featherstone, P.H., & Johnson, H. C. (1998). TA certificate programs. In M. Marincovich, J. Prostko, and F. Stout (Eds.), *The Professional Development of Graduate Teaching Assistants.* Bolton, MA: Anker.

Tice, S. K., Gaff, J. G., & Pruitt-Logan, A. S. (1998). Preparing future faculty programs: Beyond TA development. In M. Marincovich, J. Prostko, and F. Stout (Eds.), The *Professional Development of Graduate Teaching Assistants.* Bolton, MA: Anker.

Williams, L. S. (1991). The effects of a comprehensive teaching assistant training program on teaching anxiety and effectiveness. *Research in Higher Education, 32*(5), 585-598.

Wulff, D. H., Austin, A. E., Nyquist, J. D., & Sprague, J.. (2004). The development of graduate students as teaching scholars: A four-year longitudinal study. In D. H. Wulff, A.E. Austin, and Associates (Eds.), *Paths to the Professoriate: Strategies for Enriching the Preparation of Future Faculty* (pp. 46-73). San Francisco: Jossey–Bass.

Lauren Miller Griffith, Ph.D., is an instructor of anthropology at Northern Arizona University, where she teaching undergraduate courses in cultural and linguistic anthropology. Her research interests include performance, education, and tourism/pilgrimage.

Valerie Dean O'Loughlin, Ph.D., is an associate professor of anatomy and cell biology in medical sciences at the Indiana University School of Medicine, where she teaches undergraduate human anatomy, medical gross anatomy, and al methods in health sciences. Her research interests are in anatomy and teaching assistant pedagogical development.

D. Kearns, Ph.D., is a consultant in the Center for Innovative Teaching and Learning at Indiana University, where she helps faculty members and graduate student instructors design and implement courses that promote long-term learning. Before coming to IU, she taught introductory biology and mentored graduate students. As a graduate student in ecology, she received two university awards for her instruction of undergraduates and was a teaching assistant mentor for her college.

Mark Braun, M.D., is professor of pathology in the Medical Sciences Program at the Indiana University School of Medicine. He has been involved with the teaching of medical and graduate students since 1978. His interests include the application of web-based instruction to medical education and the impact of infectious diseases among Native Americans of the pre-European and colonial periods.

Isaac Heacock is a Ph.D. student in the Department of Sociology at Indiana University. His research interests include the Scholarship of Teaching and Learning and the intersection of culture of policy.

Section 3
The Challenges Involved in the Education of Future Faculty

Chapter 5

Student Engagement Challenges in Teaching about Controversial Issues

Jacki Fitzpatrick, Jeremy Boden, & Erin Kostina-Ritchey
Texas Tech University

The discussion of controversial issues in college classrooms forces instructors to face common challenges, such as student resistance, inhibition, or even defiance that may be based on students' view of culture, religion, politics, media, family, or friends. A review of the literature unveils typical reasons for the dilemma and common instructor responses. The authors suggest strategies, such as working from a principle of acceptance, for addressing such challenges that are based on the literature and on their classroom teaching experiences.

Discussion of controversial issues can occur in many environments, including the classroom, yet many instructors have limited experience with controversial issues, and little (or no) experience in how to teach such issues (Fletcher & Russell, 2001). Similarly, many areas of study have controversies that should be addressed (see Payne & Gainey, 2003). The nature of the teaching demands might vary across disciplines. For example, family studies instructors need to present diverse topics without (intentionally or unintentionally) portraying one framework as superior to other frameworks (Adams, Dollahite, Gilbert, & Keim, 2001). Fields such as biology have a primary conceptual framework that instructors are expected to teach (e.g., evolution), but instructors face counterarguments from several sources (Henderson, 2007). Colleagues in fields such as political science (Badley, 2007), science (Carter, 2004) and management (Sinclair, 2005) have to address various forms of controversy as well.

According to Johnson and Johnson (1979), educational controversy occurs when two or more individuals have incompatible ideas or theories, and they attempt to address the incompatibility. Controversy occurs when the incompatibility is sufficiently intense to (a) arouse conflict or uncertainty, (b) promote curiosity or (c) resolution is gained through new information (learning). Thus, controversy would not likely develop about trivial issues (e.g., lunch preferences), but might occur in the face of more complex issues (e.g., assisted suicide).

Instructors certainly have to teach important topics, but their preconceptions and limited skills can hinder their effectiveness (Fowler, 1996). Thus, new instructors need to understand the general teaching process (Bellows, 2008) as well as specific techniques for addressing student reactions to controversial topics. The purpose of this paper is to describe common challenges in student resistance and inhibition. Although some examples of controversial topics will be noted, these topics are not the focus of this paper. Rather, the focus is on the processes of resistance and inhibition. In addition, specific pedagogical suggestions are offered as tools for instructors to address these processes.

Student Resistance

Resistance occurs when students refuse to participate, complain, defy or actively challenge instructors (e.g., Felder & Brent, 1996). According to Weimer (2002), resistance is more likely to occur when instructors address controversial topics or use more active teaching techniques. In Weimer's model, resistance can occur when (a) students feel afraid or threatened by new information, (b) new information or intellectual growth requires losses [prior beliefs, assumptions], and (c) students find the information or learning experience is beyond their comfort level.

In reference to fear or threat, some instructors struggle to address students' willingness to learn about controversial topics. Given that students might have had diverse personal histories, they bring different insights to the university (Vials, Cardozo, Ouellett, & Makker, 2008). However, the differences do not guarantee mutual acceptance (between instructor and students, among students). Although students might learn about heterogeneity in the classroom, it can be challenging to help them understand (or accept) new information if their prior life experiences have been homogeneous. Indeed, some students experience xenophobia (Allen, Floyd-Thomas, & Gillman, 2001) and their viewpoints are affected by religion, politics, media, family or friends (Fletcher & Russell, 2001). Such students might actually defy instructors' attempts to expose them to controversial information. This defiance can present a quandary to new instructors. More specifically, how do instructors address resistance while modeling tolerance? To what extent do instructors present themselves as experts whose knowledge is superior to students while still treating students with respect? To what extent do instructors have the responsibility to deconstruct students' assumptions, "a journey that often leads to discomfort, resistance, and challenges to what is defined as . . . normal and valued" (Turner-Vorbeck, 2005, p. 6)?

In reference to loss, students can perceive resistance quite differently than instructors. Rather than seeing their behavior as immature or aggressive, they can see it as an act of loyalty to familial or cultural heritage (Fitzpatrick, 2004). Meyers and Jones (1993) noted that students feel that their prior experience and knowledge are meaningful. In addition, students can assume that instructors share their values or viewpoints, so they can be dismissive that instructors have new information to share (Milam, 2009). Thus, when students are asked to accept new viewpoints or information, some students think that they are implicitly being asked to reject their values (Allen & Hermann-Wilmarth, 2004). For these students, rejection of new information can be a steadfast act of honor. In reference to comfort level, resistance occurs when they are anxious about their ability to learn skill-based knowledge, such as math (Taylor, 2003). Thus, student reactions serve a self-protective function. In all of these cases, criticism of their resistance might only validate that they are "fighting the good fight."

Allen and Hermann-Wilmarth (2004) noted that rather than accepting responsibility for the class environment, many instructors blame students for resistance and failing to become more educated. When faced with student resistance, it is common for instructors to engage in strategies to enhance student compliance. Unfortunately, many of these strategies are antisocial in nature (e.g., punishment, expressed dislike for students). Research has shown that antisocial instructor strategies were positively associated with student resistance (Paulsel & Chory-Assad, 2004). However, there are some prosocial strategies that can foster a better classroom environment for instructors and students.

In reference to fear resistance, one approach is creating a "zone of acceptance". In this approach, instructors convey that all students are respected. This approach is similar to good practice of the artist method, in which instructors provide a low level of explicit direction in order to foster student creativity and exploration (Schank & Jona, 1991). Instructors can allow students to explore issues, but instructors do not give up control of the classroom environment. Rather, they guide students through the course material to promote accurate comprehension. For example, instructors still make point deductions when students give factually incorrect information. However, the instructors clarify the difference between evaluating students' work and judging students' opinions or life experiences. To avoid judgment, students need to be assured that they will not be penalized simply because they disagree with the instructors' viewpoints (Lusk & Weinberg, 1994) on topics for which society has not reached consensus (e.g., abortion). However, it is appropriate for instructors to make point deductions if students cannot accurately identify the legal precedents related to Roe v. Wade. Thus, instructors make distinctions between judgment of work accuracy (which is graded) and judgment of students' personal values (which are not graded). Indeed, failure to create acceptance can mean that instructors inadvertently model the intolerance that many instructors oppose (Vials, et al., 2008).

Much can be learned from the clinical literature about the acceptance process. Unless client problems present a direct threat to self or others, therapists initially accept clients' definition of their problems, affirm clients' positive qualities and acknowledge their pain (Minuchin & Fishman, 1983). Therapists elicit disclosure from clients and demonstrate respect for their viewpoints. They ask guiding questions that do not openly challenge clients, but solicit a more complete picture of the clients' perspectives. As clients experience acceptance, they become open to therapists' input. It is only at this point that therapists start moving clients toward change (Vetere, 2001). Consistent with the definition of educational controversy, the therapist acknowledges incompatibilities between (a) her/his and clients' perspectives or (b) clients' actions and life goals. The acknowledgement is done in a respectful manner, such that clients do not feel demeaned or humiliated. Indeed, the therapist often attempts to create a partnership with clients to resolve the incompatibility.

Clearly, students are not clients and instructors are not therapists. However, instructors can use the same principle of acceptance. Indeed, Minuchin and Fishman (1983) argued that building a connection with others is more a matter of attitude than technique. Thus, instructors can begin courses by accepting students' viewpoints. Openness can be generated by asking students about controversial topics (e.g., assisted suicide) and noting that honorable people can have distinctly different viewpoints on such issues. When students give responses, the instructors can acknowledge various themes that students identify (religious qualms, individual rights, risk of manipulation by unscrupulous family members, dignity in death) without agreeing or disagreeing with a specific theme. Of course, instructors can set appropriate limits on classroom expression (prohibiting racist, bigoted, or demeaning language) while acknowledging students' viewpoints. During this acceptance phase, instructors can focus on the strengths of these viewpoints, then move to an analysis of the limitations (views on assisted suicide are often based on incomplete or less than current information).

Next, instructors guide discussion to the ways in which (a) limitations can be ameliorated and (b) addressing controversy as part of the amelioration process. Meyers and Jones (1993) noted that students want both validation of their past and a comparison of past experiences to new information. After this initial discussion, instructors can teach the relevant course concepts (medical ethics, legal status, economic considerations) related to the topic. Next, instructors can guide a second discussion that focuses on how course concepts can enhance analysis of controversial topics and perhaps create change (in students, professional services or society) over time. In most cases, it would be unrealistic for instructors to expect an instant transformation in students' approaches to controversial topics. However, this tiered approach allows instructors to provide validation and new information while working to reduce resistance. This approach fits with Taylor's (2003) qualitative research, which revealed that students often struggle to find meaning as they move into more challenging information and tasks.

In reference to loss resistance, instructors can focus on empowerment in the learning process. For example, students can engage in reflective writing (reaction papers, journals) as a means to make sense of course material. This approach allows individuals to take charge of the ways in which they express their emergent knowledge or attitudinal changes (Ellis & Griffin, 2000; Mio & Barker-Hackett, 2003). In contrast to other approaches, such as public disclosure of personal viewpoints (Allen, et al., 2001), reflective writing does not require that students share their thoughts with other students in a classroom setting. Removed from the potentials of group pressure, such writing might foster more openness and honesty. This can be a valuable resource for instructors to learn about the students' grasp of course concepts.

In reference to comfort level, empowerment can also occur when students engage in out-of-classroom activities. The empowerment can occur in a gradual manner, such that less intense activities occur in the beginning and more intense activities are added as the course progresses. For example, instructors can start with passive assignments in which students simply observe contexts in which course concepts might occur. Although such activities might seem trivial, they can have educational benefits. Lakin and Wichman's (2005) research revealed that students who engaged in such activities had better concept application skills than a control group, that is, students who did not engage in the activities. If students do well with simple tasks, then they can move to more active strategies over time. Active strategies allow students to participate in events or engage environments "through someone else's eyes" (Fitzpatrick, 2004). Active teaching techniques give students the opportunity to use course concepts to solve problems (Asay & Curry, 2003), see course concepts in real-life conditions (Thompson & Cooper, 2003) or engage in analyses of case studies (Hall, 2006). Research has shown that active learning techniques facilitate students' comprehension (Sanders & Armstrong, 2008). Students can even participate in community service learning activities to create social change (Giordano, 2007). These activities allow students to (a) gain exposure to individuals and settings in which they might not typically interact, (b) see the relevance of course concepts to these settings and (c) collaborate with extant organizations to foster community development (Mobley, 2007). Indeed, Mobley's study revealed that students who engaged in service learning demonstrated more self-efficacy and endorsement of social justice values than a control group. Students can also engage in artistic events (traditional dance, music) to help preserve the culture of underrepresented groups (Mackinlay, 2003). Each strategy has unique advantages, but they share the advantage of moving students beyond lecture to utilize course concepts. Of course, such activities need close monitoring from instructors and community organization leaders (Giordano, 2007). Roberts (2006) notes that instructors need to guide students to make educationally valuable choices, or students will likely stay in their comfort zone (e.g., familiar settings, people, media).

In sum, all of these strategies share the goal of helping instructors turn student resistance from a weakness into a strength in the classroom. If new instructors can stand against the temptation to automatically treat resistance as a defiance of their authority, then they might be more successful in utilizing resistance as a teachable moment. In addition, this approach allows instructors to model the openness that they are seeking from students (e.g., Mio & Barker-Hackett, 2003). Openness is a quality that can serve students well in fields such as geography (Badley, 2007), management (Sinclair, 2005) and politics (Giordano, 2007). Although openness might not be a central value in some fields, it can be an issue in post-education careers (e.g., Conley, 2006). Student resistance can actually be an effective teaching resource, if it is channeled in an appropriate manner. Nocon's (2005) field–based research on teacher-student interaction has demonstrated that initial resistance can be overcome if teachers are effective listeners and negotiators in guiding students to complete tasks. She argued that this process is particularly important with adult learners and enhances the range of teachers' skills. Thus, Nocon suggested that this process is actually "productive resistance" (p. 101).

Student Inhibition

Sometimes instructors are perplexed by students' lack of responsiveness. Lack of responsiveness might reflect students' doubts about their knowledge or concern about others' reactions (Vials, et al., 2008). In response to these doubts or concerns, students often withdraw from classroom activities. This process reflects student inhibition. In an observational study of teacher-student interaction, Walker (2008) found that inhibition or disengagement was evident when instructors were more demanding and less supportive of students. Inhibition contrasts with resistance in that inhibition is more passive and not necessarily directed toward the instructor. However, inhibition hinders learning (Notarianni-Girard, 1999) and can be just as difficult as resistance for new instructors to manage.

Student inhibition is consistent with the Spiral of Silence (SOS) theory (Noelle-Neumann, 1991) that has been used in media and persuasion studies. According to SOS, individuals recognize that they are exposed to particular information, events or objects, which is often accompanied by messages about the response that they should have (think, feel, do about the information or event). If individuals' responses are incompatible with the messages, they are likely to make negative speculations about the outcome of expressing the incompatibility (e.g., humiliation, failure, isolation). In research on adults, Neuwirth, Frederick and Mayo (2007) noted that the fear of isolation is distinct from other psychological states, such as apprehension. So, simply telling students, "don't be nervous," might not address their fears or inhibition. Rather than risk negative outcomes such as isolation, individuals choose to engage in self-censorship (Hayes, Glynn, & Shanahan, 2005). Self-censorship can occur when individuals withhold information, withdraw from interactions or do not seek information when they do not comprehend information or events (Neuwirth, et al., 2007; Taylor, 2003). This process can occur for individual students, but it can also occur for groups of students (extending even to an entire class). Research has identified that this process occurs when group members (a) become cohesive, (b) perceive that they should not challenge leaders, (c) withhold information or opposing viewpoints and (d) make poor decisions (Ahlfinger & Esser, 2001; Rosander, Stiwne, & Granström, 2006). Group members inhibit themselves if they feel coerced (implicitly or explicitly) to accept the leaders' viewpoints.

The SOS principles might be relevant to the college classroom. Students might withhold opinions, statements, or answers to questions if they perceive that (a) the risk of embarrassment is high, (b) instructors clearly favor one viewpoint on a controversial issue or (c) their experience or knowledge does not easily fit the course constructs. For example, students from minority groups might perceive that they are expected to serve as "ambassadors" or experts to others who do not share their culture (Suskind, 2005). In anthropological projects, some individuals cannot trace their ancestors because families withhold historical information to protect family members from pain (Gates, Grant, Kunhardt, & McGee, 2008). Some students might be reluctant to share because they are concerned about the reactions from classmates (Suskind) if they reveal inadequacies or make mistakes. This premise fits with Schor, Pilpel and Benbassat's (2000) research on medical students' hesitation to disclose uncertainty about their decisions (diagnoses, treatment choices). Their research revealed that hesitation was distinct from stress about whether the students had made the right medical decisions. The findings suggested that inhibition might be more about classroom dynamics than knowledge for some students. Finally, some students might simply lack experiences that they consider relevant to the class topics. For example, one undergraduate in a family studies course explained that he had no context to complete a course assignment because he was raised in an orphanage and never developed a sense of family. In art studies, Beckman (2007) noted that many students have not had much exposure to entrepreneurship, so they do not know how to approach this aspect of professional development.

The Spiral of Silence can be particularly difficult for students in academic programs that favor active discussion. For example, feminist studies courses focus on self-disclosure in the classroom as an important element of the teaching experience (Allen & Farnsworth, 1993). Students in political science, criminal justice, and geography commonly discuss issues such as the death penalty, the Confederate flag, and gun control (Leib, 1998; Payne & Gainey, 2003). In biology and environmental sciences, there can be discourse about ethical issues, such as stem cell research or the extent of endangered species protection (Brickman, Glynn, & Graybeal, 2008; Dresner & Blatner, 2006). If instructors engage in high levels of self-disclosure about controversial issues, then they should be aware that they risk limiting student involvement. If the students perceive the disclosure as a definitive statement, then they can feel that other viewpoints are not equally valid. In other fields, (e.g., computer science, math), students might not be expected to engage in disclosure about themselves, but can be expected to discuss how they solve problems. In an observational study conducted in physics courses, Lund and Baker (1999) found that the most common teacher-student interaction was dialogue about the students' problem-solving processes.

Fortunately, there are strategies that instructors can use to reduce inhibition and break a spiral of silence. For example, if instructors pose problems, then they do not need to begin offering a solution immediately. Rather, they can ask students about the nature of the problem and ways that solutions might be derived. If students are not initially responsive, then instructors can prompt students to address information they understand about the problem and move more slowly to a focus on solutions.

In reference to the risk of imposed viewpoints, instructors can present course information in an order that does not reinforce stereotypes or restrictive views. Of course, some courses (e.g., calculus) might need a strictly sequential order of presentation for students to learn increasingly more difficult material. However, this limitation is not true in every field. There can be fields in which the presentation order is dictated more by habit than necessity. For example, the traditional family structure (heterosexual couple with biological children) remains an overarching model in family studies, such that it is treated as the benchmark of normalcy. In a study of acceptance of family structures, Anyan and Pryor (2002) found that students were aware of several structures, but most frequently endorsed traditional families. Instructors can inadvertently reinforce this stereotype if they present the traditional family structure before other structures (single parent family, childfree family, gay/lesbian family). Other family structures can then be seen as deviant or variant, in comparison to the traditional structure. This premise is consistent with research on primacy effects. For example, Kerstholt and Jackson's (1998) experiment on memory indicated that recall (and judgments based on recalled information) was affected by the order in which information was presented. One way to avoid this problem is to alter the order of presentation, such that traditional families are presented in the middle of all family structures. This reorganization of presentation order might expand students' views of "normal" families.

Issues of presentation have also been noted in fields such as history and economics (Colander, 2004). In a qualitative study of students' perceptions of history topics, Epstein (2000) found that African-American and Euro-American students responded to the same topics quite differently. Epstein recommended that instructors be mindful of the order in which they present Euro-American and African-American historical figures, as order might affect students' views of equality and justice. Similarly, the movement away from Western civilization as the standard by which other civilizations are judged can foster more complex viewpoints in World History courses (Don, 2003). In fields in which topics are less amenable to changes, there has been discussion about ways to expand integration of various learning styles. For example, the styles of Aboriginal culture have been integrated into science (Aikenhead, 2002) and music education (Mackinlay, 2003). The Aboriginal culture emphasizes a collectivistic view in which people are a small part of the natural world (Harris, 1988 in Fogarty & White, 1994), rather than architects of the natural world. Thus, discussions of science might place more emphasis on the preservation and adaptation to environments. In addition to standard lectures, instructors should also be mindful of the presentation order in case studies, problems, media, and discussion questions.

Another way to build a more open learning environment is the scaffolding of course topics. In this approach, instructors introduce less controversial information before more controversial information. For example, instructors might discuss the advantages of wealth before they discuss the advantages of white privilege in US society (Giordano, 2007). Alternatively, instructors might discuss events on which there is consensus (e.g., criticism of Japanese internment camps during World War II) before discussing events with less consistent support (e.g., criticism of current immigration policies). In a qualitative study of a diversity educational program, McAllister and Irvine (2002) reported that students responded favorably to the progression from low-risk topics to high-risk topics. Instructors can also provide some psychological distance by making an issue more hypothetical (e.g., "What might some people think about the link between violent games and rape?" rather than "Do you think that violent game manufacturers are responsible for some rapes?"). This form of scaffolding focuses on instructors relaying information to students.

Alternatively, scaffolding can be reversed. That is students could relay information to instructors. This process can be achieved by utilizing a think-pair-share technique (Chizmar & Walbert, 1999; Lyman, 1981). In typical TPS assignments, instructors convey questions or problems to students. Students individually think about the question and begin to compile a response. The students then pair with classmates to discuss their responses. In this way, students can collaborate, learn from each other and generate their best ideas. Student pairs then share their responses with other student groups or the whole class. In chemical engineering, this technique helps students learn by doing relevant tasks (Felder & Brent, 2003). In other fields, this technique can be used to get students engaged in discussion of controversial issues. This approach allows students to "test the waters" of public reaction with peers before sharing with a larger student group. In addition, it allows students to gather their thoughts so that they can articulate viewpoints, rather than speaking extemporaneously (if instructors call on them for comment). TPS can be used to facilitate discussion, reduce conflict and enhance learning (Meyers, 2003). Compared to a control group, Cortright, Collins, and DiCarlo (2005) found that students who used such techniques demonstrated better comprehension of concepts and were more proficient at identifying novel solutions to problems. Thus, the technique can facilitate academic benefits beyond reduction of inhibition.

Another consideration is that students might have an inaccurate perception of their degree of inhibition. For example, it is possible that students overestimate (e.g., "I always talk.") or underestimate (e.g., "I never get a chance to ask questions or solve problems.") their participation. Thus, it might be helpful to have students track their degree of participation. This practice might help students identify trends in their learning process (never asks questions when a new unit begins, is more inhibited in group assignments than individual assignments). In addition, research has shown that self-evaluation of participation for each class period is associated with increases in attendance, class participation, assignment completion and self-awareness (Zaremba & Dunn, 2004). If instructors collect the self-evaluations, then they can give students feedback about the accuracy of their perceptions (overestimation, underestimation). The shared information might also facilitate a dialogue between instructors and students about course dynamics. This premise fits with other teaching techniques that foster students' self-awareness when exposed to diversity or controversy (e.g., Fitzpatrick, 2004).

If inhibition is not due to psychological dynamics, such as group pressure or lack of self-awareness, then it might be due to a lack of comprehension. Students might be reticent if they are concerned about revealing ignorance, frustrations, or challenges in comprehending concepts or solving problems (Schor, et al., 2000). One tool to address such issues is brief inclass writing assignments, such as "muddiest point papers" (MPPs). In contrast to participation records, MPPs do not focus on the students' assessment of their degree of participation. Rather, MPPs focus on students' comprehension of concepts and information that they seek to learn. Originally developed by Mosteller (1989) to facilitate statistics education, the papers have been adapted for use in many academic areas, such as economics (Chizmar & Walbert, 1999), geology (McConnell, Steer, & Owens, 2003) and nutrition (Schmidt, Parmer, & Javenkoski, 2002). The basic principle of MPP is that students identify the (a) key concepts that they learned, (b) concepts that were least clear [muddiest] for them, and (c) concepts about which they wished that they had learned more information. The students provide this written information in reference to a specific lecture or class meeting (Mosteller). The papers provide immediate feedback to instructors, and allow them to engage in corrective action (review concepts more slowly, repeat experiments). In a course case study, Mosteller reported that MPP enhanced student comprehension. Using an experimental design, McConnell, et al. found that students who engaged in such learning activities demonstrated deeper understanding of course concepts than control group students. These benefits can empower students (particularly in large classes) to engage more actively in the classroom dynamics (Schmidt, et al., 2002), and demonstrate that student feedback is given serious consideration by the instructor.

A final strategy is for instructors to engage in a particular form of self-disclosure. More specifically, instructors might admit when they make mistakes or struggle with issues (Bryant, 2003). It is understandable that new instructors might hesitate to make such admissions. This could be particularly difficult for instructors in fields in which they are expected to present themselves as experts, such as math. Thus, some instructors might reject this option. An alternative viewpoint on this option is that such admissions can actually foster the learning environment. For example, it can demonstrate to students that thoughtfulness about controversial issues is a process rather than a single event (Sherrill, 2007). It also allows students to see at least one example of a developmental pathway to understanding the course concepts. If students can identify with the instructors' pathway, then they might be less likely to think that their own growth processes are unique (or even aberrant). If self-aberrance is a source of inhibition, then this particular form of instructor disclosure might reduce inhibition. As previously noted, too much instructor disclosure can increase student inhibition. So, instructors must be mindful not to overwhelm students with information.

In sum, the students are less likely to gain from class if they feel inhibited. Instructor self-disclosure can open communication with students, but it is easy for instructors to engage in a disproportionate amount of disclosure. Indeed, instructor disclosure can have a dampening effect in which students do not maximize their learning potential (e.g., Adams, et al., 2001). Thus, this form of communication should be used judiciously (Cayanus, 2004). In addition, instructors can use multiple strategies to decrease the risk of groupthink, allow students to move through material in a scaffold format, and increase students' self-evaluation of their roles in the class communication process. Such strategies fit the argument that instructors should use interactive techniques (rather than simply didactic lecture techniques) to promote student learning (Johnson, 2001).

Conclusion

Teaching is a challenge, responsibility, and privilege. Instructors have a responsibility to address controversial issues, but to do so in a manner that engages rather than distances students (Leib, 1998). We have listed several strategies that colleagues use to address controversial issues. The strategies empower students to express their viewpoints or demonstrate their knowledge in a productive classroom environment (Mio & Barker-Hackett, 2003). According to Brookfield (1995), "the hope that undergirds our efforts to help students learn is that doing this will help them act toward each other, and toward their environment, with compassion, understanding, and fairness" (p. 1). In this way, instructors facilitate the professional development of the next generation of scientists, teachers and professionals (Bellows, 2008; Vials, et al., 2008).

The strategies also empower instructors by offering them tools to address typical struggles in early teaching experiences. Although new instructors are commonly told what to teach (course content), they are less commonly told how to teach or deal with teaching problems (classroom dynamics). Yet, the issues of classroom dynamics are arguably as important as course content (Allen, et al., 2001). Indeed, Morris' (2001) research has revealed that when instructors struggle with the differences between their teaching beliefs and classroom actions, they attribute the struggles to lack of adequate training. When utilizing engagement techniques, instructors will quickly learn that each class has unique dynamics and the same techniques might not work from semester to semester. Thus, instructors would do well to be flexible in their use of techniques to address resistance or inhibition. Melles (2008) noted that instructors have to learn how to manage issues of fact, emotion, and identity to teach effectively. Good instructors engage in self-reflection to identify the ways in which they are managing classroom dynamics.

In addition, instructors might need to consider the ethical dimensions of addressing controversial topics. Some instructors maintain that the mention of controversial topics is bound to create discomfort or is an imposition for students and therefore, the more ethical choice is to avoid controversy. This approach is consistent with the "do no harm" principle that has been applied to various dimensions of teaching (Haydn & Barton, 2007) and is in its own way, an ethical stand on behalf of students. In contrast, some instructors maintain that students will face controversy throughout their careers. In a qualitative study of racial equity in the law, Conley (2006) reported that some law firms found the problems to be intractable. If racial issues are going to be part of lawyers' experiences, then Conley recommended that such issues be addressed in educational settings before students enter the profession. This advice can apply to instructors' preparation of students in many fields. Indeed, some programs integrate dilemmas and controversies through each year of an academic program (e.g., Goldie, Schwartz, McConnachie, & Morrison, 2002). From this perspective, instructors would have the right (and possibly the responsibility) to address controversy in their fields.

If instructors choose to address controversial issues, then they should consider the ethical dimensions of how they address the issues. For example, some instructors might want to set limits on the types of speech, actions and gestures that would be permissible during discussions or class activities. Others might not want to set such limits, but give students adequate notice that intense discussion might occur. In addition, instructors might want to consider whether they want to allow an "out clause," that is, students can refuse participation, leave the room, or not complete an assignment if they consider it too intense. If instructors know that they are going to address controversial topics in a course, then they could notify the students of this issue on the first day of class. If students choose to remain enrolled in the course, then they cannot claim at a later date that such notification was absent.

For example, one of the authors uses the following syllabus statement:

> Given the dynamics of individual, relational and familial development, HDFS [Human Development and Family Studies] courses address many sensitive issues. This course is no exception. Lifespan and relational issues occur in the context of sexual, racial/ethnic, political, spiritual/religious, economic/social class and disability/challenge concerns. The discussion of such issues will increase the student's knowledge of developmental conditions in the modern world, but the information can be emotionally intense. It is also likely that the student will be exposed to a diversity of viewpoints; some viewpoints might differ substantially from the student's personal views. If the student chooses to remain in class, then she/he will be expected to respect the diverse viewpoints represented in course material, as well as the viewpoints of his/her classmates. If the student is easily offended by discussion of such issues, then he/she should consider whether to remain enrolled in the course.

Another resource for classroom management is university guidelines for civil behavior. Many colleges and universities have guidelines about civil (appropriate) student behavior in the classroom (see http://ic.ucsc.edu/CTE/teaching/tips-civility.html for sample guidelines). These guidelines apply across topics or courses, so students cannot usually claim that their uncivil behavior was permissible because a class meeting was intense. If universities enforce penalties for uncivil behavior, then the instructors have a resource to help them manage a classroom environment. Of course, if instructors expect civility from their students, then they need to engage in self-awareness of their behaviors in the classroom (Sorcinelli, 2002). There is an ethical concern if instructors expect civility, but do not practice it.

In general, teaching assistant training and faculty development programs can assist new instructors by addressing systematically the issues of classroom dynamics and student engagement (Bellows, 2008; Bryant, 2003). In addition to traditional issues (lecture development, exam construction), programs can provide training in skills such as initiation, engagement, negotiation, constructive leadership, and conflict management. According to Wolhuter (2006), "any education system stands or falls by the quality of its teaching profession, and therefore, by implication, the quality of its teacher training programmes" (p. 124). If programs fail to provide training in addressing controversial issues, then new instructors are left to "sink or swim" their way through the teaching process. This can be a powerful incentive for instructors to work hard, but it does not necessarily promote a high-quality experience for instructors or their students. In contrast, programs that train instructors to teach about controversies increase the likelihood of an effective teaching and learning experience. The investment in good training benefits students, instructors, and educational systems (Allen & Hermann-Wilmarth, 2004; Wolhuter).

References

Adams, R. A., Dollahite, D. C., Gilbert, K. R., & Keim, R. E. (2001). The development and teaching of the ethical principles and guidelines for family scientists. *Family Relations, 50*, 41-48.

Ahlfinger, N., & Esser, J. (2001). Testing the groupthink model: Effects of promotional leadership and conformity predisposition. *Social Behavior and Personality, 29*, 31-42.

Aikenhead, G. (2002). Cross-cultural science teaching: "Rekindling traditions" for Aboriginal students. *Canadian Journal of Science, Mathematics, and Technology Education, 2*, 287-304.

Allen, K., & Farnsworth, E. (1993). Reflexivity in teaching about families. *Family Relations, 42*, 351-356.

Allen, K. R., Floyd-Thomas, S. M., & Gillman, L. (2001). Teaching to transform: From volatility to solidarity in an interdisciplinary family studies classroom. *Family Relations, 50*, 317-325.

Allen, J., & Hermann-Wilmarth, J. (2004). Cultural construction zones. *Journal of Teacher Education, 55*, 214-226.

Anyan, S., & Pryor, J. (2002). What is in a family? Adolescent perceptions. *Children and Society, 16*, 306-317.

Asay, S., & Curry, B. (2003). Implementing and assessing a critical thinking problem solving project. *Journal of Teaching in Marriage and Family, 3*, 375-398.

Badley, G. (2007). For and against diversity in higher education. *Teaching in Higher Education, 12*, 781-785.

Beckman, G. (2007). "Adventuring" arts entrepreneurship curricula in higher education: An examination of present efforts, obstacles and best practices. *Journal of Arts Management, Law and Society, 37*, 87-112.

Bellows, L. (2008). Graduate student professional development: Defining the field. *Studies in Graduate and Professional Student Development, 11*, 41-58.

Brickman, P., Glynn, S., & Graybeal, G. (2008). Introducing students to cases. *Journal of College Science Teaching, 37*, 12-16.

Brookfield, S. D. (1995). *Becoming a critically reflective teacher*. San Francisco, CA: Jossey-Bass.

Bryant, L. (2003). Becoming a better teacher: Learning from our mistakes. *Communication Studies, 54*, 130-135.

Carter, L. (2004). Thinking differently about cultural diversity: Using postcolonial theory to re(read) science education. *Science Education, 88,* 819-836.

Cayanus, J. (2004). Effective instructional practice: Using teacher self-disclosure as an instructional tool. *Communication Teacher, 18,* 6-9.

Chizmar, J., & Walbert, M. (1999). Web-based learning environments guided by principles of good teaching practice. *The Journal of Economic Education, 30,* 248-259.

Colander, D. (2004). The art of teaching economics. *International Review of Economics Education, 3,* 63-76.

Conley, J. (2006). Tales of diversity: Lawyers' narratives of racial equity in private firms. *Law and Social Inquiry, 31,* 831-853.

Cortright, R., Collins, H., & DiCarlo, S. (2005). Peer instruction enhanced meaningful learning: Ability to solve novel problems. *Advances in Physiology Education, 29,* 107-111.

Don, P. (2003). Establishing world history as a teaching field: Comments from the field. *The History Teacher, 36,* 505-525.

Dresner, M., & Blatner, J. (2006). Approaching civic responsibility using guided controversies about environmental issues. *College Teaching, 54,* 213-219.

Ellis, D., & Griffin, G. (2000). Developing a teaching philosophy statement: A special challenge for graduate students. *Journal of Graduate Teaching Assistant Development, 7,* 85-92.

Epstein, T. (2000). Adolescents' perspectives on racial diversity in U.S. history: Case studies from an urban classroom. *American Educational Research Journal, 37,* 185-214.

Evans, R., Avery, P., & Pederson, P. (1999). *Taboo topics: Cultural restraint on teaching social issues.* Retrieved February 25, 2008 from http://web.ebscohost.com/ehost/pdf?vid=2&hid=4&sid= c4b9193e-be62-4d99-b405-11f67edf9f90%40SRCSM1.

Felder, R., & Brent, R. (1996). Navigating the bumpy road to student-centered instruction. *College Teaching, 44,* 43-47.

Felder, R., & Brent, R. (2003). Learning by doing. *Chemical Engineering Education, 37,* 282-283.

Fitzpatrick, J. (2004, June). *Explorations of differentness and invisibility: A media diary teaching activity on cross-national cultures.* Paper presented at the 2004 Family Science and Northwest Council on Family Relations Joint Conference, West Yellowstone, Montana.

Fletcher, A. C., & Russell, S. T. (2001). Incorporating issues of sexual orientation in the classroom: Challenges and solutions. *Family Relations, 50,* 34-40.

Fogarty, G., & White, C. (1994). Differences between values of Australian Aboriginal and non-Aboriginal students. *Journal of Cross-Cultural Psychology, 25,* 394-408.

Fowler, B. (1996). Increasing the teaching skills of teaching assistants through feedback from observation of classroom performance. *Journal of Graduate Teaching Assistant Development, 3,* 95-103.

Gates, H., Grant, W., Kunhardt, P., & McGee, D. (2008). *African American Lives 2* [Television Series]. New York, NY: WNET.

Giordano, E. (2007, February). *Southeast Asian-American political participation: Engaging students to educate voters.* Paper presented at the American Political Science Association's Conference on Teaching and Learning, Charlotte, NC.

Goldie, J., Schwartz, L., McConnachie, A., & Morrison, J. (2002). The impact of three years' ethics teaching, in an integrated medical curriculum, on students' proposed behavior on meeting ethical dilemmas. *Medical Education, 36,* 489-497.

Hall, S. (2006). Promoting active learning: The marital scenario project. *Journal of Teaching in Marriage and Family, 6,* 100-120.

Haslam, S., Ryan, M., Postmes, T., Spears, R., Jetten, J., & Webley, P. (2006). Sticking to our guns: Social identity as a basis for the maintenance of commitment to faltering organizational projects. *Journal of Organizational Behavior, 27,* 607-628.

Haydn, T., & Barton, R. (2007). First do no harm: Developing teachers' ability to use ICT in subject teaching: Some lessons from the UK. *British Journal of Educational Technology, 38,* 365-368.

Hayes, A., Glynn, C., & Shanahan, J. (2005). Validating the Willingness to Self-Censor Scale: Individual differences in the effect of the climate of opinion on opinion expression. *International Journal of Public Opinion Research, 17,* 443-455.

Henderson, J. (2007). Teaching evolution to creationists. *Sociological Viewpoints, 23,* 73-84.

Johnson, D., & Johnson, R. (1979). Conflict in the classroom: Controversy and learning. *Review of Educational Research, 49,* 51-70.

Johnson, P. (2001). Changing roles for the teaching assistant: A workshop plan. *Journal of Graduate Teaching Assistant Development, 8,* 33-35.

Kerstholt, J., & Jackson, J. (1998). Judicial decision making: Order of evidence presentation and availability of background information. *Applied Cognitive Psychology, 12,* 445-454.

Lakin, J., & Wichman, A. (2005). Applying social psychological concepts outside the classroom. *Teaching of Psychology, 32,* 110-113.

Leib, J. (1998). Teaching controversial topics: Iconography and the Confederate battle flag in the South. *Journal of Geography, 97,* 229-240.

Lund, K., & Baker, M. (1999, July). *Teachers' collaborative interpretations of students' computer-mediated collaborative problem solving interactions.* Paper presented at the International Conference on Artificial Intelligence and Education, Le Mans, France.

Lusk, A. B., & Weinberg, A. S. (1994). Discussing controversial topics in the classroom: Creating a context for learning. *Teaching Sociology, 22,* 301-308.

Lyman, F. (1981). The responsive classroom discussion: The inclusion of all students. In A. Anderson (Ed.), *Mainstreaming Digest* (pp.109-113). College Park, MD: University of Maryland Press.

Mackinlay, E. (2003). Performing race, culture and gender in an indigenous Australian women's music and dance classroom. *Communication Education, 52,* 258-272.

McAllister, G., & Irvine, J. (2002). The role of empathy in teaching culturally diverse students: A qualitative study of teachers' beliefs. *Journal of Teacher Education, 53,* 433-443.

McConnell, D., Steer, D., & Owens, K. (2003). Assessment and active learning strategies for introductory geology courses. *Journal of Geoscience Education, 51,* 205-216.

Melles, G. (2008). Producing fact, affect and identity in architecture critiques – a discourse analysis of student and faculty discourse interaction. *Art, Design and Communication in Higher Education, 6,* 159-171.

Meyers, S. (2003). Strategies to prevent and reduce conflict in college classrooms. *College Teaching, 51,* 94-98.

Meyers, C., & Jones, T. (1993). *Promoting active learning: Strategies for the college classroom.* San Francisco, CA: Jossey-Bass.

Milam, R. (2009, September). *Teaching controversial subjects.* Workshop conducted at the Texas Tech University Teaching Learning and Technology Center, Lubbock, Texas.

Minuchin, S., & Fishman, H. (1983). *Family therapy techniques.* Cambridge, MA: Harvard University Press.

Mio, J., & Barker-Hackett, L. (2003). Reaction papers and journal writing as techniques for assessing resistance in multicultural courses. *Journal of Multicultural Counseling and Development, 31,* 12-19.

Mobley, C. (2007). Breaking ground: Engaging undergraduates in social change through service learning. *Teaching Sociology, 35,* 125-137.

Morris, M. (2001). Factors affecting the congruence of beliefs about teaching and classroom practices of GTAs in elementary foreign language courses. *Journal of Graduate Teaching Assistant Development, 8,* 45-53.

Mosteller, F. (1989). The muddiest point in the lecture as a feedback device. *On Teaching and Learning: The Journal of the Harvard-Danforth Center, 3,* 10-21.

Neuwirth, K., Frederick, E., & Mayo, C. (2007). The spiral of silence and fear of isolation. *Journal of Communication, 57,* 450-468.

Nocon, H. (2005). Productive resistance: Lessons from after school about engaged noncompliance. *American Journal of Education, 111,* 191-210.

Noelle-Neumann, E. (1991). The theory of public opinion: The concept of the Spiral of Silence. In J. A. Anderson (Ed.), *Communication Yearbook 14,* (pp. 256-287). Newbury Park, CA: Sage.

Notarianni-Girard, D. (1999). Transfer of training in teaching assistant programs. *Journal of Graduate Teaching Assistant Development, 6,* 119-147.

Paulsel, M., & Chory-Assad, R. (2004). The relationships among instructors' antisocial behavioralteration techniques and student resistance. *Communication Reports, 17,* 103-112.

Payne, B., & Gainey, R. (2003). Understanding and developing controversial issues in college courses. *College Teaching, 51,* 52-58.

Roberts, J. (2006). Responding to student resistance. *Medical Education, 40,* 711.

Rosander, M., Stiwne, D., & Granström, K. (2006). "Bipolar groupthink": Assessing groupthink tendencies in authentic work groups. *Scandinavian Journal of Psychology, 39,* 81-92.

Sanders, D., & Armstrong, K. (2008). Understanding students' perceptions and experience of a tourism management field trip: The need for a graduated approach. *Journal of Hospitality & Tourism Education, 20,* 29-37.

Schank, R., & Jona, M. (1991). Empowering the student: New perspectives on the design of teaching systems. *The Journal of Learning Sciences, 1,* 7-35.

Schmidt, S., Parmer, M., & Javenkoski, J. (2002). Sharing our experiences with writing-for-learning techniques in a large introductory course: The daily microtheme. *Journal of Food Science Education, 1,* 28-33.

Schor, R., Pilpel, D., & Benbassat, J. (2000). Tolerance of uncertainty of medical students and practicing physicians. *Medical Care, 38,* 272-280.

Sherrill, K. (2007, February). *Teaching and learning about LGBT politics.* Paper presented at the American Political Science Association's Conference on Teaching and Learning, Charlotte, NC.

Sinclair, A. (2005). Body and management pedagogy. *Gender, Work and Organization, 12,* 89-104.

Sorcinelli, M. (2002). Promoting civility in large classes. In C. Stanley & M. Porter (Eds.), *Engaging large classes: Strategies and techniques for college faculty* (pp. 44-57). Bolton, MA: Anker Publishing.

Suskind, R. (2005). *A hope in the unseen: An American odyssey from the inner city to the Ivy League.* New York, NY: Broadway Books.

Taylor, A. (2003). Transforming pre-service teachers' understandings of mathematics: Dialogue, Bakhtin and open-mindedness. *Teaching in Higher Education, 8,* 333-344.

Thompson, S., & Cooper, D. (2001). Grand rounds: Not just for doctors. *Action in Teacher Education, 23,* 84-88.

Turner-Vorbeck, T. A. (2005). Expanding multicultural education to include family diversity. *Multicultural Education, 13,* 6-10.

Vetere, A. (2001). Structural family therapy. *Child Psychology and Psychiatry Review, 6,* 133-139.

Vials, C., Cardozo, K., Ouellett, M., & Makker, K. (2008). Thinking beyond the department: Professional development for graduate students of color. *Studies in Graduate and Professional Student Development, 11,* 29-40.

Walker, J. (2008). Looking at teacher practices through the lens of parenting style. *Journal of Experimental Education, 76,* 218-240.

Weimer, M. (2002). *Learner-centered teaching: Five key changes to practice.* San Francisco, CA: Jossey-Bass.

Wolhuter, C. (2006). Teacher training in South Africa: Past, present and future. *Education Research and Perspectives, 33,* 124-139.

Zaremba, S., & Dunn, D. (2004). Assessing class participation through self-evaluation: Method and measure. *Teaching of Psychology, 31,* 191-193.

Jacki Fitzpatrick, Ph.D., has taught more than 18 distinct courses at the undergraduate and graduate level at two universities. In collaboration with a Department Chair, Dr. Fitzpatrick generated a teacher training program for graduate instructors in a social science field. Dr. Fitzpatrick has completed several conference presentations and manuscripts on college teaching topics. All inquiries about this paper should be sent directly to Jacki.Fitzpatrick@ttu.edu.

Jeremy Boden, M.S., is a full-time faculty member at Utah Valley University, where he teaches marriage & relationship courses and family life education courses. He is a Ph.D. candidate in the Department of Human Development and Family Studies at Texas Tech University. He has a few years of teaching experience at the college level.

Erin Kostina-Ritchey, M.A., is a graduate student in both the Human Development & Family Studies Department and Biligual Education/Diversity Studies Program at Texas Tech University. In addition to teaching undergraduate courses at Texas Tech University, she has taught university-level courses in Russia and Hungary.

Appendix

Sample Books on Teaching Techniques

Brookfield, S., & Preskill, S. (1999). *Discussion as a way of teaching: Tools and techniques for democratic classrooms*. San Francisco, CA: Jossey-Bass.

Hamon, R. (2006). *International family studies: Developing curricula and teaching tools*. New York, NY: Haworth.

B. Jacoby & Associates (1996). *Service learning in higher education: Concepts and practices*. San Francisco, CA: Jossey-Bass.

Meyers, C., & Jones, T. (1993). *Promoting active learning*. San Francisco, CA: Jossey-Bass.

Nilson, L. (2003). *Teaching at its best: A research-based resource for college instructors* Bolton, MA: Anker.

Stanley, C., & Porter M. (2002). *Engaging large classes: Strategies and techniques for college faculty.* Bolton, MA: Anker.

Weimer, M. (2002). *Learner-centered teaching: Five key changes to practice*. San Francisco, CA: Jossey-Bass.

Chapter 6

Students' Perception of Lesson Objectives in Introductory Mathematics Courses Taught by Teaching Assistants

Jeff Meyer, Matt Elsey & Vilma Mesa
University of Michigan

We report on an investigation within calculus reform courses of the alignment of TAs' stated lesson objectives with perceived lesson objectives by students and external observers. We contrasted the objectives stated by TAs prior to the lesson, objectives as understood by observers viewing the lesson, and objectives reported by students immediately following the lesson. We found discrepancies between those objectives that point to a mismatch between TAs' intended objectives and what actually occurs in the classroom; students' objectives are aligned with classroom activities but not with TAs' stated objectives. We make suggestions to assist TAs in building lesson plans for reform-oriented classes.

Graduate student teaching assistants [TAs] who have full responsibilities for teaching (e.g., planning, teaching, and assessing students), play an important role in teaching introductory-level undergraduate mathematics courses in research universities. Often, however, TAs receive very limited training before entering the classroom as instructors; they have little opportunity to learn how to teach in ways they have not experienced and may very well have never experienced a calculus reform-type course. As such, the limited training can be especially problematic when the TAs are asked to teach classes with a significant focus on in-class group work and problem solving, as advocated by the calculus reform movement (Speer, Gutman, & Murphy, 2005).

Since the beginning of the calculus reform movement in the late 1980s, there have been numerous studies documenting and comparing student progress in reform and classically taught courses. Over the long term, the data support the claim that reform-type classroom activities are more effective in helping students realize their teachers' learning goals. In summarizing the results of 127 NSF projects at 110 institutions between 1988 and 1994, Susan Ganter remarks:

> Evaluations conducted as part of the curriculum development projects mostly concluded that students in reform courses had better conceptual understanding, higher retention rates, higher confidence levels, and greater levels of con-

tinued involvement in mathematics than those in traditional courses. (Ganter, 1999, p. 234).

In this exploratory study, we investigated the alignment (or misalignment) of what a TA teaching a calculus reform class perceives to be the most important parts of a lesson with what his or her students perceive to be the instructor's goals for the lesson. We define "objectives" as what we want students "to learn as a result of our teaching" (Anderson, et al., 2001). We examined how students' perceptions of their TAs' objectives differed from the TAs' intended objectives. We considered the TAs' stated objectives (as obtained from pre-lesson interviews), objectives as understood by an observer viewing the lesson, and objectives as reported by students immediately following the lesson. Ideally, these objectives would be one and the same, but we found that this was not the case.

We used a now-classical model for studying curriculum that has been developed in the mathematics education literature (Travers & Westbury, 1989). This model posits that there are three different versions of curriculum. First, the *intended* curriculum refers to the aims, intentions, goals, and objectives for mathematics that are envisioned for learning at a national, regional, or local level, that is, guidelines in state standards, textbook content, or master syllabi outline the content, processes, and skills that we want students to learn. Second, the *enacted* curriculum is what results from enacting those guidelines in the classroom, via lectures, discussions, or activities that teachers plan so that their students learn the material in the classroom. Third, the *attained* curriculum describes what students learned, and it is usually measured via standardized tests or other forms of assessments, such as quizzes, homework, and examinations.

The model is represented in Figure 1. The arrows in the model indicate that each version of the curriculum affects the next version of the curriculum. The model is useful because it acknowledges that intentions, enactments, and learning might be different; that enactments of similar intentions can vary from classroom to classroom; and that what students learn depends on both the intended and the enacted curriculum.

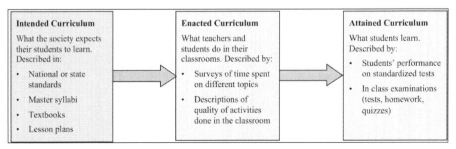

Figure 1: Model for describing different versions of curriculum. Adapted from Travers and Westbury (1989).

In this paper, we investigate how TAs' objectives (i.e., their intentions for the lesson) were realized in the classroom (i.e., the enacted lesson) and how the enactment related to what their students understood these intentions to be (i.e., a weak version of attained curriculum). This framework allows us to describe alignments and discrepancies that occur in teaching from the starting point of lesson objectives. Objectives are "explicit formulations of the ways in which students are expected to be changed by the educative process" (Anderson, et al., 2001, p. 1). There are numerous definitions of objectives in the field (Bloom et al., 1956; Gagné, et al., 2005; Gerlach & Ely, 1980) but all share a description of an "observable student behavior or action that will demonstrate learning, the conditions under which the behavior/action is to occur, and the standard against which the behavior/action will be evaluated" (Sleep, 2009, p. 29). Words such as "appreciate," "know," and "understand" are considered ambiguous because it is not clear what is meant by these verbs and they cannot be directly observed. Rather instructors are encouraged to determine what it would look like (e.g., what students would be able to do) if they appreciated, knew, or understood (Diamond, 2008, p. 148-149). That there are discrepancies between intended and enacted objectives is a common theme in the K-12 mathematics education literature, but the phenomenon has not been studied in higher education, where the literature indicates that what matters is the formulation of clear objectives. Although defining clear objectives is an important first step, we argue that aligning intended objectives with the objectives as enacted in the classroom is not a trivial process in teaching, especially for TAs who need to learn to teach using reform-oriented techniques. Alignment seems to be a crucial goal, as it would support students' opportunities to learn.

"Opportunity to learn" describes the content students have been exposed to in class and allows researchers to make judgments about students' performance on tests relative to their in-class experiences. For example, students who were not given opportunities to learn about derivatives conceptually— either because the conceptual explanations were not in their textbooks or because their instructors did not teach derivatives conceptually in the classroom— are more likely to perform poorly on a test of the conceptual underpinnings of derivatives than students who were exposed to derivatives in a conceptual form. In K–12 educational research, "opportunity to learn" has become a general notion that includes not only content and instructors' enactment of the curriculum, but also school factors that most directly affect student learning (e.g., availability of graphing calculators, qualified teachers, or good textbooks). For a historical description of the evolution of this notion from a research to a policy tool, see McDonnell (1995) and Tate and Rousseau (2006).

Methods

Data were collected in Fall 2008. Our sample consisted of seven TAs, selected as a convenience sample from a pool of approximately fifty who had prior experience teaching introductory-level mathematics at a large research university. Five of the TAs were teaching Calculus I, one was teaching Pre-Calculus, and one was teaching an introductory Interest Theory class. All of the TAs were pursuing graduate studies in mathematics. Six had at least two semesters of college teaching experience and the seventh had two semesters of teaching experience in a high school mathematics scholars program affiliated with another university. None of the observed TAs spoke English as a second language. The seven classes included a total of 146 students.

At this university, Pre-Calculus and Calculus I are taught in small sections (32 students or less) rather than in large lectures. TAs teach the majority of these sections, with a few sections taught by faculty. The vast majority of sections meet three times a week in 80-minute blocks. Instructors are expected to make use of the small class sizes by offering a combination of short mini-lectures, classroom discussions, and individual and group work sessions during class. Homework assignments and exams are standardized across all sections to ensure comparability of all sections. The interest theory course is an introductory course on the mathematical concepts and techniques employed by financial institutions such as banks, insurance companies, and pension funds. It has one section per semester and is taught by a TA. These sections meet three times a week in 50-minute blocks and have enrollments of under 30 students. The TA determines how class time is spent and designs the homework and exams. Although the TAs teaching this class go through the same rigorous training, they are not bound by the need to use reform-oriented techniques in their teaching. This lesson served, in some ways, as a contrast for the reform-oriented classes in our sample.

Seymour (2005) reports that it is common for TAs to attend a "generic one- or two-day workshop that is held before the start of the academic year and that provides a general orientation consisting largely of information on university policies and procedures," (p. 250) and that it is key for TAs to receive assistance in learning to use interactive methods (p. 275). All the TAs observed in this study participated in a rigorous weeklong professional development program immediately prior to their first semester of teaching. The program included practice teaching sessions (videotaped and discussed), sessions on administrative policies, and sessions geared towards techniques particular to reform-style calculus classes. For example, there were sessions titled "Planning and Managing an Interactive Classroom," "Cooperative Learning Techniques in the Classroom," and "Setting Up and Running Homework Teams." As the semester progresses, they also participate in ongoing training in the form of weekly course meetings where course information is shared and TAs can discuss issues arising in their sections. First-semester TAs are also observed at least twice during their first semester of teaching and receive feedback from students and the observer as an outcome of the observation. By all standards, this training gives students substantial support in learning to use the interactive teaching method that is required for the calculus program.

The first two authors contacted each TA and requested permission to (1) conduct an individual interview prior to one of his or her lessons, (2) observe that lesson, and (3) have his or her students respond to a questionnaire at the end of that lesson.

TA Interviews. Our goal was to learn about the TA's teaching experience as well as his or her specific objectives for the lesson that we would observe. The interviews were short (approximately 10 minutes) and informal. We asked them, "What are your objectives for the upcoming lesson?" If the TA had difficulty responding to this prompt, we rephrased the question to clarify our usage of "objective" or provided examples. An objective given by one Calculus I instructor was "for students to develop skill in computing implicit derivatives."

Observations. Our goal was to see the ways in which the TA communicated his or her objectives for the lesson to the students. To this end, either Matt Elsey or Jeff Meyer observed each lesson. We qualitatively recorded events in the lesson using a classroom observation protocol, a modified version of a protocol used in a study of mathematics instruction in community colleges (Mesa, 2009, in turn adapted from Grubb & Associates, 1999). This protocol allowed us to collect information on classroom activities, time spent on those activities, student engagement, and board work. Six lessons were 80 minutes long and the seventh lesson (from the interest theory course) was 50 minutes long.

Student Questionnaire. Our goal was to see what the students could recall at the end of the lesson. The questionnaire had two prompts: (1) "List the major ideas emphasized in today's class," and (2) "Suppose one of your teammates missed this class and they later asked you to tell them what they missed. How would you describe the major ideas emphasized in today's class and how they fit in the context of this course?" The purpose of this questionnaire was to determine what students perceived the objectives of the lesson to be without explicitly cueing them that we were after the objectives. We assumed that by using the term "emphasis," we would target the objectives of the lesson.

Data Analysis

In order to get a sense of the relative emphasis of conceptual versus procedural knowledge in the lessons, we classified the TAs' objectives as either pertaining to conceptual knowledge [C] or procedural knowledge [P] (see Table 1). This is an important categorization, because calculus reform is concerned with conceptual understanding, and at the same time, calculus requires substantial procedural work (Thompson, 1994; Thompson & Silverman, 2008). For example, we coded the objective "Students should understand the accuracy of linear approximations," as conceptual, using the key word "understand" as an indication of interest in deepening meaning, while we coded the objective "Developing skill and proficiency with the Fundamental Theorem of Calculus" as procedural, using the terms "skill" and "proficiency" as an indication of interest in developing methods and techniques.

Reform-oriented classes are designed to include a significant amount of group work and discussion between the instructor and students instead of the traditional lecture format. Because it was germane to our analysis, we parsed our class observation notes into events in which the role of the participants clearly changed; we had three categories, lecture (L), discussion between the TA and students (D), and group or individual work (G/I). We labeled a presentation by the TA that introduced new material to be a "lecture" when there were no questions, answers, or comments formulated by the students. We labeled the presentation as a "discussion" when there was substantial engagement in the form of questions and answers by both the TA and the students. Segments were labeled "group work" or "individual work" when the TA assigned problems to the students and he or she walked around asking or answering questions. We determined the general level of student engagement, which we classified as either "High," "Moderate," or "Low," depending on the number and type of instructor-student and student-student interactions. In particular, we referred to comments in the sections of our notes regarding the frequency and types of student-student interactions such as "students excited about

Table 1: Dimensions of Knowledge: Conceptual and Procedural (Anderson et al., 2001).

Conceptual Knowledge: The interrelationships among the basic elements within a larger structure that enable them to function together.	
Types of Conceptual Knowledge	Examples
C1. Knowledge of classifications and categories	Periods of geological time, forms of business ownership
C2. Knowledge of principles and generalizations	Pythagorean theorem, law of supply and demand
C3. Knowledge of theories, models, and structures	Theory of evolution, structure of Congress
Procedural Knowledge: How to do something, methods of inquiry, and criteria for using skills, algorithms, techniques, and methods.	
Types of Procedural Knowledge	Examples
P1. Knowledge of subject-specific skills and algorithms	Skills used in painting with watercolors, whole-number division algorithm
P2. Knowledge of subject-specific techniques and methods	Interviewing techniques, scientific method
P3. Knowledge of criteria for determining when to use appropriate procedures.	Criteria used to determine when to apply a procedure involving Newton's second law, criteria used to judge the feasibility of using a particular method to estimate business costs

group work" or "student texting" (indicating that a student was using their cellular phone during class rather than engaging with the discussion) to make decisions about level of engagement. We also recorded whether the TA ever explicitly wrote down the lesson objectives on the blackboard.

In Figure 2 we show an example of a summary of class events, recorded during the observation of TA2's class. The summary shows the type of objective formulated by the instructor and how the events in the class corresponded to each objective, from the observer's perspective. The summary also gives the time spent on each event.

Each student response was classified in relation to his or her TA's objectives as Detailed, Nominal, Vague, or Unrelated. Consider the objective "Students should gain proficiency in computation of tangent line approximations" (formulated by TA2). A "detailed" response closely matched the instructor's statement, for example, *"We use linear approximation to approximate $f(a)$ at a point a. This is done by finding the tangent line using the formula, $y - f(a) = f'(a)(x - a)$."* In a "nominal" response the student referred to the objective by name (e.g., *"linear approximation"*). A "vague" response was one that approached the objective but that either showed considerable confusion or was too general (e.g., *"We learned how to approximate functions with lines"*). A response was coded as "unrelated" to an objective if no mention was made of that particular objective. This coding was agreed upon by the observers then independently applied. To calibrate the coding, two tests of inter-rater reliability were conducted; first a full set of students' responses for one TA was coded by both of the first authors and the agreement established as a proportion of agreements to total items coded. This agreement was 66%. The review of the disagreements revealed that they were mostly with contiguous categories (for example, between Vague and Nominal). After discussing the disagreements, a better understanding of the coding categories was developed and agreed upon. Second, another full set of students' responses was recoded

Objective	Type	Events				
		1	2	3	4	5
Students should gain proficiency in computation of tangent line approximations	P		✓	✓	✓	
Students should understand the accuracy of such approximations	C		✓			
Events:						
1. Discussion of homework regarding implicit differentiation. (23 min)						
2. Lecture-based introduction to tangent line approximation with questioning of students. (10 min)						
3. Group exercise: "Find tangent line to $\sqrt{x}$ at x = 1." (8 min)						
4. Group exercise: Two book problems, "What is tangent line approximation to e^x near x = 0" and a problem using the local linearization to approximate derivatives. (20 min)						
5. Group assignment: "Write a potential quiz question on the material from this and the previous section." (7 min)						

Figure 2: Example of event coding for TA2's class.

independently and this time the agreement reached 73%. Given the complexity of the coding system and the nature of the data, we deemed this moderate level adequate for the purposes of this paper, and used the agreed upon definitions to code the remaining student data.

Results

We start with a general summary of the data that we collected, providing numerical information that is useful in characterizing the data; next, we present our three main claims and use data from different aspects of our study to substantiate them.

Summary and Characterization of Data

Table 2 shows a summary of the main characteristics of the lessons taught by the seven TAs. A total of 146 students responded to the questionnaires.

In general the classes observed followed the expected emphasis for the different types of events, with less time devoted to lecture than to discussion or group and individual work. The TAs indicated that the classes observed were representative of their teaching and that there were not unusual events occurring (e.g., exam review or an in-class quiz) on the day on which the observation took place.

Table 3 presents the synthesis of our data concerning the reported TA objectives, class events, and student responses. Eight observations can be derived from the table. First, as a group, the 7 instructors stated 17 objectives; more than half (9) were conceptually oriented. Second, with the exception of TA3, all the TAs stated at least one conceptual objective, and with the exception of TA6, all the TAs stated at least one procedural objective. Only one

Table 2: Characteristics of the Observed Lessons.

Lesson by	Class Size	Student Engagement	Time Allocation by Class Events (min)			Objectives Written on Board
			D	L	G/I	
TA 1	19	Moderate	25	35	15	No
TA 2	21	Moderate	40	10	25	No
TA 3	26	High	40	5	25	No
TA 4	20	Low	25	35	15	Yes
TA 5	22	High	24	28	16	No
TA 6	22	High	13	22	39	No
TA 7[a]	16	High	11	26	6	No
Average[b]	21	-	28	23	23	-

[a] This class was 50 minutes long. All other classes were 80 minutes long. Five to eight minutes were taken from each class to administer the student survey. Time devoted to administrative tasks (e.g., reporting change in office hours) was not included.
[b] Because the 7th observation was shorter, this average does not include it; the average is rounded to the nearest integer.

Table 3: Objectives, Class Events, and Students' Responses in the Seven Lessons Observed.

Class, Number of Stdents in Class, Type of Objective, Stated TA Objective	Event Type[a]	Time (%)[b]	Detailed	Nominal	Vague	Unrelated
						(Students' Responses[c])
TA1 (19 Students)						
1. **[C]** Reinforce the concept of inverse function with the example of inverse trigonometric functions.	D, L	14	11	5	0	3
2. **[P]** Develop skill/proficiency with computations related to inverse trigonometric functions.	D, G	34	7	1	2	9
3. **[C]** Introduce the concept of the tangent function.	D, G, L	13	8	9	0	2
TA2 (21 Students)						
4. **[P]** Students should gain proficiency in the computation of tangent line approximations.	D, G, L	40	9	12	0	0
5. **[C]** Students should understand the accuracy of such approximations.	D, I	7	0	0	2	19
TA3 (26 Students)						
6. **[P]** Demonstrate mathematical modeling of functions based on non-mathematical problem descriptions.	D, G	71	15	4	2	5
7. **[P]** Understanding/recalling/applying the procedure for solving optimization problems.	D, G	14	16	9	1	0
TA4 (20 Students)						
8. **[C]** Understand connection between area under velocity curve and final position.	G, L	13	4	3	4	9
9. **[P]** Proficiency with basic computations using graphs and tables of velocities.	D, G, I	49	11	3	5	1
10. **[P]** Familiarity with notation.	-	0	0	0	0	20
TA5 (22 Students)						
11. **[C]** Understand/Remember statement of Fundamental Theorem of Calculus	D, L	22	5	15	1	1
12. **[P]** Develop skill/proficiency with computations related to the Fundamental Theorem of Calculus.	L	7	0	2	6	14
TA6 (22 Students)						
13. **[C]** Understand the definite integral as a signed area under curve.	D, G, L	66	2	12	3	5
14. **[C]** Understand velocity $v(t)$, position $s(t)$ relationship extends to $f(x)$, $f(x)$ relationship.	-	0	0	0	1	21
15. Have fun	G	69	1	0	0	21
TA7 (16 Students)						
16. **[C]** Understand concept of IRR, in particular how it helps them decide if they should invest.	D, I, L	32	11	4	0	1
17. **[C-P]** Understand and be able to compute some basic probabilities.	D, L	47	11	5	0	0

[a] D: discussion, G: group work; I: individual work; L: lecture. [b] Percentage of minutes of the class devoted to the given events; [c] number of students who gave each type of response; in each row, the numbers add up to the number of students in the class

instructor (TA6) stated an objective that was not cognitively oriented ("15. Have fun"). Third, the majority of the TAs' objectives were addressed in a variety of formats throughout the lessons, but there were two objectives (stated by TA4 and TA6) that were not addressed during the observed classes. Fourth, excluding TA7's class, which was 50 minutes long, on average the TAs spent more time on procedural objectives (31 minutes) than on conceptual objectives (19 minutes); in addition, there was wider variation of time spent on the conceptual objectives (ranging from 7 minutes to 66 minutes).

Fifth, detailed responses about objectives were not very common. Only in the class taught by TA7 (the interest theory course) did a high percentage of the students (near 70%) provide a detailed response for both of the objectives that the TA stated. In TA3's class, about 60% of students provided detailed responses to both objectives. There were six objectives (all of TA6's, one each of TA2, TA4, and TA5's) that were described in detail by less than 10% of the students. It is difficult to determine whether this is a result of low extrinsic motivation for the students to answer the questions carefully (no grade was given and the response was anonymous), the students' difficulties in understanding the lessons, their lack of experience in answering these questions, or their TAs' lack of coherent lesson plans. The students were asked to write their responses immediately following the lessons, while the lessons were still fresh in memory; thus the students had no opportunity to review their notes or try problems on their own prior to responding. As a result, there was no additional opportunity for students to make sense of the material beyond what was provided by the TA during the lesson, which may explain why so few detailed responses were given to match the TAs' objectives. However, the large number of detailed responses provided for some objectives (particularly for TA3 and TA7) suggests that students did have the ability to answer the questionnaires.

Sixth, only 6 of the 17 objectives were identified with detailed or nominal responses by 85% or more of students (both of TA7's, and one each of TA1, TA2, TA3, and TA5's). However, in all classes, at least one student mentioned in detail at least one TA objective.

Seventh, the correlation between time spent on each objective and the number of detailed responses to the objective given by students, was positive $(r = .31, t(15) = 1.28, p < .10)$, which suggests that the more time a TA spent on an objective, the more likely it was that the objective was recalled in detail (or vice versa, the more detailed responses were from objectives on which the TA spent the most time). Conversely, the correlation between unrelated responses and time spent on an objective was negative $(r = -.28, t(15) = -1.13,$ n.s.), which suggests that the less time a TA spent on an objective, the more likely it was for students to provide an unrelated response for that objective. The sample size is too small for making definite claims, but the numbers do suggest an important trend in the data, namely that there is a positive correlation between in-class time spent on an objective and students' recognition of the objective.

In addition, some students described in their responses main ideas that were not stated by their TAs as objectives of the lesson. In Table 4 we list the ideas that at least 50% of the students shared in each class yet were not provided by TAs as objectives. The case of the lesson taught by TA6 is interesting. This TA listed two conceptual objectives, but about half of the students gave detailed or nominal responses about a procedural objective not stated by the TA, an objective that, according to our observation records, was addressed throughout the whole lesson (74 minutes). At the same time, in this class very few students provided detailed or nominal responses regarding the TA's stated objectives (compare with Table 3).

Key Observations

The analysis of the qualitative data allows us to propose three major claims that would merit further investigation with a larger sample. First, and foremost, we found that students listed ideas and techniques related to activities done in the class as objectives of that class, regardless of those activities' relationship to the instructor's intended objectives. Second, student responses differed from TAs' responses in multiple ways. Third, students' engagement alone is not enough to determine how well the objectives perceived by students will match the TA's intended objectives.

Table 4: Main Ideas Described in Detail or Nominally by Students but Not Proposed as Objectives by Their TAs.

Objective	Event	Time (%)	# of Detailed or Nominal Responses
TA2 (21 Students)			
Review of implicit differentiation.	D	27	11 (52%)
TA4 (20 Students)			
Integration.	D	27	12 (60%)
TA5 (22 Students)			
Average of a function over an interval.	L	13	14 (64%)
Integration	D	27	15 (68%)
TA6 (22 Students)			
Develop skill/proficiency with approximating area with rectangles.	D, G	74	17 (77%)

Observation 1: Students listed ideas and techniques related to activities done in the class as objectives of that class, regardless of those activities' relationship to the instructor's intended objectives.

An interesting phenomenon was the wide range of main ideas that students listed in their questionnaires. Some ideas matched their TA's stated objectives very closely, others were slightly related, and many were not related at all (see Table 3). TA7 was the ideal case, with 69% of the students giving detailed responses matching TA7's objectives. The lesson was primarily lecture but punctuated frequently with short individual activities (primarily computation and problem solving) that matched the TA's objectives particularly well. The students were engaged during lecture and on-task during the individual activities. In the end, nearly all of the students' listed objectives matched TA7's. Student responses in TA3's class also matched well with TA3's pre-class interview; in this case, the class consisted primarily of (1) setting up and (2) solving optimization problems, both activities aligning well with the TA's objectives. In contrast, one of the three objectives named by TA6 was nominally matched by about two-thirds of the students, while the other two objectives received in total only one response coded as either "detailed" or "nominal." Time in this lesson was primarily spent on two long segments of group work. For each segment, TA6 assigned several problems out of the text from the same section; however, there was no obvious theme relating any of them. During the second long segment of group work, most groups lost focus within ten minutes and began discussing non-course related material; in spite of this, the segment continued for another eleven minutes. In the students' responses, 14 out of 22 were detailed or nominal matches for the first objective, the only cognitive objective that TA6 spent time on. In addition, the students' responses were mostly unfocused and referred to a wide variety of topics unrelated to TA6's stated objectives.

While TA6 was an extreme case, the students of other TAs provided a variety of responses as well. TA1, using lecture and discussion, introduced the new concept of the tangent function in the last eight minutes of class. TA1 indicated in the interview that this objective was secondary; however, nearly 90% of the students listed the introduction of the tangent function as one of the main ideas of the lesson. After completing a lecture on the Fundamental Theorem of Calculus, TA5 gave out a worksheet that required the use of conceptual knowledge about the integral. Many of the students (about 68%) then listed as an objective for that class "problem solving with the integral," as opposed to problem solving using "computations related to the Fundamental Theorem of Calculus," as had been intended by the instructor.

In summary, students consistently listed ideas and techniques related to activities they engaged in as objectives of that class. This is significant because TA1, TA2, TA5, and TA6 conducted activities requiring ideas and techniques not directly related to their intended objectives, and their students listed those ideas and techniques in their responses (refer to Figure 2 and Tables 3 and 4).

Observation 2: Students' responses differed from TAs' responses in multiple ways. In addition to the students' reporting ideas related to activities done in the class, we noticed three other discrepancies between students' responses and their TAs' intended objectives for their lessons. We list these three discrepancies below.

Focus on review material: In their responses, students consistently included concepts and techniques related to review material from past lessons. We observed that TAs generally spent the first part of the lesson going over past material. In particular, two of the seven classes observed spent 20 minutes or more of the lesson reviewing homework problems. TA2 spent 27% of the lesson reviewing implicit differentiation, and more than half the students in that class reported implicit differentiation as a main idea on their questionnaires.

Procedural vs. Conceptual Knowledge: We also found that the TA objectives most frequently matched by detailed student responses were those pertaining to procedural knowledge, such as TA2's, "Students should gain proficiency in the computation of tangent line approximations." Conversely, objectives pertaining to conceptual knowledge, such as TA2's, "Students should understand the accuracy of such approximations," had fewer detailed student responses (9 of 21 versus 0 of 21). One possible explanation is that, in this lesson, more class time was spent on the procedural objective than on the conceptual objective (30 minutes to 5 minutes). Another possibility is that the benefit of the computational process is immediately obvious to the student—in order to solve the basic problems in the associated section, one must be able to perform the computational procedure, and if students feel confident about those procedures they might be able to describe that confidence in procedural terms. Furthermore, we suspect students have more facility for recognizing and remembering procedures than concepts due to the nature of K–12 mathematical education. To pursue these explanations further interviews with individual students after both conceptual and procedural activities are given would be necessary.

Name of Topic as an Objective: Students uniformly reported the topic of the lesson or the name of the related section in the textbook as a major idea of the day's lesson. In contrast, the TAs reported objectives that were more specific. Consider TA2's first objective: "Students should gain proficiency in the computation of tangent line approximations." All twenty-one students reported "linear approximation," yet only nine of them reported something related to the "computation" of linear approximations as an objective of the lesson.

These discrepancies may be due in part to the differences in the ways in which we asked TAs and students about the objectives of the lesson. The TAs gave their intended objectives in an interview while the students answered preprinted questionnaires, thus while TAs had the opportunity to clarify their objectives, the students did not. While a different method may have been useful, it is unclear that it would have reduced the wide range of responses students gave. The impact of the method for collecting data could be investigated in a follow-up study, but we anticipate that unless the objectives match the activities in the classroom there would still be great variation in student responses.

Observation 3: Student engagement alone is not sufficient to determine how well the objectives perceived by students will match the TA's intended objectives.

Even if the class events emphasized the TA's objectives, low student engagement may prevent the objectives from being internalized by the students. The responses provided by the students of TA4 (the only TA observed with student engagement coded as "low") varied greatly and did not match their TA's stated objectives. Most notably, TA4 concluded class by writing the major objective of the lesson on the board ("Conclude: The area under the curve = distance traveled"). It remained on the board during the time the students filled out their questionnaires. Yet only 55% of TA4's students mentioned this objective in any form in their responses.

At the same time, student responses in classes with high student engagement still may not match the objectives of their TA. For example, the student engagement in TA5's class was coded as "high," yet, as mentioned in Observation 1, there was a significant misalignment between the objectives described by the TA in the interview and the objectives described in the student responses. Thus low engagement can naturally prevent students from learning in class, but high engagement in activities that are unrelated to the class objectives can be also problematic.

Discussion

Few would dispute that in order to be an effective teacher of a calculus reform class, a TA must come to each lesson with a lesson plan that includes activities reflecting the objectives chosen for that lesson. However, our findings suggest that there is more subtlety than one might have originally thought in the relationship between what TAs would like their students to get out of a lesson and what students say were its main points in these reform-oriented classes. Each of the TAs observed came to class with a clear idea of what he or she wanted the students to learn, as well as a lesson plan that he or she thought reflected those goals; that is, they had a clear idea of their 'intended curriculum' for the lesson. However, immediately following the lesson, students generally did not share with their TAs the same ideas about the main mathematical ideas of the lesson, which points to discrepancies in the 'attained curriculum.' As suggested by the Travers and Westbury (1989) model, implementation of the TA's goals in teaching (the 'enacted curriculum') determines the attained curriculum in important ways.

Our first observation is a corroboration of the curriculum model; students reported more frequently what they had the opportunity to learn as the important points of the lesson, independently of what instructors had in mind. This idea appears obvious, in hindsight. But it is important to be aware of, as these TAs clearly had good intentions and a clear idea of what was key for the lessons they were teaching. Yet we observed that the enactments of their plans were not well tied with those objectives. We see here important opportunities for TA development, in terms of assisting TAs in developing activities that match the objectives they have for a particular lesson. TAs need to be exposed to explicit descriptions of the relationship between intentions, enactment, and students' learning, and to the importance of designing objectives that are observable and attainable (Anderson, et al., 2001; Diamond, 2008). A complementary activity to this training is to repeat the process outlined in this paper with TAs, that is, ask them to formulate objectives; observe their lesson, taking notes on how time is used and spent; ask the students for input on main points of the lesson; and then contrast the three pieces of evidence in a mutual discussion. Planning and enacting lessons that fit a given set of purposes are not straightforward activities; TAs must have practice and feedback in order to improve in these skills.

Although TAs were aware that they were going to spend some of their lesson time reviewing past lessons, they did not report ideas in the review as objectives of that day's lesson. It seems that the time spent reviewing was more important in shaping students' understanding of the lesson than instructors recognized. This suggests that TAs might need to spend more time preparing this segment of the lesson and incorporate the ideas treated in the review into their objectives for the lesson.

Often TAs are told that a major key to successful teaching is keeping students engaged in the classroom activities. They are given a wide variety of techniques and suggestions aimed at achieving and maintaining high student engagement. However, it seems that student engagement alone does not necessarily ensure that students will have a clearer idea of what their TA wants them to know at the end of the lesson. While disengaged students are unlikely to learn much from even a well-planned lesson, it is necessary to ensure that the class events that students engage in are also specifically geared toward the TAs' objectives.

To us, the most striking finding was that students consistently listed ideas and techniques related to activities they did individually or in groups as objectives of that class, regardless of their relationship to the instructor's intended objectives. When students were given activities whose completion required auxiliary concepts other than the one being emphasized, the students were later unable to distinguish the primary concept from these auxiliary concepts. For example, TA6's conceptual objective (Table 3) was to "Understand the definite integral as a signed area under curve." Immediately after presenting the concept of signed area and the example $\int_0^{2\pi} \sin(x)dx = 0$, TA6 gave the students five problems to do in groups. The first of these problems asked the students to use a table of data representing the (monotonically decreasing) rate that a chemical is leaking out of a vat to approximate the amount that had leaked out of the vat over several time intervals. In Table 4, we see that 77% of students in this class listed "Develop skill/proficiency with approximating area with rectangles" as an objective of the class, which reflects the techniques associated with completing this activity. Although related, these objectives are mismatched: whereas the students focused on the process of finding the areas, the TA expected them to focus on the nature of that area. This finding is important because the reform movement in calculus places substantial emphasis on peer-to-peer interaction in the classroom; thus this finding makes the need to plan lessons with activities that reflect and emphasize the desired objectives more salient. With this in mind, it appears to be warranted to suggest that for each lesson, TAs choose activities whose completion depends primarily on the application of the concept or skill just introduced.

Finally, and connected to this last point, we see the potential for focused training in designing activities that emphasize students' conceptual development; our observations point to little emphasis in this area in the enacted lessons, and in the students' reports. This area is key, as one of the most important goals of the reform in calculus was to attend to conceptual development.

Limitations

We mention two limitations of the study. First, this is an exploratory study conducted with a convenience sample of seven willing TAs who were aware that we were observing their lesson in advance, and therefore the results are to be interpreted cautiously. These TAs are probably more confident than others about their teaching because they were willing to have others observe and scrutinize their practice. However, the large proportion of students in several of the classes who stated objectives that differed from those of their TAs, suggests that this difference is likely to also be present in a more carefully chosen sample. The TAs were told that we were observing the alignment of objectives between the instructor, classroom events, and students. This knowledge might have affected the lessons, as TAs would have been more purposeful in making the lesson align to their objectives; yet we still observed a significant misalignment between lesson objectives and enactment. If there were such an effect, it would just show that the misalignment would be larger in standard conditions.

Second, students had a short time period to respond to the questionnaire (five to ten minutes at the end of class) and lacked familiarity with the format. This could have had an impact on the quality of the responses they produced, some of which were very short and unelaborated. In addition, there were no tangible incentives for the students to respond with attention and detail, because their participation was anonymous, voluntary, and had no implications for their own standing, we suspect that some students might not have taken the questionnaire seriously. At the same time, we think that for these reasons students gave us a more valid and candid account of what they perceived had happened in the lesson. This format also can be systematically used by instructors to assess the extent to which their lesson objectives match students' perceptions of those objectives, and thus, we felt satisfied with this choice of format.

Conclusion

In spite of the limitations of our exploratory study, our findings reflect an important discrepancy between the objectives conceived by the TA and the objectives perceived by the students in reform-oriented classes. The objectives perceived by students were directly related to what was enacted in the lesson and not with the TAs' intentions for that lesson. Thus when TAs' objectives aligned well with their class enactment, the students had more opportunities to engage with the intended content of the lesson. Although this result appears obvious, there is more we need to understand about *how* exactly the process of stating objectives and aligning instruction takes place; as our results point out, not all the TAs manage to align lesson objectives and enactment despite the rigorous training they received.

Our study suggests that TA training programs need to emphasize not only the importance of setting objectives for lessons but also to reflect on the process of choosing activities that adequately address those objectives. Workshops that illustrate why certain activities might be more appropriate than others in meeting lesson objectives would be fundamental; this kind of work requires expertise in the discipline and knowledge of students' learning processes (Speer, Strickland, Johnson, & Gucler, 2006) which underscores the importance of content-based TA and faculty development.

Besides this emphasis on planning, TAs can be encouraged to ask students at the end of some classes questions similar to the ones we asked in order to determine the extent to which their students agree with the goals they have set for the lesson. This feedback can be productive in helping TAs to create lessons that are more coherent—from intended, to enacted, to attained objectives. Doing so may increase the number of opportunities students have to learn the content of the course and potentially result in greater student achievement.

Authors' Note

This paper is a part of a research study conducted by the first two authors while taking a class on college teaching across science, technology, mathematics, and engineering taught by the third author. Preliminary reports on this work were presented at the *Mathematics Teaching Seminar* at the University of Michigan, February, 2009.

References

Anderson, L. W., Krathwohl, D. R., Airasian, P. W., Cruikshank, K. A., Mayer, R. E., Pintrich, P. R., et al. (Eds.). (2001). *A taxonomy for learning, teaching, and assessing*. New York: Longman.

Bloom, B., Englehart, M. D., Furst, E. J., Hill, W. H., & Krathwohl, D. R. (1956). *Taxonomy of educational objectives: Handbook I, cognitive domain*. New York: McKay.

Diamond, R. M. (2008). *Designing and assessing courses and curricula: A practical guide*. San Francisco, CA: Jossey-Bass.

Gagné, R. M., Wager, W. W., Golas, K. C., & Keller, J. M. (2005). *Principles of instructional design*. Belmont, CA: Wadsworth.

Ganter, S. (1999). An evaluation of calculus reform: A preliminary report of a national study. In B. Gold, S. Z. Keith & W. A. Marion (Eds.), *Assessment practices in undergraduate mathematics* (Vol. 49, MAA Notes, pp. 233-236). Washington, DC: Mathematical Association of America.

Gerlach, V. S., & Ely, D. P. (1980). *Teaching and the media: A systemic approach* (2nd ed.). Englewoods Cliffs, NJ: Prentice Hall.

Grubb, N. W., & Associates. (1999). *Honored but invisible: An inside look at teaching in community colleges*. New York: Routledge.

McDonnell, L. M. (1995). Opportunity to learn as a research concept and a policy instrument. *Educational Evaluation and Policy Analysis, 17*, 305-322.

Mesa, V. (2009, April). *An analysis of classroom interaction in mathematics classrooms in a community college*. Paper presented at the Annual Meeting of the American Educational Research Association, San Diego.

Seymour, E., & Associates. (2005). *Partners in innovation: Teaching assistants in college science courses*. Lanham, MD: Rowman & Littlefield.

Sleep, L. (2009). *Teaching to the mathematical point: Knowing and using mathematics in teaching*. Unpublished PhD Dissertation. University of Michigan, Ann Arbor, MI.

Speer, N., Gutman, T., & Murphy, T. J. (2005). Mathematics teaching assistant preparation and development. *College Teaching, 53*, 75-80.

Speer, N., Strickland, S., Johnson, N., & Gucler, B. (2006). *Mathematics graduate students knowledge of undergraduate students' strategies and difficulties: Supporting concepts for derivative*. Paper presented at the Tenth Research in Undergraduate Mathematics Education Conference, San Diego.

Tate, W. F., & Rousseau, C. (2006). Engineering change in mathematics education. In F. K. Lester (Ed.), *Second handbook for research in mathematics teaching and learning* (pp. 1209-1246). Reston, VA: National Council of Teachers of Mathematics.

Thompson, P. W. (1994). Images of rate and operational understanding of the fundamental theorem of calculus. *Educational Studies in Mathematics, 26,* 229-274.

Thompson, P. W., & Silverman, J. (2008). The concept of accumulation in calculus. In M. Carlson & C. L. Rasmussen (Eds.), *Making the connection: Research and teaching in undergraduate mathematics* (pp. 43-52). Washington, DC: Mathematical Association of America.

Travers, K. J., & Westbury, I. (1989). *The IEA study of mathematics 1: Analysis of mathematics curricula.* Oxford: Pergamon Press.

Jeff Meyer is a graduate student of pure mathematics at the University of Michigan where he has been teaching introductory calculus courses since 2007. He received a B.S. in mathematics and a B.A. in physics from the University of Chicago. His current research is in the area of algebraic groups over local fields. Address: 2074 East Hall, 530 Church Street, Ann Arbor, MI 48109-1043, e-mail: jmeyster@umich.edu.

Matt Elsey is a graduate student in the Applied and Interdisciplinary Mathematics Ph.D. program at the University of Michigan. He received his B.S. and M.S. in Mathematics from the University of Michigan. He studies algorithms for interfacial motions and has interests in mathematics education and in computer science.

Vilma Mesa is an assistant professor in the School of Education. She has a B.S. in computer sciences and a B.S. in mathematics from the University of Los Andes in Bogotá, Colombia, and a master's and a Ph.D. in mathematics education from the University of Georgia. She studies the role that resources play in developing teaching expertise in undergraduate mathematics and she has been involved in several evaluation projects that analyze the impact of innovative teaching practices in mathematics for students in STEM fields. Currently she is studying mathematics instruction in community colleges.

Chapter 7

Effectiveness of Online Case-based Instruction on International Teaching Assistants' Presentation and Active Listening Strategies

Shenghua Zha
James Madison University

Gail Fitzgerald
University of Missouri

This quasi-experimental study examined the effectiveness of online case-based instruction using asynchronous peer discussion through a comparison with face-to-face instruction using peer discussion. Results reveal that online case-based instruction using asynchronous peer discussion is as effective as its face-to-face format in improving international teaching assistants' effective use of presentation and active listening strategies. Based on the positive results of this study, the authors recommend the use of online case-based instruction facilitated through asynchronous peer discussion in training for international teaching assistants so that more time can be devoted to practicing the use of classroom English.

The number of international teaching assistants (ITAs) in United States (U.S.) universities has increased over the past twenty years (De Berly, 1995; Finder, 2005; Hoekje & Williams, 1992; Rounds, 1987; Rubin, 1993; Smith & Simpson, 1993; Yule & Hoffman, 1990). The importance of ITA training has been recognized by the general public as well as by faculty in universities. Typical ITA training offered by U.S. universities includes a one-semester language and culture course, short-time seminars, and workshops (Tang & Sandell, 2000; Yule & Hoffman, 1990). However, insufficient attention to teaching context and role, the lack of time for training, and the shortage of ITA training experts, continue to be problems in ITA training programs (Gorsuch, Stevens, & Brouillette, 2003; Guthrie, 2000; Hoekje & Williams, 1992).

Effective use of presentation strategies and active listening strategies is an important part of successful classroom teaching (Di Leonardi, 2007; Gordon, 1974; Helterbran, 2008; Straits, 2007). Presentation strategies refer to the language strategies that instructors use in class to organize and deliver information effectively (Meyers & Holt, 2002). Active listening strategies are the language strategies that instructors use proactively to elicit students' feedback, acknowledge and rephrase their responses, and reply to their questions for the purpose of improving mutual understanding (Charles, 1999; Gordon, 1974). A recent survey collected from 1310 undergraduate students in a western urban university found that, in students' perceptions, ideal instructors are those who not only are knowledgeable and care about students but also present knowledge in a clear and comprehensible manner (Strage, 2008). Langham (1989) examined the use of language strategies by American and international teaching assistants in their teaching situations. Data collected from students in those TAs' classes showed that the most effective teaching assistants were those who elicited responses from students, listened to students proactively, and replied to students' feedback. Evidence from these studies suggested that ITAs should be given substantive opportunities to learn and practice necessary presentation and active listening strategies in their role as teachers. However, no empirical studies have been reported to investigate the implementation of an approach or a module that effectively enhances ITAs' use of presentation strategies and active listening strategies.

A review of the literature shows that studies on ITA training have been intermittent since the early 1990s when technology-integrated learning first showed its great potential in teacher education and language education (Crumley, 2010; Liu, Moore, Graham, & Lee, 2002). Although discussions and descriptions of technology integration can be easily found on ITA training program web sites or ITA special interest group discussions, to date there are no empirical studies on the effectiveness of technology use in ITA training (Crumley, 2010).

Case-based Instruction

Case-based instruction is an active-learning pedagogy that presents episodes of an event that has or supposedly has happened. Students analyze the resources and contexts provided in the case and discuss issues that were raised in the case before they solve problems and reach conclusions (Stepich, Ertmer, & Lane, 2001). This pedagogy has been widely used in professional areas like business, law, medicine and teacher education (Bramorski, 2002; Flynn & Klein, 2001; Riedel, Fitzgerald, Leven, & Toenshoff, 2003; Semrau & Fitzgerald, 1995; Stepich, Ertmer, & Lane, 2001; Weiss & Levison, 2000). Studies in case-based instruction provide sufficient evidence that it is an effective pedagogy in improving students' problem-solving abilities, knowledge acquisition, and even learning attitudes in a short period of time (Cliff & Wright, 1996; Fitzgerald & Semrau, 1998; Fitzgerald et al., 2006; Tillman, 1995).

Most ITAs in the U.S. do not have teaching experience in postsecondary institutions prior to attending ITA training. Without scenarios presented to them about what classroom teaching looks like, it is difficult for ITAs to transfer what they learn in ITA training to their classroom teaching (Hoekje & Williams, 1992; Kolodner & Guzdial, 2000). By using case-based instruction in ITA training, novices can have the opportunity to confront their conceptions of class-room teaching from multiple perspectives, identify what they need to learn, and think about how the lessons learned from the cases can be utilized in future teaching situations (Kolondner & Guzdial, 2000).

Online Asynchronous Peer Discussion versus Face-to-Face Peer Discussion

Class discussion is key in case-based instruction (Flynn & Klein, 2001; Levin, 1995; Tillman, 1995). After reading or watching cases, either the instructor facilitates case discussions or the students analyze cases with other peers in small groups. Studies revealed that peer discussion worked much better than teacher-led or mentor-led discussion. It promoted participants' mutual responses, improved their understanding of the content, helped them to acquire new strategies, and increased their knowledge of language and language production as well (Beauvois, 1994; Burgstahler, 1997; Droge & Spreng, 1996; Flynn & Klein, 2001; Forman & Cazden, 1985; Hyland, 2000; Kear, 2004; Kern, 1995; Miller, 1995; Myers, 1998; Singhal, 1998; Warschauer, 1996).

Results of some studies suggest that online asynchronous peer discussion facilitates students' active participation and higher-order cognitive processing and is an ideal instructional method in case-based instruction (Bonk & King, 1998; Harasim, 1990; Heckman & Annabi, 2005). A two-year research project on pre-service teachers' use of multimedia case-based instruction found that teachers in online asynchronous discussions had greater conceptual changes than those in face-to-face discussions (Fitzgerald, et al., 2006; Mitchem et al., 2008). However, other studies countered the effectiveness of online asynchronous peer discussion in case-based instruction. For example, students in Kamhi-Stein's (2000) study were found to make fewer evaluative comments in online asynchronous peer discussion than they did in face-to-face peer discussion groups. Likewise, a study done by Angeli, Valanides, and Bonk (2003) showed that students' online peer discussion did not reach a high level of critical thinking and the majority of their discussions only involved the sharing of personal experiences. Research findings also indicated that some students' interest and engagement in asynchronous online discussions decreased over time, which may interfere with the development of learning communities (Angeli, Valanides, & Bonk, 2003; Hammond, 2000). Based on the literature reviewed for this study, there is no conclusive answer about the effectiveness of online asynchronous peer discussion compared to face-to-face synchronous peer discussion.

One challenge in improving ITAs' oral English is the lack of support from their peer groups (Smith, 1993). ITAs are usually friends with students who come from the same ethnic background and who speak the same language. Constant communication in their native language reduces their practice in the use of oral English. Additionally, time spent in face-to-face ITA training provided by universities is short, and provides little opportunity for ITAs to communicate and build social networks with other teaching assistants. Therefore, a broad social mix of teaching assistants may help them to use English to discuss and solve teaching problems outside training sessions and allow them to increase their practice of English.

The purpose of this quasi-experimental study is to explore the effectiveness of online case-based instruction facilitated through asynchronous peer discussion on international teaching assistants' use of presentation and active listening strategies. The effectiveness was measured by comparing changes in their effective use of presentation and active listening strategies in online asynchronous peer discussion with that in face-to-face peer discussion in pre- and post-assessments. The research questions are:

1. Is case-based instruction using peer discussion effective in improving ITAs' effective use of presentation and active listening strategies?

2. Is the online format (case-based instruction using asynchronous online peer discussion) as effective as the face-to-face format (case-based instruction using face-to-face peer discussion) in improving ITAs' use of presentation and active listening strategies?

Methods

Participants

Due to the limited number of ITAs enrolled in the course, a convenience sampling method was selected that included all the 22 ITAs in the two classes of the course on Communication and Culture for American College Teaching in a mid-western university in the Fall semester 2005. One class of ITAs ($N=12$) was assigned to participate in face-to-face instructional activities while the other class of ITAs ($N=10$) was assigned to participate in online instructional activities. All of them had taken the Oral Proficiency Test prior to the course. Their scores fell in the intermediate language proficiency level (lower than 4 out of 5). The same instructor taught the same course content to the two participating classes. Among them, ten were male students and 12 were female students. Students' ages ranged between 20 and 40. The majority were Asians ($N=19$). The rest were African ($N=1$) and Caucasians ($N=2$). The two Caucasians came from Italy.

Research Design

The course instructor agreed not to teach the presentation and active listening strategies that were implemented in this study. The researcher, who also had academic and teaching background in Teaching English as a Second Language (TESL) and had used the Blackboard Learning System™ for several years, was responsible for the delivery and organization of the online and face-to-face instructional activities in this study.

Instructional Activities

One class of ITAs participated in face-to-face instructional activities, which took place in the last class of the week prior to a microteaching presentation (Table 1). The 12 ITAs in this class had to watch the video cases, complete their discussion, and turn in their group solutions. The length of the activities on each topic was around 75 minutes. All the instructional activities in this class were done in the classroom setting.

The other class of ITAs (10 individuals) participated in online instructional activities (Table 1). The ten ITAs could watch the video cases, participate in discussions, and turn in their group solutions anytime within three weeks on each topic. All the instructional activities in this class were conducted in the Blackboard Learning System™. In the first week of the study, ITAs in this class were taught how to log in/off the Blackboard Learning System™, navigate between different sections, download and print materials, and post and edit discussion messages.

Starting with the second week, ITAs in each class were divided into three small groups. Six short videos were viewed in small groups. They included episodes about ITAs' problems in communicating with students, preparing for a class, and engaging students in classroom lecture. After ITAs watched the videos, they were provided with guided questions for group discussion. Questions focused on the use of presentation and active listening strategies in the video cases. After group discussions, ITAs were asked to summarize their group answers, and present the summaries to the whole class or post to the discussion board.

Presentation strategies and active listening strategies were covered in ITAs' instructional activities in chronological order.

Topic 1. Classroom Presentation Strategies. Presentation strategies, such as, word choice, emphasis on key points, explicitness and comprehensibility of the presentations, and organization of the presentations were discussed in this section. Problems displayed in the video cases were related to the introduction to the class, preparation for a class, and students' lack of comprehension of instructions. Guiding questions focused on ITAs' interpretation of inappropriate or insufficient use of presentation strategies in the video cases.

Topic 2. Active Listening Strategies. This section involved discussion of listening, questioning, and answering strategies that a teacher might use in class. Problems presented in the video cases included classroom disruptions and students' miscommunication with instructors. Students in small groups discussed solutions to problems of inappropriate or insufficient use of active listening strategies demonstrated in the video cases.

After each topic, there was a required videotaped microteaching in which each ITA did a teaching presentation in their specialization areas in class. The members of the class, including the course instructor, acted as students, listening to the presentations and asking questions (Table 1).

Data Collection

The Evaluation Sheet for ITAs' Use of Presentation and Active Listening Strategies was used by the course instructor to evaluate ITAs' effective use of presentation and active listening strategies in the microteaching presentations (Appendix A). It was adapted from a five-point Likert scale evaluation sheet that was created and has been used in the ITA program at the university for many years. The Evaluation Sheet for ITAs' Use of Presentation and Active Listening Strategies measures ITAs' effective use of presentation and active listening strategies from seven key elements. They were (1) vocabulary and word/phrase choice, (2) emphasis on key points, (3) explicitness of directions, (4) comprehensibility of presentations, (5) organization of lectures, (6) eliciting students' input, and (7) responding to students' questions. Among them, the

Table 1. Schedule of the Study

Wk	Schedule of Face-to-face Activities Conducted in One Class	Schedule of Online Activities Conducted in the Other Class
1		Training on the use of Blackboard
2	Microteaching as pre-test on use of presentation strategies	
3		
4		Topic 1. Classroom Presentation
5	Topic 1. Classroom Presentation Strategies (75 minutes)	Strategies (three weeks)
6	Microteaching as post-test on use of presentation strategies and pretest on use of active listening strategies	
7		
8		Topic 2. Active Listening Strategies
9	Topic 2. Active Listening Strategies (75 minutes)	(three weeks)
10	Microteaching as post-test on use of active listening strategies	

first five elements were focused on presentation strategies while the last two elements were focused on active listening strategies.

A pre-testing assessment was conducted in the beginning of the course through a microteaching presentation to measure ITAs' initial level of use of presentation strategies. The same instrument was administered at the end of the second microteaching presentation after the instructional activities on presentation strategies. They were used as a post-test measure for ITAs' use of presentation strategies and a pre-test for their use of active listening strategies. The post-test of ITAs' use of active listening strategies was conducted in the third microteaching presentation after the instructional activities on active listening strategies (Table 1).

A pilot test was conducted in the summer semester of 2005 as a basis for this formal study. Results of the pilot study indicated that the inter-rater reliability was very low when the course instructor and the researcher co-evaluated ITAs' performance in the microteaching presentations (á=0.20). Therefore, it was decided that the course instructor would be the only rater to evaluate ITAs' effective use of presentation and active listening strategies in the microteaching presentations in the formal study. Validity and reliability of the Evaluation Sheet for ITAs' Use of Presentation and Active Listening Strategies were investigated in the pilot study. Results showed adequate reliability (á=0.93) and validity for this instrument.

Analysis and Results

Data obtained from the pre- and post-testing were collected to determine the improvement of ITAs' use of presentation and active listening strategies in teaching situations. Repeated measures analysis of variance (ANOVA) and t-test were used to analyze the significance of changes in ITAs' use of presentation strategies and active listening strategies after they completed online or face-to-face instructional activities, and whether these changes were significantly different between participants in the online and face-to-face sessions.

Effectiveness of the Module

The Effectiveness of Case-based Instruction Using Peer Discussion on ITAs' Use of Presentation and Active Listening Strategies

Analysis of repeated measures ANOVA showed that ITAs, in both online and face-to-face instructional activities, had significant improvement ($F=5.387$, $p<.05$) on their use of presentation strategies after the instructional activities.

Analysis of the pre and post-test results also showed that ITAs, in both online and face-to-face instructional activities, had significant improvement on their use of active listening strategies after the online/face-to-face instructional activities ($F=25.651$, $p<.05$).

Comparison of Face-to-Face Format to Online Format

Results of a t-test analysis suggested that there was no significant difference in the use of presentation strategies between the participants in the online and face-to-face instructional activities at the beginning of the study ($p_{presentation\_strategies} > .05$). However, those who participated in face-to-face activities used active listening strategies more effectively than ITAs in online activities in the pre-test ($p_{active\_listening\_strategies} < .05$).

After the online/face-to-face instructional activities, the gap in the usage of presentation strategies between participants in online instructional activities and those in face-to-face instructional activities was narrowed from 1.7 points in the pre-test to .12 points in the post-test (Table 2, Figure 1). However, this difference was not significant between the two classes ($F=1.092$, $p>.05$).

Results of the use of active listening strategies demonstrated that the participants in face-to-face instructional activities significantly outperformed their peers in online instructional activities in the post-test ($F=7.119$, $p<.05$). Since those in face-to-face instructional activities had significantly better use of active listening strategies than those who participated in online instructional activities in the pre-test as well, an improvement rate was computed to see which class of participants had higher improvement on their use of active listening strategies. The improvement rate (IR) was calculated by dividing the difference of the participants' average score in pre- and post-tests by their average in the pre-test ($IR=(M_{post}-M_{pre})/M_{pre}$). Results showed that when com-

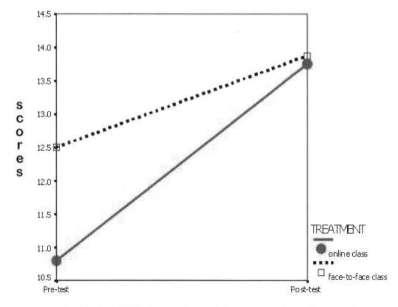

Figure 1. ITAs' Efficient Use of Presentation Strategies

pared to the results in the pre-test, ITAs in online instructional activities improved their use of active listening strategies by 33.7% while ITAs in face-to-face instructional activities improved their use of active listening strategies by 24.8% in the post-test (Table 2, Figure 2).

Discussion

The significant improvement of ITAs' use of presentation and active listening strategies in the pre- and post-tests showed that case-based instruction with peer discussion was an effective approach in improving ITAs' presentation and active listening strategies regardless of its delivery format. As this study measured which learned strategies had been transferred and used in ITAs' micro-teaching presentations, the participants' significant improvement

Table 2. Means of ITAs' Use of Presentation and Active Listening Strategies

	Pre-test		Post-test	
	Presentation strategies	Active listening strategies	Presentation strategies	Active listening strategies
ITAs in online activities (N=10)	10.8	4.3	13.75	5.75
ITAs in face-to-face activities (N=12)	12.5	5.8	13.87	7.24

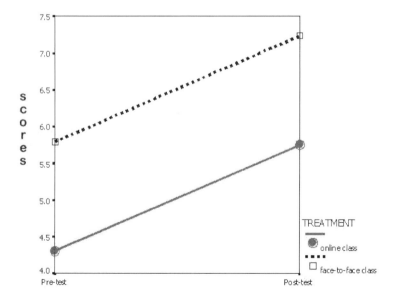

Figure 2. ITAs' Use of Active Listening Strategies

in the pre- and post-tests also revealed that case-based instruction with peer discussion helped them to transfer the presentation and active listening strategies that they learned in cases and discussions to real-world presentations. Previous studies indicate as well that peer discussion and analysis of cases strengthen participants' awareness of the discussed topics and facilitate their transfer of knowledge (Fitzgerald, et al, 2006; Kolondner & Guzdial, 2000; Zha, Tsai, & Fitzgerald, 2008).

Results of this study indicated that the online case-based instruction facilitated through asynchronous peer discussion was as effective as the case-based instructional activity via face-to-face peer discussion in improving ITAs' use of presentation and active listening strategies. This resonates with findings from other studies that endorsed the use of online asynchronous peer discussions in case-based learning (Bonk & King, 1998; Fitzgerald, et al., 2006; Harasim, 1990; Heckman & Annabi, 2005). While face-to-face classroom discussions are short and difficult to monitor by one instructor, online peer discussion offers ITA trainers an opportunity to assess the quality of individual ITAs' discussion and to extend their practice of using English in the role of teachers. A variety of positive teaching cases, as well as negative teaching cases with solutions, can give ITAs clear ideas of how the appropriate use of presentation and active listening strategies will affect teaching and what good teaching situations look like. However, a larger sample study is needed to demonstrate statistical significance in the changes in ITAs' use of presentation and active listening strategies between the online and face-to-face formats.

Limitations

As the inter-rater reliability on the use of presentation and active listening strategies was very low between the instructor and the researcher in the pilot study and it was not possible to employ more raters, the instructor was the only rater in this study. Therefore, lack of objectivity in ratings is a possible limitation for this study. The instructor's interaction with ITAs and impression of their participation and classroom demeanor may affect the instructor's scoring of ITAs' use of presentation and active listening strategies (Allen & Lambating, 2001). It is suggested that an outside, independent observer or a panel of well-trained observers make ratings in similar studies in the future.

Conclusion

Most of ITA training programs are concentrated on accuracy of pronunciation and grammar, which is hard to improve in the short period of time that ITA training programs usually are offered (Hoekje & Williams, 1992; Guthrie, 2000). Given the shortage of time and personnel in ITA training programs and the nature of ITAs' role in classroom teaching, it would be much more efficient to teach novice ITAs to learn how to use presentation and active listening strategies to convey their thoughts and stay in conversation with students. This study proposed a module that integrated asynchronous online peer discussion and case-based instruction into ITAs' learning of presentation and active listening strategies. Findings of this study demonstrated that the combination of these pedagogical elements in an online format was as effective as its face-to-face format in improving ITAs' use of presentation and active listening strategies. Given that the two formats are equally effective, the online method offers an excellent alternative to traditional face-to-face instruction and may provide additional efficiencies in teaching asynchronously across multiple sites and scheduling restrictions. Although a larger sample study is needed to examine statistical significance, the module provides ITA trainers with research-based recommendations for offering ITAs an alternative format to practice and improve their use of English in the role of a teacher using case-based discussions in an online format.

Acknowledgements

Appreciation is given to Monica McCrory, the instructor of the course *Communication and Culture for American College Teaching*, who allowed me to conduct the study in her classes, supported my study, and provided suggestions as an expert in ITA training program.

References

Allen, J. D., & Lambating, J. (2001). *Validity and reliability in assessment and grading: Perspectives of preservice and inservice teachers and teacher education professors*. Paper presented at the Annual Meeting of the American Educational Research Association, Seattle, WA.

Angeli, C., Valanides, N., & Bonk, C. J. (2003). Communication in a web-based conferencing system: The quality of computer-mediated interactions. *British Journal of Educational Technology, 34*(1), 31-43.

Beauvois, M. H. (1994). E-talk: Attitudes and motivation in computer-assisted classroom discussion. *Computers and the Humanities, 28*(5), 177-190.

Bonk, C. J., & King, K. S. (1998). *Electronic collaborators: learner-centered technologies for literacy, apprenticeship, and discourse*. Mahwah, NJ: Lawrence Erlbaum Associates.

Bramorski, T. (2002). The use of cases in teaching business courses in Central and Eastern Europe and the United States. *Journal of Teaching in International Business, 13*(3), 41-55.

Burgstahler, S. (1997). Peer support: What role can the Internet play? Retrieved October 25, 2004, from http://www.rit.edu/~easi/itd/itdv04n4/article2.html

Charles, C. M. (1999). *Building classroom discipline* (6th ed.). New York: Addison, Wesley, and Longman.

Cliff, W. H., & Wright, A. W. (1996). Directed case study method for teaching human anatomy and physiology. *Advances in Physiology Education, 15*(1), S19-S28.

Crumley, H. (2010). Instructional technology in International Teaching Assistant (ITA) programs. *CALICO Journal, 27*(2), 409-431.

De Berly, G. (1995). *The ITA trainer: Advocate or adversary.* Paper presented at the Annual Meeting of the Teachers of English to Speakers of Other Languages, Long Beach, CA.

Di Leonardi, B. C. (2007). Tips for facilitating learning: The lecture deserves some respect. *Journal of Continuing Education in Nursing, 38*(4) 154-163.

Droge, C., & Spreng, R. (1996). Enhancing involvement and skills with a student-led method of case analysis. *Journal of Marketing Education, 18*(3), 25-34.

Finder, A. (2005). When the teacher has mastered all but English. *International Herald Tribune.* Retrieved November 20, 2006, from http://www.iht.com/articles/2005/06/24/news/assistant.php

Fitzgerald, G. E., & Semrau, L. P. (1998). The effects of learners differences on usage patterns and learning outcomes with hypermedia case studies. *Journal of Educational Multimedia and Hypermedia, 7*(4), 309-331.

Fitzgerald, G., Tsai, H., Koury, K., Mitchem, K., Hollingsead, C., & Miller, K. (2006). *Supporting case-based instruction in higher education through technology: What works?* Paper presented at the International Conference on e-Learning, Bangkok, Thailand.

Flynn, A. E., & Klein, J. D. (2001). The influence of discussion groups in a case-based learning environment. *Educational Technology Research & Development, 49*(3), 71-86.

Forman, E. A., & Cazden, C. B. (1985). Exploring Vygotskian perspectives in education: The cognitive value of peer interaction. In J. W. Wertsch (Ed.), *Culture, communication, and cognition* (pp. 323-347). New York: Wiley.

Gordon, T. (1974). *Teacher effectiveness training.* New York: Peter H. Wyden.

Gorsuch, G., Stevens, K., & Brouillette, S. (2003). Collaborative curriculum design for an international teaching assistant workshop. *Journal of Graduate Teaching Assistant Development, 9*(2), 57-68.

Guthrie, E. (2000). New paradigms, old practices: Disciplinary tensions in TA training. In B. Rifkin (Ed.), *Mentoring foreign language teaching assistants, Lecturers, and adjunct faculty: AAUSC 2000 volume* (pp. 19-39). Boston: MA: Heinle.

Hammond, M. (2000). Communication within on-line forums: the opportunities, the constraints and the value of the communicative approach. *Computers & Education, 35*, 251-262.

Harasim, L. (1990). *Online education: Perspectives on a new medium.* New York, NY: Prager/Greenwood.

Heckman, R., & Annabi, H. (2005). A Content analytic comparison of learning processes in online and face-to-face case study discussions. *Journal of Computer-Mediated Communication.* Retrieved October 10, 2006, from http://jcmc.indiana.edu/vol10/issue2/heckman.html

Helterbran, V. R. (2008). Professionalism: Teachers taking the reins. *The Clearing House, 81*(3), 123-127.

Hoekje, B., & Williams, J. (1992). Communicative competence and the dilemma of international teaching assistant education. *TESOL Quarterly, 26*(2), 243-269.

Hyland, F. (2000). ESL writers and feedback: Giving more autonomy to students. *Language Teaching Research, 4*(1), 33-54.

Kamhi-Stein, L. D. (2000). Looking to the future of TESOL teacher education: Web-based bulletin board discussions in a methods course. *TESOL Quarterly, 34*(3), 423-455.

Kear, K. (2004). Peer learning using asynchronous discussion systems in distance education. *Open Learning, 19*(2), 151-165.

Kern, R. G. (1995). Restructuring classroom interaction with networked computers: Effects on quantity and characteristics of language production. *The Modern Language Journal, 79*(4), 457-476.

Kolodner, J. L., & Guzdial, M. (2000). Theory and practice of case-based learning aids. In D. H. Jonassen & S. M. Land (Eds.), *Theoretical foundations of learning environments* (pp. 215-242). Mahwah, New Jersey: Lawrence Erlbaum Associates, Inc.

Langham, C. K. (1989). *Discourse strategies and classroom learning: American and foreign teaching assistants.* Unpublished doctoral dissertation, University of California at San Diego, San Diego, California.

Levin, B. B. (1995). Using the case method in teacher education the role of discussion and experience in teachers' thinking about cases. *Teaching and Teacher Education, 11*(1), 63-79.

Liu, M., Moore, Z., Graham, L., & Lee, S. (2002). A look at the research on computer-based technology use in second language learning: A review of the literature from 1990-2000. *Journal of Research on Technology in Education, 34*(3), 250-272.

Meyers, C., & Holt, S. (2002). *Success with presentations.* Burnsville, MN: Aspen Productions.

Miller, S. M. (1995). Vygotsky and education: The sociocultural genesis of dialogic thinking in classroom contexts for open-forum literature discussions. Retrieved July 27, 2004, from http://psych.hanover.edu/vygotsky/miller.html

Mitchem, K., Fitzgerald, G., Hollingsead, C., Koury, K., Miller, K., & Tsai, H. (2008). Enhancing case-based learning in teacher education through online discussions: Structure and facilitation. *Journal of Interactive Learning Research, 19*(2).

Myers, S. A. (1998). GTAs as organizational newcomers: The association between supportive communication relationships and information seeking. *Western Journal of Communication, 60*(1), 54-73.

Riedel, J., Fitzgerald, G. E., Leven, F., & Toenshoff, B. (2003). The design of computerized practice fields for problem solving and contextualized transfer. *Journal of Educational Multimedia and Hypermedia, 12*(4), 377-398.

Rounds, P. L. (1987). Characterizing successful classroom discourse for NNS teaching assistant training. *TESOL Quarterly, 21*(4), 643-671.

Rubin, D. L. (1993). The other half of international teaching assistant training: Classroom communication workshops for international students. *Innovative Higher Education, 17*(3), 183-193.

Semrau, L. P., & Fitzgerald, G. E. (1995). Interactive case studies in behavioral disorders: Looking at children from multiple perspectives. *Education and Treatment of Children, 18*(3), 348-359.

Singhal, M. (1998). Computer-mediated communication (CMC): Technology for enhancing foreign language/culture education. Retrieved March 28, 2005, from http://www.cltr.uq.edu.au/oncall/singhal121.html

Smith, K. S. (1993). A case study on the successful development of an international teaching assistant. *Innovative Higher Education, 17*(3), 149-163.

Smith, K. S., & Simpson, R. D. (1993). Becoming successful as an international teaching assistant. *The Review of Higher Education, 16*(4), 483-497.

Stepich, D. A., Ertmer, P. A., & Lane, M. M. (2001). Problem-solving in a case-based course: Strategies for facilitating coached expertise. *Educational Technology Research & Development, 49*(3), 53-69.

Strage, A. (2008). Traditional and non-traditional college students' descriptions of the "ideal" professor and the "ideal" course and perceived strengths and limitations. *College Student Journal, 42*(1), 225-231.

Straits, W. (2007). "She's teaching me": Teaching with care in a large lecture course. *College Teaching, 55*(4), 170-175.

Tang, L., & Sandell, K. (2000). Going beyond basic communication issues: New pedagogical training of international TAs in SMET fields at two Ohio universities. *Journal of Graduate Teaching Assistant Development, 7*(3), 163-172.

Tillman, B. A. (1995). Reflections on case method teaching. *Action in Teacher Education, 17*(1), 1-8.

Time series analysis and forecasting with SPSS trends 9.0. (1999). Chicago, IL: SPSS Inc.

Warschauer, M. (1996). Comparing face-to-face and electronic discussion in the second language classroom. *CALICO Journal, 13*(2), 7-26.

Weiss, L. B., & Levison, S. P. (2000). Tools for integrating women's health into medical education: Clinical cases and concept mapping. *Academic Medicine, 75*(11), 1081-1086.

Williams, J. (1992). Planning, discourse marking, and the comprehensibility of second language speakers. *TESOL Quarterly, 26*, 693-709.

Yule, G., & Hoffman, P. (1990). Predicting success for international teaching assistants in a U.S. university. *TESOL Quarterly, 24*(2), 227-243.

Zha, S., Tsai, H., & Fitzgerald, G. (2008). *The impact of online interactions on individual transfer of knowledge in case-based discussion.* Paper presented at the Poster Session at the Annual Conference of Association for Educational Communications and Technology (AECT), Orlando, FL.

Shenghua Zha, Ph.D., works as an Instructional Technologist in the Center for Instructional Technology at James Madison University. Her research interests include online asynchronous communication, peer collaboration, group dynamics, case-based instruction, and knowledge transfer in distance education.

Gail Fitzgerald, Ph.D., is a Professor in the School of Information Science and Learning Technologies at the University of Missouri-Columbia. Her main fields of research are design and evaluation of multimedia case-based learning environments, electronic support systems for students with disabilities, classroom observation research, and online communities.

Correspondence concerning this article should be addressed to Shenghua Zha at zhasx@jmu.edu MSC 4602, James Madison University, Harrisonburg, VA 22807.

Appendix A

The Evaluation Sheet for ITAs' Use of Presentation and Active Listening Strategies

Name of the presenter: _____ Date:_____(mm/dd/yy)

Please circle the number which you think best describes the presenter's use of language as a teacher.

	Very ineffective←————————→Very effective				
1. Vocabulary and word/phrase choice	1	2	3	4	5
2. Emphasis on key points	1	2	3	4	5
3. Explicitness of directions	1	2	3	4	5
4. Comprehensibility of presentations	1	2	3	4	5
5. Organization of lectures	1	2	3	4	5
6. Eliciting students' input	1	2	3	4	5
7. Responding to students' questions	1	2	3	4	5

Section 4

Models in Context: Educating Graduate Students for Future Roles as Academics

Chapter 8

An Interdisciplinary Approach to Graduate TA Training: A Reflection of Best Practice

Barbi T. Honeycutt, Miriam Ferzli, Tamah Morant, & Sarah Egan Warren
North Carolina State University

Universities face the challenge of preparing graduate students to teach in most disciplines. Campus collaborations that share resources, staff, and expertise are necessary. The implementation of a collaborative interdisciplinary model for GTA training based upon recommendations from current literature has allowed the large research university featured here to meet diverse challenges. The model integrates a centralized university-wide developmental program with individualized discipline-specific training programs to address GTA training at a research institution not only more effectively but also more efficiently. The current program is now sustainable, scalable, and repeatable to other departments across campus.

Introduction

Graduate Teaching Assistants (GTAs) are often on the "front lines" in college classrooms. In some colleges and universities, GTAs teach more than 35 percent of introductory courses, and many universities rely heavily on GTAs to support other levels of undergraduate and graduate courses as well (Bettinger & Long, 2004; Prieto & Meyers, 2001). GTAs represent a unique population on a university campus since their job description requires them to successfully balance the responsibilities of their own degree requirements while simultaneously learning how to be effective teachers. One of the most important services a campus can provide is the opportunity to create a "community of practice" for educators to share resources and experiences (Hutchings, 2008). GTAs should be part of these communities of practice, and universities should provide opportunities for GTAs from across disciplines to engage in interdisciplinary conversations and learn from each other.

Research in GTA training and development has been ongoing since the

1960's (Abbott, Wulff, & Szego, 1989). Despite these efforts, many GTAs are still being placed in the classroom without proper training or guidance to ensure quality educational experiences (Robinson, 2008). GTAs are often the first point of contact for many college students, and they have a direct impact on undergraduate education. Developing quality GTA training programs has been considered one of the most valuable contributions a university can make (Hardé, Ferguson, Bratton & Johnson, 2008; Lambert, 1993). The combination of student development theory and pedagogical training should be considered when designing GTA training experiences (Weidman, Twale, and Stein, 2001). The most successful GTA training models combine the vision and resources of a centralized unit with discipline-specific training and mentoring to maximize competence and effectiveness in the classroom while also considering the stages of development, experiences of GTAs, and recognition for their achievements (Border, 2006; Meyers, 2001; Nyquist & Sprague, 1998; Tice, 1998).

According to Border's (2006) nine principles of best practice, effective GTA programs should: (1) include appropriate levels of administrative support, (2) encourage across-campus liaison, (3) encourage campus-wide GTA development efforts, (4) require departmental GTA training, (5) encourage active faculty supervisors or mentors, (6) encourage graduate students to engage in their own professional development, (7) promote diversity, (8) support application of theory, and (9) encourage effective program evaluation.

In another recent study, Pchenitchnaia and Cole (2009) focused on essential *faculty* development programs in research-extensive universities. The

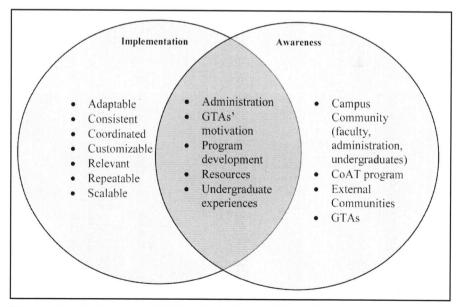

Figure 1. Challenges of GTA Training and Development

eight essential topics for faculty development programs can also serve as a guide for GTA development programs. The eight topics are: (1) enhancing teaching strategies, (2) designing the course and syllabus, (3) evaluating student performance, (4) assessing student learning outcomes, (5) addressing issues specific to teaching in college, (6) developing strategies for active and cooperative learning, (7) designing strategies for student-centered learning, and (8) teaching large classes.

University leaders are recognizing the need to provide training and support for GTAs, but it is often difficult to transfer all of these best practices and comprehensive development models into successful interdisciplinary programs. Articles have been published on implementation and evaluation of specific training and development models, but few have discussed an interdisciplinary approach to GTA training (Davis & Kring, 2001; Hollar, Carlson, & Spencer, 2000; Nicklow, Marikunte, & Chevalier, 2007; Prieto & Scheel, 2008). The purposes of this article are to describe a collaborative interdisciplinary model for GTA training which addresses issues of both implementation and awareness (Figure 1) and to reflect on its alignment with Border's (2006) principles of best practice and Pchenitchnaia and Cole's (2009) findings. Our interdisciplinary efforts provide support for GTAs interested in balancing both the general pedagogical practices and discipline-specific training with an added incentive of university recognition.

Background

Prior to 2006, GTAs at our university were introduced to teaching through a half-day orientation coordinated by the teaching center and the Graduate School. Some GTAs were fortunate to find additional training and resources within their departments either through formal courses or a seminar series. Resources and experiences were fragmented and diverse, with varied levels of support and training offered from one department to another. While these approaches were solid efforts to provide support to GTAs, they were not the most effective ways to provide consistency, share resources, or create opportunities for university recognition.

In 2005, our university's teaching center created a pilot program to determine the types of resources GTAs needed to support their professional development in teaching. Fifteen GTAs were paid a stipend to participate in the pilot program and provide recommendations for program development. The feedback indicated a need for a centralized GTA training program that could connect with individual departments to provide a launching base for GTA training. Using Border's (2006) principles of best practice as a guide, the Certificate of Accomplishment in Teaching (CoAT) program was created and implemented as a first step towards meeting this need. The CoAT program was formally established in 2006 in the university's teaching center and is now the only campus-wide teaching certificate program at our institution that offers GTAs a chance to demonstrate their commitment to teaching excellence through training, evaluation, and recognition. The program is designed to provide training workshops, individual consultations, and teaching observations for GTAs from any department. Through critical reflection and application, participants learn the fundamental components of pedagogy and enrich their personal growth and professional development in teaching and learning.

Since its inception in 2006 and through 2009, the CoAT program has gradually shifted from a "shopping bag" approach, where participants selected random workshops based on their immediate needs, to a more intentionally designed developmental model. Participants now complete a series of structured workshops, write reflections, and engage in transfer of knowledge by demonstrating their ability to apply concepts learned throughout their participation in the program. As part of the CoAT program requirements, participants: (1) attend an orientation session, (2) attend and complete reflection assignments for six workshops, (3) complete two semesters of teaching experiences, (4) participate in two teaching observations, and (5) create a teaching portfolio.

Participants who complete CoAT receive a certificate, transcript notation, and an official letter of recommendation, all of which give legitimacy and credibility to the program. The program design gives consistency to GTA training and development and encourages participants to become self-reflective throughout their growth as teachers. The teaching observation and the portfolio assignment serve as documentation of professional and personal development GTAs may use for future positions in academia. In 2008, it was determined CoAT could best serve GTAs by being centralized in the Graduate School as part of a new professional development initiative. The program now represents all of the academic colleges and departments within the university. Since GTAs are often isolated on campus as they focus on their area of specialization, the CoAT program connects them with each other to create a network of support and resources to share effective teaching practices.

Creating a Collaborative Interdisciplinary Model

As the CoAT program was evolving during its first two years, representatives from hard sciences, social sciences, and humanities integrated with the CoAT program to launch a collaborative interdisciplinary model for implementing GTA training. While adhering to the guiding principles in the literature, this informal scholarly community aimed to design and implement a sustainable program that honors both pedagogical training and discipline-specific expertise. The top priorities were to share resources and establish a mutually beneficial and collaborative relationship to maximize GTAs' experiences in the classroom.

In our university, like many others, GTAs' responsibilities range from grading to serving as lead instructors for a course. Findings from a campus-wide survey conducted in 2007-2008 confirmed a range of responsibilities within and across departments. Our interdisciplinary approach emerged from the need to address these variations in GTAs' responsibilities and now provides a foundation for general training and serves as a springboard for building discipline-specific structures.

In the following section, we highlight three GTA training programs, which have been designed using this interdisciplinary approach as a guide to balance pedagogical training with discipline-specific expertise: Biology, Economics and the Professional Writing Program (PWP). Table 1 shows how the CoAT program and the three disciplines collaborate to integrate various components of GTA training.

Discipline-Specific Programs

As mentioned above, the different programs in each department have varied roles for their GTAs. GTAs in biology teach the laboratory sessions and provide a crucial service in large introductory courses that house hundreds of students by teaching course content, safety, and procedural protocols. They also provide support to the lecturing faculty in the form of exam proctoring and grading. In the economics program, GTAs impact, either through grading or classroom instruction, approximately 3,000 students each academic year. GTAs are assigned one of three categories with varying levels of responsibility: Graders, who either have little to no direct student contact; lab section leaders who conduct review sessions for a faculty member's lecture course; and, indepen-

Table 1. Integration of CoAT and Departmental Components of GTA Training

	Biology Dept.	Economics Dept.	Professional Writing Program
Summer Workshop	--	Department	--
Orientation	CoAT	--	CoAT
CoAT Workshops	CoAT	CoAT	CoAT
Classroom Observations	Department	Department	Department
Reflections	CoAT/Department	CoAT/Department	CoAT/Department
Peer Observations	Department	Department	--
Seminars	Department	--	Department
Mentoring	--	Department	Department
Self Evaluation	Department	--	--
Observing Faculty	Department	Department	Department
Teaching	Department	Department	Department
Portfolio	CoAT	CoAT	CoAT
Recognition	CoAT	CoAT/Department	CoAT

dent instructors who teach a full course. The GTAs in the Professional Writing Program (PWP) become instructors of record for junior/senior level writing-intensive courses with enrollment between 200-500 students per year.

Prior to partnering with CoAT, each department/program prepared and delivered some form of GTA training. However, GTAs and the faculty mentors recognized that additional training would benefit the GTAs, the students, and the faculty. In biology, GTAs attend a weekly lab prep meeting during which they run through lab experiments and focus on safety and procedures leaving little time to emphasize pedagogical knowledge and skills. A series of informal departmental teaching workshops was created to supplement the prep meeting training. In economics, GTAs who lead the lab sections received guidance and mentoring from their supervising faculty. Although valuable, this guidance was not formalized and did not help GTAs who were graders or individual course instructors. Since there are numerous faculty members providing independent guidance, this type of training was inconsistent and it did not provide any instruction for GTAs before they entered the classroom. It also required a significant investment of faculty time. In the PWP, GTAs received training through an informal mentoring relationship with a faculty member and by observing experienced teachers. Although this process had been mostly successful, just like in economics, it was time-intensive for the faculty mentor. Because the responsibility for training GTAs rotated, GTAs received different information, support, and resources each year.

Biology, economics, and the PWP partnered with the CoAT program to integrate their own discipline-specific training with CoAT's comprehensive pedagogical training. As a result of this collaboration, GTAs became part of a larger campus-wide community of practice. Through interactions with peers in other disciplines, they realize that although some of their concerns may be discipline-specific, there are fundamental teaching issues that all GTAs share. Below, we discuss how the three different department/programs integrate CoAT into their training models.

"Teaching Life Sciences in the College Classroom," a credit-only seminar followed by a one-semester practicum, was created in biology to integrate teaching in a laboratory with the general pedagogical knowledge and skills in the CoAT program. The course helps GTAs learn teaching methods and self-evaluation skills. Participants have the opportunity to demonstrate their own teaching while receiving group feedback. As part of the group feedback process, GTAs learn how to evaluate their peers using specific evaluation tools. Regular weekly assignments include reflective writing as well as more concrete, objective-driven tasks.

During the second semester, GTAs enroll in a credit-only practicum which allows them the opportunity to implement their new teaching skills and obtain feedback through peer and self-evaluation protocols. During this part of the program, GTAs work in pairs to videotape each other and to follow a specific evaluation process that culminates in a plan of action for improvement. A follow-up evaluative session targets the plan for improvement and provides the GTAs with concrete data on their growth as a teacher.

The economics department's three-tiered model provides a range of basic to advanced training based on the GTAs' level of responsibility and interest in the teaching profession. The first tier requires that all new lab section leaders and course instructors begin with a three-day summer workshop designed to prepare them for the first day in the classroom beginning the fall semester. GTAs develop a lesson plan for a predetermined topic. They are videotaped while presenting to their peers and to faculty. Afterwards, the GTAs receive immediate feedback from both peers and faculty and use the videotape for self-evaluation. During the fall semester, GTAs attend one CoAT workshop and complete a classroom observation and follow-up evaluation.

GTAs interested in further training in teaching may opt to continue the program into the spring semester by completing the second tier of the model. The second tier requires GTAs to attend two additional CoAT workshops and participate in a second classroom observation. During this observation, it is expected that the GTA addresses the areas noted for improvement in the previous semester's follow-up evaluation. Tier three of the model allows GTAs who are interested in continuing their training in teaching to enroll in the CoAT program. The three CoAT workshops completed in tiers one and two transfer into the CoAT program making it possible for the GTA to complete CoAT requirements in one additional academic year.

The PWP model is a seminar program that is repeatable, scalable, and customizable so that any faculty member can implement the model without needing to re-create new materials, schedules, or resources. In addition, it allows faculty members the ability to adapt the training to a varying number of GTAs. The program is customizable since PWP GTAs have different teaching backgrounds and levels of experience (some have never taught; others have been corporate trainers, high school teachers, or GTAs at other universities). GTAs without teaching experience complete their training in two semesters while those with teaching experience complete their training in one. GTA seminars are held weekly or bi-monthly and cover information specific to teaching in the PWP. GTAs can choose any three CoAT workshops; however, they are encouraged to select workshops that complement the PWP seminars.

GTAs in the PWP participate in observations with experienced instructors. During their first semester, GTAs attend as many instructors' classes as possible to get a broad overview of the different teaching styles and techniques. In the second semester, the GTA spends an entire semester with one experienced instructor and gradually assumes some responsibilities in the classroom. Once the GTA begins teaching, a faculty mentor observes the individual's classroom teaching. A second classroom observation ensures that suggestions from the first observation have been implemented.

Program Evaluation

Border's (2006) principles for best practice provided an excellent foundation for the design and development of the CoAT program. Over time, we have assessed, adapted, and adjusted our approach to develop a comprehensive program more aligned with all of Border's (2006) recommendations. In just three years, the interdisciplinary design within the CoAT program meets six of the nine recommended principles of best practice for GTA development (Border, 2006). Participants in the interdisciplinary GTA training programs benefit from the six principles outlined by Border (2006). The six principles met are:

- Includes appropriate levels of administrative support: Both the departments and the Graduate School share administrative processes. The Graduate School coordinates all administrative tasks for the CoAT program, and departments coordinate all administrative tasks for individual GTA positions.
- Encourages campus-wide GTA development efforts: Both the CoAT program and the individual departments integrate the annual graduate student TA orientation into existing program structures. Experienced GTAs facilitate breakout sessions during orientation.
- Requires departmental GTA training: Each of the three disciplines integrates their own departmental-specific training into the CoAT program to provide balance and context.
- Encourages graduate students to engage in their own professional development: The CoAT program is self-paced, and it is not connected to graduation requirements. Successful participants are self-motivated, self-directed, and eager to find opportunities to enhance their teaching skills. For every workshop CoAT participants complete, they must write a reflection paper exploring their personal reactions to how the workshop will influence their teaching. This reflection assignment allows them the opportunity to discuss their strengths, limitations, and plans for continued professional development as it relates to their career path. In the final assignment for CoAT, the teaching portfolio serves as a document, not only to capture their teaching experience, but to show their professional development and journey since their first day as a GTA.
- Supports application of theory: CoAT workshops are designed to introduce participants to general pedagogy. Workshops are designed to focus on reflection and application of theoretical processes.
- Encourages effective program evaluation: In the first three years, faculty in the CoAT program, biology, economics, and the PWP have carefully monitored students' experiences, collected feedback, and re-structured program

requirements to meet the needs of GTAs. Ongoing discussions have led to more formalized processes for collecting data through workshop evaluations and the CoAT exit survey.

Since participation in the CoAT program also provides teaching preparation for many GTAs seeking faculty positions, we examined our interdisciplinary approach through the lens of Pchenitchnaia and Cole's (2009) findings relating to faculty development. We have found that the CoAT program's interdisciplinary approach aligns itself closely with these findings and serves as a strong foundation for preparing GTAs for future faculty positions.

With the exception of promoting separate programs for international GTAs and new faculty, which does not fall within the goals of the CoAT program or the Graduate School, our interdisciplinary approach addresses all eight of Pchenitchnaia and Cole's (2009) essential topics for successful faculty development programs. The eight topics are:

- Enhancing teaching strategies: All of the workshops for the CoAT program emphasize effective teaching strategies. Workshops are designed to give GTAs the opportunity to see the strategies "in action" and allow for instant application to their course(s) during their teaching experience.
- Designing the course and syllabus: In the "Introduction to Teaching" workshop, GTAs are introduced to lesson planning, learning outcomes, and course design. In the "Writing Effective Learning Outcomes" workshop, GTAs critique a syllabus and re-write learning outcomes for their own course(s).
- Evaluating student performance: In the "Evaluation and Grading" workshop, GTAs practice giving feedback using different types of assessment tools. During their teaching experience, many GTAs have the opportunity to be involved in both formal and informal assessment for the course(s) they teach.
- Assessing student learning outcomes: In the "Evaluation and Grading" and the "Writing Learning Outcomes" workshops, GTAs learn how to write effective outcomes and assess student performance. For many GTAs, they are given the opportunity to assess students' learning, both formally and informally, in the course(s) they teach.
- Addressing issues specific to teaching in college: GTAs have different needs from faculty, and the CoAT program address these through workshops, reflection assignments, and the teaching portfolio. In 2009, we offered workshops on "Establishing Credibility and Authority in the Classroom" and "Classroom Management" which helped GTAs learn how to separate themselves from the students they teach and establish a professional identity in the classroom.
- Developing strategies for active and cooperative learning: In the "Collaborative Learning and Group Work" and "Active Learning" workshops, GTAs

learn how to design effective collaborative learning activities in their courses and integrate active learning strategies into the lectures and labs they teach.

- Designing strategies for student-centered learning: Several of the CoAT workshops address student-centered learning teaching strategies. Workshops on "Active Learning," "Effective Questioning Techniques," "Learning Styles," and "Motivational Teaching Strategies" help GTAs think about designing learning experiences centered around who their students are as learners and what they can bring to the learning environment.
- Teaching large classes: Many of our GTAs are teaching in large, introductory course settings that have unique challenges worthy of a separate series of workshops. In 2009, the CoAT program partnered with the university's faculty development office which offered a year-long series of workshops on teaching large classes. These workshops were open to both graduate students and faculty.

The CoAT program and the individualized discipline-specific programs have evolved together to provide support for and address the responsibilities faced by GTAs across and within disciplines. Based on Border's (2006) recommendations and Pchenitchnaia and Cole's (2009) findings, we continue to refine the CoAT program to improve resources and training for GTAs and to enhance the foundation they need to become successful faculty members. While we recognize that the programs will continue to develop, we are pleased with how the overall structure and vision we have established for our campus connects to the principles of best practice in GTA development.

Discussion

The CoAT program is intentionally designed to be flexible and adaptable, allowing each departmental program opportunities to customize and integrate appropriate components. In our interdisciplinary approach, the CoAT program in the Graduate School manages the records, schedules workshops, and coordinates the overall administrative responsibilities of program implementation. The discipline-specific programs are coordinated by a faculty member who serves as the essential link between the types of support and training GTAs need and which programs fit within existing departmental structures and expectations. Disciplines are able to set standards, establish policies, and formalize requirements for GTAs within their departments.

This interdisciplinary approach also contains both discipline-specific context and general pedagogical training, allowing for a more balanced training experience for GTAs. Our approach allows us to share resources, knowledge and experiences which continues to help us learn from each other and maintain momentum in GTA training and development. Integrating our strategies has also helped us focus on the most important components of GTA training while providing consistency and quality. GTAs in these programs select workshops from the same list of topics, and the individual departments do not need to re-create workshops that are already being offered at the centralized level.

The integration with the Graduate School also allows for an approach that is now sustainable, scalable, and repeatable to other departments across campus, and all of the participants can benefit from the breadth of experiences offered by both the CoAT workshop facilitators and the individual experts within each discipline. Stepping outside of the discipline has become one of the most important lessons for GTAs, allowing them to build a learning community and support group that crosses disciplinary boundaries.

This type of interdisciplinary approach also allows us to raise awareness within the campus community. Justification for GTA development programs must reach the entire campus community, including the GTAs themselves, their mentors, their advisors, the administration, and the undergraduate students. For these reasons, there are numerous benefits to combining the perspectives of the discipline-specific programs and the centralized university-wide program.

In our design, the Graduate School organizes the publicity and marketing for GTA training opportunities. GTA training is part of a larger initiative on our campus to prepare future leaders for careers in industry, academia, and government. CoAT is one of five other professional development programs, and the Graduate School packages this story in all materials for promoting, recruiting, and retaining talented graduate students. Being part of a larger institutional movement gives individual departments and their supporting faculty credibility and justification for their efforts to support this work.

As a centralized unit, the Graduate School is effective in program management from a "big picture" perspective. The Graduate School has the capability to contact each individual graduate student to promote upcoming workshops, professional development opportunities, and application deadlines for programs. The Graduate School also oversees all of the workshop registration, attendance records, and program application processes, and it distributes all of the certificates and transcript notations for GTAs who successfully complete the CoAT program. Finally, the Graduate School sponsors a campus-wide ceremony to provide formal recognition to GTAs who have earned the teaching certificate.

The Graduate School, although centralized, must form partnerships with individual departments to serve the needs of their GTAs and to integrate training experiences into existing structures. Without the support of the individual departments and programs, the Graduate School would not be successful in capturing the awareness of the GTA population. Similarly without the general framework that CoAT offers, it would be nearly impossible for our individual departments/programs to implement the level of quality and consistency in GTA training we are able to provide under this partnership. GTAs need to know they have support from their mentors and advisors, and ongoing communication between the Graduate School and the individual department is critical to this collaborative process.

Conclusions

Although this article is not meant to be a blueprint for how to design GTA training experiences, we hope it inspires others to work collaboratively and think innovatively as they create models for helping GTAs become effective teachers. By using recommendations from the literature on best practice, we developed and implemented a cohesive interdisciplinary program for GTA training on our campus that connects GTAs across disciplines and scaffolds their development as teachers and learners. Participants who completed the exit survey indicated that one of most beneficial components of the CoAT program is the opportunity to exchange ideas with other GTAs and workshop facilitators. Some of the workshops and discussions CoAT participants valued the most included handling challenging classroom situations, incorporating technology into the classroom, organizing lesson plans and lectures, sharing active learning strategies, designing creative assignments, creating classroom policies, and asking effective questions. GTAs indicated that writing the teaching philosophy, writing reflections from each of the workshops, and participating in the classroom observation process were some of the components that had the greatest impact on their professional development in teaching.

Although our program has been successful in its initial implementation, we acknowledge the need to formally track GTA participants to study the long-term impacts on their careers. Coupled to this effort would be a study of the impacts of GTA training on undergraduate education and the overall undergraduate experience. We are also interested in studying the role that CoAT participants play in mentoring other GTAs in their departments. One other area that we find both interesting and disconcerting, and that warrants further study, is the apparent lack of awareness that some GTAs have concerning the importance of proper training in teaching. Based on conversations with GTAs, many do not realize the need or benefits of participating in training experiences. It is critical for departments to explain their expectations with respect to teaching in the department. From our experiences, we know GTAs come to training opportunities with varying levels of motivation and commitment. Regardless of their motivation, the combination of university recognition combined with the department's expectations and the GTAs' responsibilities can be designed to benefit the learning process for all involved.

In addition to our goals for formal studies, we recognize that there are various limitations to face when implementing GTA programs. At our campus, the three main ones are: budget limitations, GTA motivation, and campus community engagement. Due to campus budget limitations, there is a reduction in the number of GTA positions which will ultimately result in fewer numbers of CoAT participants. The budget challenges are also affecting current GTAs who are expected to maintain their current level of responsibility while meeting their department's expectations and teaching larger classes with limited resources. We also need to consider GTAs' motivation for participating in training and development experiences. Some are internally motivated to pursue training opportunities, and others are externally motivated to receive a certificate or transcript notation. We need to consider how to reinforce participation and help GTAs understand the impacts of their contribution to undergraduate education and student success.

Finally, although we have generated interest from the GTA community, we continue to seek campus-wide support for GTA training and development. We would like to formally connect with other departments and programs to expand the resources and opportunities available to all interested graduate students. Our collaboration has allowed us to share resources, discuss ideas, and engage in scholarly activities to improve the quality of GTA training and development on our campus. To formalize our work and to attract other faculty members to the discussion, we have formed iCATT, the Interdisciplinary Consortium for Advancing TA Training. Our goals are to (1) advance training opportunities, programs, and resources to support the development of graduate students, (2) improve the educational experience for undergraduate students; and (3) increase awareness of the importance of effective GTA training and development. We hope to make an impact on the institutional commitment to GTA training since this population is increasingly finding itself responsible for crucial courses in the disciplines.

As we reflect on the past three years, our vision for change is to design a developmental process for GTA training by offering varied levels of programs and opportunities ranging from individualized consultations to mentoring experiences to peer facilitated workshops led by experienced GTAs. This will be a new venture for our campus, and we are dedicated to pursuing this mission while maintaining our commitment to creating interdisciplinary partnerships. With these types of collaborations, the centralized unit and the individual departments can work together to maximize resources and offer a variety of programs to meet the motivations and goals of each GTA.

References

Abbott, R., Wulff, D.,& Szego, C. (1989). Review of research on TA training in Nyquist, J. D., Abbott, D., & Wulff, D. H. (eds.) Teaching assistant training in the 1990's. *New Directions for Teaching and Learning*, 39, 111-123.

Bettinger, E. & Long, T. (2004). Do college instructors matter? The effects of adjuncts and graduate assistants on students' interests and success. *NBER Working Paper No. 10370.*

Border, L. L. B. (2006). Two inventories for best practice in graduate student development. *Journal on Excellence in College Teaching, 17*(1 & 2), 277-310.

Davis, S. & Kring, J. (2001). A model for training and evaluating graduate teaching assistants. *College Student Journal, 35*(1), 45.

Hardé, P., Ferguson, C., Bratton, J, & Johnson, D. (2008). Online professional development for TAs: What they need, what they have, what they want. Journal of Faculty Development, *22*(1), 11-20.

Hollar, K., Carlson, V., & Spencer, P. (2000). 1+1=3: Unanticipated benefits of a co-facilitation model for training teaching assistants. *The Journal of Graduate Teaching Assistant Development, 7*(3), 173-181.

Hutchings, P. (2008) A different way to think about professional development. *Carnegie Perspectives.* Retrieved June 15, 2009, from http://www.carnegiefoundation.org/perspectives/sub.asp?key=245&subkey=2768

Lambert, L. M. (1993). Centralized TA programs and practices. In L. M. Lambert & S. L. Tice (Eds.), *Preparing graduate students to teach: A guide to programs that improve undergraduate education and develop tomorrow's faculty* (pp. 13-60). Washington, DC: American Association for Higher Education.

Meyers, S. (2001). Conceptualizing and promoting effective TA training. In Prieto, L. R. &

Meyers, S. (Eds.) *The teaching assistant training handbook: How to prepare TAs for their responsibilities* (pp. 3-23). Stillwater, OK: New Forums Press, Inc.

Nicklow, J., Marikunte, S., & Chevalier, L. (2007). Balancing pedagogical and professional practice skills in the training of graduate teaching assistants. *Journal of Professional Issues in Engineering Education and Practice*, (2007, April), 89-93.

Nyquist, J. & Sprague, J. (1998). Thinking developmentally about TAs. In Marincovich, M., J. Prostko, & Stout, F. (Eds.) *The professional development of graduate teaching assistants* (pp. 61-88), Boston, MA: Anker Publishing Company, Inc.

Pchenitchnaia, L. & Cole, B. (2009). Essential faculty development programs for teaching and learning centers in research-extensive universities. In L. B. Nilson & J. E. Miller (Eds.) *To Improve the Academy*. Vol. 27. *Resources for faculty, instructional, and organizational development* (pp. 287-308). San Francisco: Jossey-Bass.

Prieto, L. & Meyers, S. (2001). *The teaching assistant training handbook: How to prepare TAs for their responsibilities.* Stillwater, OK: New Forums Press, Inc.

Prieto, L. & Scheel, K. (2008). Teaching assistant training in counseling psychology. *Counseling Psychology Quarterly*, 21(1), 49-59.

Robinson, J. (2008). How to Create Terrible Professors. Retrieved on June 22, 2010 from http://www.popecenter.org/commentaries/article.html?id=2099

Tice, S., Featherstone, P., & Johnson, H. (1998). TA certificate programs. In Marincovich, M., J. Prostko, & Stout, F. (Eds.), *The professional development of graduate teaching assistants* (pp. 263-274), Boston, MA: Anker Publishing Company, Inc.

Barbi Honeycutt, Ph.D., is the Director of Graduate Teaching Programs in The Graduate School and an adjunct faculty member in the Department of Leadership, Policy, Adult and Higher Education at North Carolina State University.

Miriam Ferzli, Ph.D., is a Teaching Assistant Professor in the Biology Department at North Carolina State University.

Tamah Morant, Ph.D., is the Director of the Economics Graduate Program and a Teaching Associate Professor in the Department of Economics at North Carolina State University.

Sarah Egan Warren is a Senior Lecturer and Assistant Director of the Professional Writing Program in the Department of English at North Carolina State University.

Chapter 9

One Process, Two Contexts: Designing Professional Development for Graduate Student Educators

Michele M. Welkener
University of Dayton

Graduate students charged with taking on the role of educator in the higher education environment often need assistance with adopting new habits of mind that will help them realize their potential. These habits frequently call for a qualitatively different type of meaning-making than what they needed to be successful undergraduate students. How can we design professional development activities that will help graduate students meet the challenges that face them? This article provides a theoretically-grounded process and set of principles that can be used to promote graduate students' growth, and the outcomes from employing this strategy in two different institutional settings.

Results from a research project conducted at the University of North Carolina at Chapel Hill "indicate a clear need to assist graduate students to perform effectively in both academic and non-academic professional settings" (Poock, 2001, p. 1). The complexity of our work to help graduate students meet the demands of professional life requires, at minimum, innovative approaches. The academy often expects graduate students to be able to assume the role of educator upon arrival on campus—for some, only weeks away from undergraduate life and with no prior preparation or experience. This shift is not an easy one, and it necessitates intentionality on the part of mentors, trainers, and faculty/TA developers involved in facilitating the transition.

In this paper, I will present a process used in two completely different environments that had a similar purpose—to promote the professional development of graduate students who had educational responsibilities at their institutions. More specifically, I will share how instructional design and adult development theories were used to shape practice to promote this transformation and the unique models of professional development that emerged from this collaborative process. In order to accomplish these goals, first, I will share some important components of instructional design and adult development theories to provide a backdrop for their applications. Second, I will spotlight two exemplars to show how these theories were used to inform professional development activities for graduate students in different contexts. Finally, I will address the importance of campus partnerships for making these professional development programs possible. For the purposes of this paper, I focus mainly on the complex *process* of developing such programs.

Principles from Instructional Design: Driving the Process

A rich conversation related to the systematic design of effective learning experiences has been occurring in the instructional design field for some time. Unfortunately this conversation has not often reached administrators or faculty in higher education, especially in the past decade. The ever-growing call for delivering web-based courses has frequently required specialists in this area to redirect their efforts from addressing general teaching issues to working on the challenges and possibilities of designing practice in the online environment.

What is instructional design? The assumptions outlined by Gagné, Wager, Golas and Keller (2005) help us understand the nature of this approach.

> First, we adopt the assumption that instructional design must be aimed at aiding the process of learning rather than the process of teaching. Instructional design is also aimed at 'intentional' learning as opposed to 'incidental' learning.... Second, we recognize that learning is a complex process affected by many variables.... Third, instructional design models can be applied at many levels. Principles of instructional design can be of immediate value to a teacher or trainer who is planning a lesson for a day's activity, a trainer preparing a three-day workshop, or a curriculum developer designing a course of study.... Our fourth assumption is that design is an iterative process.... The fifth assumption is that instructional design itself is a process consisting of a number of identifiable and related subprocesses. At the simplest level, instructional design is aligning desired outcomes, instructional methods, and student assessments..... Our sixth and final point...is that different types of learning outcomes call for different types of instruction. (pp. 2-3)

Walter Dick and Lou Carey's (1996) "systems approach" model, one of several models within what is called Instructional Systems Development (ISD), has offered steps to guide the learning process. They have asserted that "there are a number of models that bear the label 'systems approach,' and all of them share most of the same basic components.... Typically the major phases of ISD are analysis, design, development, implementation, and evaluation" (p. 4). While often referred to as a behaviorist model, the most recent revisions to Dick and Carey's work have included an assessment of learner needs that allow it to be interpreted as more harmonious with the tenets of constructivism and contemporary psychological approaches (Deubel, 2003). Terence O'Connor and I developed an adaptation of Dick and Carey's model that can act as a basic design structure to guide practice, and was utilized in the two applications this article presents. Consistent with the themes of ISD mentioned above, the steps of this simplified model (see Figure 1) include: analyzing learner needs/contexts, identifying appropriate learning goals, selecting guiding philosophies/assumptions, developing an instructional plan, and performing an evaluation of instructional effectiveness in relation to stated learning goals. Directional arrows are included to illustrate the reevaluation that needs to occur throughout the entire design process. For example, the first two steps are represented as reciprocal because in order to create suitable learning goals one must know some things about the learners and the context in which they are learning. In addition, after an evaluation occurs, feedback should be incorporated into the redesign.

For each phase of the process, we developed some questions for designers to consider in order to ensure that deliberate linkages are made between steps and focus is maintained. These questions are:

- Analyzing learner needs and contexts—What variables will inform how you go about reaching your goal? Who are your learners; what specific information, needs, demands are important to bear in mind? What is the context like; what about it is important to recognize?
- Identifying goal(s)—What is the overarching goal of this program/activity/lesson? Specifically, what do you hope to accomplish/have learners gain?
- Selecting a design philosophy/strategy—What theory(ies) will best inform your approach to the goal? Why choose that framework given your design considerations (remembering that theory is value-laden)? What assumptions/principles from this theory will help you guide learners toward the goal?
- Designing and implementing an instructional plan—How will you go about applying principles from theory in a way that drives learners toward the goal? What methods will you use to deliver the program? Why might these delivery methods be the most effective given your goal?

Figure 1. Design Steps Adapted from Dick and Carey (1996)

- Evaluating instructional effectiveness—How will you know if your instructional plan was successful? What approaches will you take to find out if your design has been successful in helping participants reach the goal? How and what will you revise based on your findings?

Echoing the assumptions of Gagné, et al. (2005), it is expected that these steps and prompts can be equally useful for designing a large-scale, year-long University program as well as a small-scale, ten-minute learning activity.

Principles from Adult Development: Driving Philosophies

Another type of theory that has the potential to revolutionize the teaching and learning enterprise in higher education is student and adult development theory. However, like instructional design theory, too few faculty and administrators have discovered this body of literature that can help us better understand our students and how to meet their learning needs. The two theories I have found most helpful are described as "constructive-developmental." Constructive developmental theory, according to Robert Kegan (1994), "looks at the growth or transformation of how we construct meaning" (p. 199). He went on to say

> The general idea of 'ways of knowing' derives from the tradition of constructivism. It implies that we are active in our apprehension of reality. We do not just passively 'copy' or 'absorb' already organized reality; instead, we ourselves actively give shape and coherence to our experience. Constructivism implies that there is a consistency or holism to our meaning-making. Each apprehension on our part is not merely a response to a momentary stimulus. Instead, from moment to moment and across different spheres of living, our ways of knowing share the design of a common organizing principle or system. (p. 199)

Constructivism assumes that humans actively construct reality. Studying development presumes an interest in the progression of these ways of knowing over time and with experience. Kegan was one of the first and few scholars to attend to not only the intellectual dimension of human meaning-making in his theory of the evolution of human "consciousness," but also interpersonal relationships and identity, and claimed that these dimensions are inextricably intertwined. His view of how humans develop was based on what he called "subject-object" transformations, or shifts in consciousness that occur when what is "subject" to our awareness (unrecognized) becomes "object" of our awareness (recognized) (p. 32).

In addition to the work of Kegan that helps us appreciate the nature of development across the life span, some researchers have focused specifically on college students and adults. Baxter Magolda, in a text titled *Knowing and Reasoning in College* (1992) shared results from a longitudinal study on college students' development that has served as the foundation for continuing research with the same participants who are now in their early 40s, providing helpful insight into the transition between undergraduate and post-college life. In the process of following these students' college and adult development, she discovered conditions that can serve as a framework for promoting "self authorship," or the ability to compose, evaluate, and mediate one's experience. This framework, now the basis of the "learning partnerships model" (Baxter Magolda and King, 2004) includes empirically-based assumptions and principles to guide practice. The assumptions that Baxter Magolda found were evident in environments that promoted development are: viewing "knowledge as complex and socially constructed... [recognizing that] self is central to knowledge construction...[and] that authority and expertise [are] shared in the mutual construction of knowledge among peers" (2001, p. *xx*). These assumptions, when translated into principles for designing practice, can guide educators in creating learning experiences that promote adult students' development. Baxter Magolda defined these principles as: "validating learners' capacity to know...situating learning in learners' experience... [and] mutually constructing meaning" (p. *xxi*).

Application #1: The Indiana State University TA/GA Professional Development Model

When I was a new faculty developer, I was made responsible for the Teaching Assistant (TA) development program at Indiana State University (ISU). Inspired by the collaborative spirit and concern for graduate students our departmental liaisons (faculty partners from various disciplines who were TAs' advisors) shared, I chose to ask the group to take a decidedly strategic approach to designing our TA development plans. This approach included assessing the knowledge, skills, abilities and dispositions—competencies— TAs needed in order to be successful professionals. Using competencies as a vehicle for focusing educational efforts, while debated in some circles (Gilbert, Balatti, Turner & Whitehouse, 2004) is flourishing in undergraduate (AAC&U, 2002) and graduate (Nyquist, 2002) curricular reform in America.

What resulted from this approach and subsequent dialogue (which included two committees, numerous campus offices and departments, the Graduate School, and an endorsement by the Provost) was a campus-wide, comprehensive program for Graduate and Teaching Assistants that outlined the competencies desired and commitments of all parties involved in supporting graduate student professional development. In the following sections, mirroring the design process used, I will share some details about the context, learners, purpose/goals and competencies that informed the program design. A discussion of the application of adult/student development theory and decisions related to evaluation will be provided in a later section since program designers in both institutional examples in this paper employed similar practices.

Context and Learners

In our Center for Teaching and Learning there was a growing interest in moving away from *informative* professional development models to those that were *transformative*, integrative, learning-centered (Barr & Tagg, 1995), developmental, and holistic. Thus, it made sense for us to begin by investigating our students' lives and needs.

There was no such thing as a "typical" graduate student at Indiana State. In fact, when our group set out to study ISU's graduate learner profiles, we found more diversity than commonality. Men and women students reflected a range of ages, races, ethnicities, disciplines, and expectations. Some were recent graduates, some were returning students. Some were new to professional life, some came with years of experience. Students traveled to attend ISU from as near as only blocks away and as far as across the globe. Some held employment in addition to their assistantship, and some did not. The only two major themes shared among graduate students were that all were juggling multiple roles (for example: student, educator, daughter/son, partner, parent, friend, employee, volunteer), and a majority of students, both at the Master's and doctoral level, were not planning to become college faculty members. Instead, they were pursuing degrees to prepare to be better researchers, specialists, managers, administrators, leaders—professionals in their chosen field.

Since the graduate students that we served often did not plan to pursue the professoriate, a professional development program aimed at refining teaching-related transferable skills was more appropriate than a Preparing Future Faculty (PFF) program for this community of learners. Along the way, we also discovered that our colleagues in Student Affairs were training their Graduate Assistants (GAs) on issues similar to those we identified as important for TAs. Given my own graduate education in student development and student affairs, I suggested that we bring together TAs from academic departments and GAs from student affairs since they all carry educational responsibilities (related to in- or out-of-class learning)—fairly new territory for a teaching and learning office (Welkener, 2003).

Purpose/goals & Competencies

Our primary goal, as stewards of students' undergraduate as well as graduate education, was to help these TAs/GAs learn how to understand and meet their undergraduate students' complex learning needs. In order to accomplish this, we set out to promote the personal, social, intellectual and professional development of our graduate students, hoping to provide them with a broader base of transferable skills, a larger sense of community within the institution, and a more complex understanding of themselves and their relationships with others.

Groups of students, faculty, department chairs, campus administrators in academic and student affairs, and staff from the Center for Teaching and Learning contributed to a list of competencies that defined an ideal professional. After developing this list, we examined where, when, and how these competencies were already being addressed by various campus offices and curricula. A group of two committees refined this list, using processes similar to qualitative data analysis, to develop categories. The categories were then negotiated in a way that everyone who already had a role in the development of graduate students (Center for Teaching and Learning—CTL, individual departments, the graduate school, academic affairs—AA, and student affairs—SA) retained that role, but we eliminated some duplication of efforts, worked with each other, and relied on expertise in appropriate areas rather than "reinventing the wheel" in each of our offices and departments. See Figure 2 for a visual representation of the TA/GA professional development model competencies and campus commitments to training and development. This diagram indicates individual office responsibilities within academic and student affairs as well as opportunities for collaboration.

Application #2: The Ohio State University SPA Professional Development Model

I used a similar process to create a program for TAs and GAs who were graduate students in Higher Education and Student Affairs (HESA) at the Ohio State University. HESA students who served in assistantships through the Student Personnel Assistantship (SPA) program could be in positions in Academic or Student Affairs that required them to act as judicial officers, housing coordinators, classroom instructors, academic and career advisors, campus activities programmers, diversity specialists, and more (and sometimes multiple roles simultaneously). When I became a HESA faculty member and Coordinator of the SPA program, some of the Master's students approached me about helping them create a professional development program to complement the experiences they were having via their coursework and assistantships/internships. We formed a working group consisting of students and supervisory staff, and, like the ISU partners, began the process by acknowledging our learners' design considerations and developing a fairly exhaustive list of competencies students needed in order to be effective professionals.

Context and Learners

The HESA and SPA programs have been home to MA and PhD students studying to be professionals and scholars in the higher education context. The philosophy of these programs is focused on theory-to-practice, emphasized in the assistantship environments, in classes, and in additional internships.

An analysis of learners revealed that OSU graduate students in the HESA/ SPA program were as diverse as those at ISU. Due to higher education and student affairs programs' interdisciplinary qualities, and because undergradu-

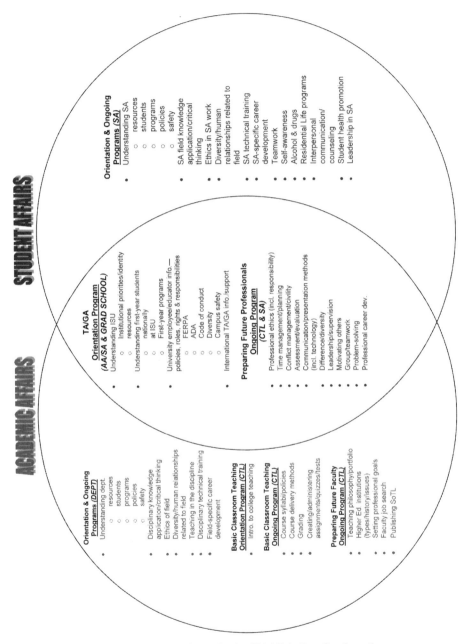

Figure 2: Indiana State University's TA/GA Professional Development Plan—Academic/Student Affairs Partnership

ate studies in this area are unusual, graduate students in the HESA/SPA program came from a variety of majors. Also like the ISU students, OSU students were attempting to balance the many roles that accompany being an adult graduate student between approximately 21-50 years of age. Many students held a SPA assistantship that allowed them to work part-time, while others attended classes part-time and worked full-time. They came with a variety of personal and professional experiences, expectations, identities, homelands, and aspirations. Although a majority of these students desired to become campus administrators, a few aimed to be faculty members in a similar higher education or college student personnel academic program. What these graduate students shared was an interest in making their life's work helping college students learn and grow.

Purpose/goals & Competencies

The overarching goal of the SPA professional development program was to foster HESA students' intellectual, professional, and personal growth by providing opportunities to integrate their in-class and out-of-class experiences. Resembling the ISU process, several groups were involved in developing a list of competencies considered hallmarks of an ideal professional. Alumni, students, supervisors, and faculty contributed ideas and the committee doing the design work reviewed documents, programs, and standards of the field in an effort to reach a saturation point of concepts. In a qualitative, inductive fashion, these ideas were sorted into categories and "member checking" (Lincoln & Guba, 1985) of these competencies and categories with contributors ensured that we retained the essence of their ideas. Benefits of creating our own inductively constructed competency list (rather than adopting existing models) were garnering a context-specific array of ideas and the engagement of individuals involved to promote buy-in of the resultant program.

The major categories of competencies that emerged for the OSU program were: professional/administrative, human relations, organizational dynamics, and scholarship, with a focus on understanding students and in the context of foundational commitments. Figure 3 (Welkener, Brischke, Shilling, & Hollingsworth, 2006) depicts the general categories, their relationship to one another, and the assumptions from Baxter Magolda's (2001) work that drove our practice. We then underwent a process of considering where these competencies were being addressed (in the curriculum, existing training through assistantship offices, university programs) and selectively deciding which competencies weren't being sufficiently covered and thus should be the purview of the professional development program. (For a full list of competencies and those chosen as the focus of the professional development program, see Figure 4.) Finally, we determined which graduate level(s) should be targeted for certain competencies and organized the competencies into a two-year, sequenced plan (since the MA program is two years). For example, "self-direction" programming (including self-motivation, self-awareness, flexibility/balance, and time management) was directed toward the needs of first-year MA students, while "publishing" was aimed at serving second-year MA or PhD students.

From Process to Practice—Applying Development Theory in Both Contexts

Since the goals of "helping TAs/GAs learn how to understand and meet their undergraduate students' complex learning needs" and "integrat[ing] their in-class and out-of-class experiences" imply developmental demands, we needed to find ways to offer appropriate challenge and support to graduate students through how we delivered these professional development programs. Both groups of designers agreed that the assumptions of constructive-developmental theory were congruent with what we were hoping to accomplish, and chose to use Baxter Magolda's principles as a guide to invite students into active participation. For example, in order to "validate learners [TAs/GAs] as capable knowers" we would welcome TAs/GAs as young professionals with valuable experience and skills that could be translated to educational/professional environments,

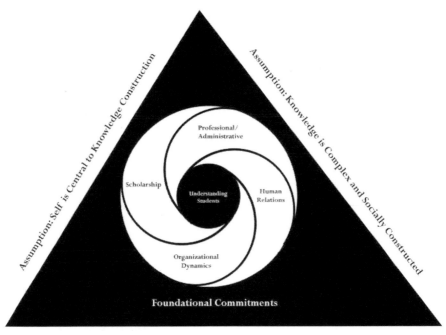

Figure 3: The Ohio State University (SPA) Professional Development Model (Illustrated by Sarah Shilling)

treat TAs/GAs with collegial respect, and value their perspectives. "Situat[ing] learning in students' [TAs'/GAs'] own experience" would necessitate starting conversations about good professional practice by asking participants to reflect on their experience in previous professional or educational work environments, inquiring about their professional development needs, and designing programming with these needs in mind. "Defin[ing] learning as mutually constructing meaning" would call for persons in a position of authority to take on the role of facilitator and co-learner, program participants to actively learn from each other, TAs/GAs to help design and facilitate sessions, and everyone involved to create activities that are discussion-based (where various views are heard). Such

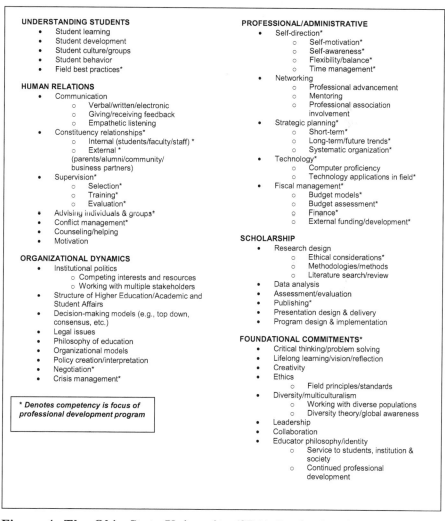

Figure 4: The Ohio State University (SPA) Professional Development Competencies

encounters with diverse others and ideas have the potential to challenge their existing beliefs and, as Kegan would contend, move what is "subject" to their consciousness to "object." By showing graduate students that they are important members of the campus learning community, have a unique set of experiences to bring to their work as educators, and "matter," we can cultivate their emerging "voice"—something Baxter Magolda (2004) claims is crucial to the development of self-authorship.

From Process to Practice—Evaluation in Both Contexts

All good design *starts* with what is desired at the *end* of the process, often (and aptly) referred to as "backward design" (Wiggins & McTighe, 2005). Setting appropriate goals at the outset of any design process will ultimately result in more effective outcomes and more accuracy when attempting to measure success. In both of these designs, formal (questionnaire, focus group) and informal (casual conversation, word of mouth) approaches to evaluation were chosen, seeking: TA/GA interest, quality of participation, reactions from students involved in the program, "knowledge, attitude, and skill changes," "practice and behavior change," and "end results" (Patton, 1997). Evaluation was considered ongoing—at the *beginning* of the program (by asking TAs/GAs for input on program content and approach); in the *middle* of the program (by asking TAs/GAs what was and was not helping their growth, what could be done to improve the program); and at the *end* of the program (by asking for feedback on the overall value of the program, what an ideal program would "look like" and how our program compared)—and was used to revise practice.

In the case of these two contexts where the program designs were medium to large-scale, an additional layer of design (that included the creation of individual modules using the same instructional design steps) aimed at specific competencies and behavioral goals (statements that point to clear, concrete outcomes—what you want students to be able to know or do) was necessary. Presenting such a level of detail, however, is beyond the scope of this paper.

Conclusion

As evidenced in these two designs, campus partnerships were crucial for making purposeful professional development experiences for graduate students possible. Not only did these collaborations benefit our graduate students for whom we designed such support programs, it accomplished several other objectives as well. Such intentional collaboration promoted a sense of shared purpose and community across divisional/disciplinary/administrative boundaries, prompted increased investment from members' immediate involvement in shaping the programs' direction, and encouraged faculty and staff to be creative in the use of theory to guide practice.

The professional development programs for graduate educators shared in this paper were transformative not only in their application of design and development theory (and innovative in their attempts to bring together graduate educators working in various campus environments), but also in the way this process shaped the individuals involved and their relationships with each other. While research to investigate approaches for their long-term effectiveness and impact on graduate students' holistic growth is needed, this work heeds the call being advanced to work across boundaries within higher education to promote student learning (AAC&U, 2002; Keeling, 2004). Patrick and Fletcher (1998) suggested that faculty developers are in an ideal position to begin shifting the culture of higher education toward increasing cooperation among its constituencies.

> If colleges and universities are to become learning organizations...higher education institutions must develop supportive cultures; create environments that value risk-taking; reward innovating exploration and implementation; and encourage collaboration, trust, and a sense of connectedness to institutions and communities. We believe that faculty developers are ideally suited to play a major role in creating such an environment. To do so they must become change agents on their campuses (p. 159).

A group of "change agents" modeling and designing strategic, cooperative learning experiences for graduate students, like in these examples, has the potential to give rise to a new generation of professionals in academic and student affairs who view the academy as a collegial community of learning partners who take very seriously the work of designing for learning and development.

References

Association of American Colleges and Universities (AAC&U). (2002). *Greater Expectations: A New Vision for Learning as a Nation Goes to College.* Washington, DC: Association of American Colleges and Universities.

Barr, R. B. & Tagg, J. (1995). From teaching to learning—A new paradigm for undergraduate education. *Change Magazine, 27*(6), 12-25.

Baxter Magolda, M.B. (1992). *Knowing and reasoning in college: Gender-related patterns in students' intellectual development.* San Francisco, CA: Jossey-Bass.

Baxter Magolda, M.B. (2001). *Making their own way: Narratives for transforming higher education to promote self-development.* Sterling, VA: Stylus Press.

Baxter Magolda, M.B., & King, P.M. (2004). *Learning partnerships: Theory and models of practice to educate for self-authorship.* Sterling, VA: Stylus Publishing.

Deubel, P. (2003). An investigation of behaviorist and cognitive approaches to instructional multimedia design. *Journal of Educational Multimedia and Hypermedia, 12*(1), 63-90.

Dick, W., & Carey, L. (1996). *The systematic design of instruction.* (Fourth ed.). New York, NY: HarperCollins.

Gagné, R.M., Wager, W.W., Golas, K.C., & Keller, J.M. (2005). *Principles of instructional design.* (Fifth ed.). Belmont, CA: Wadsworth/Thomson Learning.

Gilbert, R., Balatti, J., Turner, P., & Whitehouse, H. (2004). The generic skills debate in research higher degrees. *Higher Education Research & Development, 23*(3), 375-388.

Keeling, R. (Ed.) (2004). *Learning reconsidered: A campus-wide focus on the student experience.* Washington, DC: National Association of Student Personnel Administrators and American College Personnel Association.

Kegan, R. (1994). *In over our heads: The mental demands of modern life.* Cambridge, MA: Harvard University Press.

Lincoln, Y., & Guba, E. (1985). *Naturalistic inquiry.* Newbury Park, CA: Sage.

Nyquist, J. (2002). The PhD: A tapestry of change for the 21st Century. *Change, 34*(6), 12-20.

Patton, M. Q. (1997). *Utilization-focused evaluation: The new century text.* Thousand Oaks, CA: Sage.

Patrick, S.K., & Fletcher, J.J. (1998). Faculty developers as change agents: Transforming colleges and universities into learning organizations. *To Improve the Academy,17,* 155-169.

Poock, M.C. (2001, September 1). A model for integrating professional development in graduate education. *College Student Journal.* Retrieved August 30, 2006 from http://www.findarticles.com/p/articles/mi_m0FCR/is_3_35/ai_80744646

Welkener, M. M. (2003, October). *Advancing a New Vision: Designing a ProfessionalDevelopment Program for Teaching/Graduate Assistants from Academic and Student Affairs.* Paper presented at the meeting of the Professional and Organizational Development Network in Higher Education (POD), Denver, CO.

Welkener, M. Brischke, K., Shilling, S. & Hollingsworth, R. (2006, March). *Making a difference in the professional development of graduate students.* Paper presented at the meeting of the American College Personnel Association, Indianapolis, IN.

Wiggins, G., & McTighe, J. (2005). *Understanding by design.* Alexandria, VA: Association for Supervision & Curriculum Development.

Michele M. Welkener, Ph.D., is an Assistant Professor, Counselor Education and Human Services, and Coordinator, Ph.D. program in Higher Education for the School of Education and Allied Professions at The University of Dayton.

Author's note: This work is founded on the effort of many partners who deserve to be recognized for their contributions. From Indiana State University, these colleagues are Don Bonsall, Andy Corn, Robert Guell, Jolynn Kuhlman, Tom Johnson, David Langley, Mary Ellen Linn, Jonathon Myers, Al Perone, Rob Perrin, Missy Plew, David Worley, David Wright, and the Offices of Academic and Student Affairs. Special recognition goes to the late Terence O'Connor, former Director of the Center for Teaching and Learning. From The Ohio State University: Katie Beres, Kristy Brischke, Richard Hollingsworth, Kathy Krajnak, D'Andra Mull, Sarah Shilling, and Kathy Titus- Becker. Also the HESA/SPA students, faculty, alumni and supervisors; the School of Educational Policy and Leadership; and, the Office of Student Affairs.

Made in the USA
Charleston, SC
31 March 2011